Artificial Neural Networks: Concept Learning

Edited by Joachim Diederich

ARTIFICIAL NEURAL NETWORKS
Concept Learning

Edited by Joachim Diederich

 IEEE Computer Society Press ◆ The Institute of Electrical and Electronics Engineers, Inc.

Artificial Neural Networks: Concept Learning

Edited by Joachim Diederich

IEEE Computer Society Press
Los Alamitos, California

Washington • Brussels • Tokyo

QA
76.5
·C6182
1990

Artificial neural networks: concept learning / [edited by] Joachim
Diederich
        p.   cm.
        Includes bibliographical references (p.   )
        ISBN 0-8186-2015-3 (pbk.).--ISBN 0-8186-6015-5 (microfiche)
        1. Neural computers 2. Artificial intelligence.   I. Diederich, Joachim

QA76.5.C6183   1990
006.3--dc20   90-33580 CIP

Published by IEEE Computer Society Press
10662 Los Vaqueros Circle
P.O. Box 3014
Los Alamitos, CA 90720-1264

Cover designed by Jack I. Ballestero

Printed in the United States of America

IEEE Computer Society Order Number 2015
Library of Congress Number 89-81694
IEEE Catalog Number 90EH0308-7
ISBN 0-8186-2015-3 (paper)
ISBN 0-8186-6015-5 (microfiche)
ISBN 0-8186-9015-1 (case)
SAN 264-620X

139677

Additional copies can be ordered from:

IEEE Computer Society Press
Customer Service Center
10662 Los Vaqueros Circle
P.O. Box 3014
Los Alamitos, CA 90720-1264

IEEE Computer Society
13, Avenue de l'Aquilon
B-1200 Brussels
BELGIUM

IEEE Computer Society
Ooshima Building
2-19-1 Minami-Aoyama,
Minato-Ku
Tokyo 107, JAPAN

IEEE Service Center
445 Hoes Lane
P.O. Box 1331
Piscataway, NJ 08855-1331

THE INSTITUTE OF ELECTRICAL AND
ELECTRONICS ENGINEERS, INC.

Preface

This volume of the technology series is devoted to the emerging field of *concept learning*. The first volume of the "Artificial Neural Networks" series (Editor: V. Vemuri) includes a collection of papers on theoretical concepts of artificial neural networks (ANNs) and provides a good introduction to the foundations of neural networks.

There are currently a large number of advanced research projects on ANNs underway, and there is a need for a representative collection of papers dealing with learning in connectionist systems. Since learning is an important part of almost all neural network systems the editor of this volume decided to emphasize "concept learning," that is, learning and representation of classes of objects which are similar to one another and/or share features and attributes. Concept learning is based on the presentation of training examples and forms a concept representation either *unsupervised*, or by use of a *reinforcement* or *teaching* input. Therefore, concept learning is more complex than habituation or simple associative Hebbian learning (see the introduction to this volume for more details). In addition to "leaning by example" methods, the present volume also provides an introduction to learning techniques which use a single instruction to build a concept representation (one-trial learning).

The purpose of this volume is to give an overview which includes several of the most important ANN approaches. The consideration of research areas such as "reinforcement" and "recruitment learning," approaches which have made important contributions, but have not yet been appropriately represented in the literature, should allow a representative introduction to the field. Hinton's "Connectionist Learning Procedures" is one of the best introductions to learning in neural networks, and is therefore included as the first paper of this volume. Carpenter & Grossberg give a valuable overview of unsupervised learning (i.e., learning without teaching or reinforcement signal) by use of the "adaptive resonance theory." Two papers by Barto, Sutton and Anderson and by Williams demonstrate how reinforcement learning, which requires a signal about success or failure from the environment rather than a complete teaching input, can be applied to control tasks and can be combined with supervised learning.

I would like to thank Jerome A. Feldman and Rao Vemuri for their help in selecting valuable publications for this volume, and Gerhard Paass for his comments on previous versions of the introduction.

Joachim Diederich

Table of Contents

Introduction

Learning is one of the most important features of artificial neural networks (ANN), which are supposed to be adaptive (i.e., they can change internal representations as a response to training data, sometimes combined with a teaching input). Since all knowledge in ANNs is encoded in weights; that is, numeric values associated with links connecting network nodes (units), learning is performed by weight change. A weight represents the strength of association (i.e., the co-occurrence of the connected features, concepts, propositions, or events during a training or learning period). On the network level, a weight represents how frequent the receiving unit has been active simultaneously with the sending unit. Hence, weight change between two units depends on the frequency of both units having positive output simultaneously.

This form of weight change is called Hebbian learning (Hebb 1949), which provides a simple mathematical model for synaptic modification in biological networks. Its most general form is expressed by the equation, $\Delta w_{i,j} = y_i y_j$ (i.e., weight change is the product of the output of unit i and unit j). Several important modifications of this simple weight change rule have been proposed. The basic principle (i.e., local weight change depending on the outputs/states/potentials of the connected units) is accepted. Recently, neurophysiological evidence for synaptic changes corresponding to the Hebbian covariance rule has been found (Stanton & Sejnowski 1989. See Morris & Willshaw for a discussion of these results).

There are several additional rules for weight change in ANNs: learning should be local; that is, the only available information is the weight itself, the current input (output of the sending unit) and the potential, state or output of the receiving unit. Next, no programming is allowed; no external program or other network shall modify weights or network structures directly. Weight change is slow in most cases (i.e., the connected units have to be active simultaneously for some period to get a strong association).

The simple Hebbian learning rule can be generalized to more complex networks where some units are used to represent input and output, and some internal (hidden) units are used to encode important features of the environment (as the result of learning). Features of training instances must not be known in advance, so it is possible to "extract" features from training data. Learning is then realized by error correction procedures, for example. One possible solution is to use gradient-descent methods, where each link computes the derivative, with respect to the weight and a global performance measure (the error), and weight change is an amount proportional to $\partial E/\partial w$:

$$\Delta w_{i,j} = -e \frac{\partial E}{\partial w_{i,j}}$$

The global error E depends on the difference between the actual states of output units (in a given input-output case) and a desired state. Formally,

$$E = \frac{1}{2} \sum_{j,c} \left(y_{j,c} - d_{j,c} \right)^2$$

where $y_{j,c}$ is the state of output unit j in case c and $d_{j,c}$ is the desired state of this unit. These learning methods have been proven useful in small domains (see Hinton's paper on connectionist learning procedures for more details).

The learning techniques, which have been outlined above, represent weight-change-only methods (i.e., the network topology remains unmodified). It is also possible, and sometimes necessary, to use structure-changing learning schemes. Two methods are available: (1) Learning procedures that physically change the network topology (e.g., by simulating axon-grow) and (2), learning techniques that use weight-change-only and allocate previously unused connections and units. The latter of these methods is often called *recruitment learning*, since "free units" become "recruited" and get an assigned meaning (i.e., represent an instance, concept, proposition, or event).

A Classification for Neural Network Learning Techniques

There are obviously several ways to classify neural network learning techniques (see Figure 1). Several classification schemes have been proposed. Rumelhart & McClelland (1986) identify four *learning tasks*: pattern association, autoassociation, regularity-detection, and reinforcement learning. On the level of the *learning rules*, a distinction between correlational (Hebbian) learning, error correction learning, competitive learning, and Boltzmann machine learning is made. This classification cannot cover all the

2

approaches presented in this volume, but it emphasizes the need for cross-classification also.

Interaction with the Environment

This category, the distinction in supervised, reinforcement, and unsupervised learning, is often considered the most important one. In *supervised learning*, precise teaching data are available and are used to calculate weight change (e.g., when the training data consists of input-output pairs and the task is to predict the output given the input). The above example for error correction learning requires a "desired state," which is used to calculate the global performance of a network. In other words, the relation between input cases and their classification must be known in advance, roughly equivalent to "discriminant analysis" in statistics. Almeida, Hinton, Jordan, and Williams describe supervised learning procedures in this volume.

```
_____
A. Interaction with the environment.
      1. Supervised learning.
      2. Reinforcement learning.
      3. Unsupervised learning.

B. Topological changes.
      1. Weight-change-only.
      2. Topology-change-only.
      3. Weight and topology change.

C. Stochastic vs. deterministic learning.

D. Input requirements.
      1. Similarity-based learning ("learning by examples").
      2. Instruction-based learning ("learning by being told").
_____
```
Figure 1: A classification of ANN learning techniques.

The central idea in *reinforcement learning* is to use a global signal, which represents "award/punishment" only, and to measure how local decisions correlate with this reinforcement input. Local decisions are alterations in variables such as weights and states. The reinforcement signal is not a complex teaching input; it only represents "good" or "bad" performance (i.e., "positive reinforcement" and "punishment"). The network can perform gradient ascent (i.e., the probability distribution associated with each local variable is changed in order to increase the expected reinforcement). In general, reinforcement methods have advantages if there are a few local variables only, but they might get stuck in local minima. The two papers by Barto, Sutton, and Anderson and by Williams describe reinforcement learning methods.

Unsupervised learning is roughly equivalent to "cluster analysis" and does not require a teaching or reinforcement input. In competitive learning, a technique which is most representative for unsupervised learning, the procedure classifies a set of input vectors into disjoint clusters, in a way that elements in a cluster are similar to each other. It is called competitive learning because there is a set of hidden units that compete with each other to become active and to do the weight change. The winning unit increases its weights on input-lines with high input and decreases weights on links with small input. Since there is a constraint on each weight vector that the sum of weights has to be constant, the winning hidden unit will be selective to the input-vector where it was active, and not to other input patterns.[1]

There are a number of different versions of competitive learning. This volume includes Carpenter and Grossberg's introduction to the adaptive resonance theory (ART), an unsupervised learning technique that developed from competitive learning approaches. Diederich (1988) uses competition in the context of structure-changing learning techniques (i.e., to select a unit from a pool of free units for recruitment learning).

Topological Changes

By topological changes, one means learning methods that change a network structure as opposed to methods that perform weight-change-only. Learning techniques that physically change the network structure are rare, since it is assumed that the full neural structure is available soon after birth and topological changes are degenerative modifications only (Edelman 1986). However, topological changes by weight modifications are biologically plausible (Honovar 1989). Recent studies in brain physiology and anatomy have shown that structural modifications play an important role in learning during animal life. See Merzenich et al. (1988) for a summary of recent experimental work on cortical

---

[1]This form of unsupervised learning is a special form of supervised learning, in a way, since the built-in network architecture, or some other implicit principle, is necessary to allow clustering. In general, unsupervised means that no class or concept labels are provided with the trainings-instances.

representational plasticity and see Edelman (1986) on theoretical aspects of topographic changes in biological neural networks.

The consideration of structure-changing learning techniques is a fairly recent development. This class of methods is not totally disjoint to the weight-change models briefly discussed above. The recruitment of previously uncommitted units is also part of ART (see Carpenter and Grossberg in this volume) and it has been used in backpropagation learning (Kruschke 1988) for the allocation of new hidden units. Honavar and Uhr (1988) report technical advantages of structure-changing methods in comparison with "weight-change-only" techniques.

"Recruitment learning," as it is used in "structured connectionist systems" (e.g., Feldman 1982, Diederich 1988, this volume), is a structure-changing learning scheme for ANNs. In recruitment learning, a network consists of two classes of units: *Committed Units* are units that already represent some sort of information or function (i.e., conceptual information). Committed units are connected to other committed units and their simultaneous activation must represent a meaningful state of the network. Committed units are also connected to free units. *Free Units* form a kind of "primordial network" (Shastri 1988) and are connected to other free units as well as to committed units.

Recruitment learning is the strengthening of the connections between a group of committed units and one or more free units. This results in the transformation of free units into committed units. The term "chunking" is used if "a free node becomes committed and functions as a chunking node for the cluster [of committed units, this author] (i.e., the activation of nodes in the cluster results in the activation of the chunking node, and conversely the activation of the chunking nodes activates all the nodes in the cluster" (Shastri 1988)). It is possible to view the subnetwork of committed units embedded in the network of free units.

Stochastic vs. Deterministic Learning

The stochastic Boltzmann machine is a generalized Hopfield network; that is, it uses symmetric weights, binary units with a stochastic decision rule, and asynchronuous update. The probability that unit j gets state 1 (is on/off) is given by:

$$p_j = \frac{1}{1 + e^{-\Delta E_j / T}}$$

where $-\Delta E_j$ is the total input (note: E refers to "energy" now) received by unit j and T is the "temperature" (i.e., the extent of randomness). A network which applies this update rule will reach thermal equilibrium (i.e., the joint distribution of network states converges to a limit). By use of stochastic optimization techniques, such as "simulated annealing," the network will find low energy states with high probability. In other words, the global solution (optimum) can be found by applying the appropriate "annealing" strategy.

The stochastic Boltzmann machine is important, not only because a learning procedure which uses hidden units in an optimal way is available, but also because the stochastic Boltzmann machine is topologically unspecific. The stochastic Boltzmann machine, however, is very slow and has a number of disadvantages from a neurobiological and cognitive science perspective.

Recently, the "deterministic Boltzmann machine" was introduced to efficiently approximate the equivalent stochastic Boltzmann machine and to allow much faster learning. The deterministic Boltzmann machine uses analog units that perform a meanfield approximation. Hinton (1989, this volume) has proven that the deterministic Boltzmann machine performs steepest descent in weight-space. The discussion about the usefulness of the deterministic Boltzmann machine for large applications is undecided. The approach is important, however, and Hinton´s paper on the deterministic Boltzmann machine is included in this volume.

Input Requirements

Competitive, reinforcement, backpropagation, and Boltzmann machine learning are all "learning by examples" techniques (i.e., they require an ensemble of input vectors). One of the disadvantages of these procedures is that they make rather strong assumptions about the environment type. For example, a set of input patterns must be available to do learning. Early learning theories in psychology (e.g., Guthrie (1959)) assumed that a single co-occurrence of stimulus and response is sufficient for generating an association. Furthermore, and this is a different, more recent development, symbolic artificial intelligence knows "one-shot" learning techniques that need one training example only for concept formation (Mitchell et al. 1986). This is sometimes necessary and has advantages, for example when one single new fact is presented to the system and has to be integrated.[2] Such an "integration" procedure is difficult to realize by "learning by example" techniques only.

The term "explanation-based generalization" (EBG) is used by Mitchell et al. (1986) and refers in symbolic artificial intelligence to knowledge-intensive learning methods, which require only a single example and use domain knowledge to constrain search for a possible generalization. This involves generating a new chunk of knowledge that describes a set of features including the properties of the training example. EBG is a two-step learning method: (1) Construct an explanation of why an example fits a particular goal concept and find those features of the training example that are relevant to satisfy this goal concept, and (2) search for sufficient features of the example to build the general concept definition, the goal of the method. EBG, however, requires a strong domain theory, a precondition that is unrealistic for real-world applications. Consequently, efforts were made to use weaker domain models.

Diederich (in this volume) presents steps toward a one-shot learning method that applies recruitment learning. It is important to note that this system does not realize analytical generalization in a sense EBG does, but rather shares some of the features like input requirements and the use of built-in knowledge. Techniques like EBG require unification and deduction which remain hard to realize in connectionist networks.

Final Remarks

As mentioned in the preface, it is the intention of the editor to use the limited space in this volume for a representative overview of the most important ANN learning techniques. Undoubtedly, this overview will not be representative for a long time (if it is at all), because of rapid changes in the ANN area. A few remarks to some of these expected changes are in order.

---

[2] A good example is a representation of "tax laws." Changes in tax laws are single new facts which have to be integrated in the knowledge-base and the effects have to be propagated throughout the representation. Any form of "learning by example" is unnatural in this case (Thanks to Jerry Feldman for this analogy).

The simple, formal model of units in ANNs is neurobiologically false and too primitive and inflexible from a computational point of view. Although the introduction of various "sites" in units as locations of separate computations (i.e., for computation of input from different sources) is a step in the right direction, since it facilitates the realization of various connection patterns, unit types are much too simple and do not represent neurophysiological evidence.

"Learning from scratch," as it is currently done in almost all ANN models, is most probably not adequate for learning in large, structured domains. This point has been made several times:

"Humans are intelligent because evolution has equipped them with a richly structured brain. This structure, while serving a variety of functions, in particular enables them to learn. A certain critical degree of structural complexity is required of a network before it can become self-modifying -- no matter how sophisticated its reinforcement rules -- in a way that we could consider intelligent" (Arbib, M.A. 1987, p.70).

"However, some fundamental problems remain to be solved before flexible robots can be realized. One of these problems is scalability to realistic size. Learning strategy based on exhaustive search of full combinatorial phase spaces blow up too quickly. The solution to this problem will very likely have to be based on the introduction of a clever *a priori* structure to restrict the relevant phase spaces" (v.d. Malsburg 1988, p.26).

Significant changes in unit structure, network structures, and the types of interaction among units networks might be possible, and likely, in future ANN models.

References

Ackley, D.H., Hinton, G.E., and Sejnowski, T.J.: *A Learning Algorithm for Boltzmann Machines*. Cognitive Science 9, 1985, 147-169.

Arbib, M.A.: *Brains, Machines, and Mathematics*. Second Edition. Springer Verlag, New York, 1987.

Edelman, G.E.: *Neural Darwinism. The Theory of Neuronal Group Selection*. Basic Books Inc., Publishers, New York, 1986.

Guthrie, E.R.: "*Association by Contiguity.*" In: Koch, S. (Ed.): Psychology, the study of a science, Vol. 2, 158-195, McGraw-Hill, New York, 1959.

Hebb, D.O.: *The Organization of Behavior.* Wiley, New York, 1949.

Honavar, V.: *Perceptual Development and Learning: From Behavioral, Neurophysiological, and Morphological Evidence to Computational Models.* Technical Report #818, Computer Sciences Dept., University of Wisconsin-Madison, Madison, Wisconsin, January 1989.

Honavar, V. and Uhr, L.: *Experimental Results Indicate That Generation, Local Receptive Fields and Global Convergence Improve Perceptual Learning In Connectionist Networks.* Technical Report #805, Computer Sciences Dept., University of Wisconsin-Madison, Madison, Wisconsin, 1988.

Kruschke, J.: "*Creating Local and Distributed Bottlenecks in Hidden Layers of Backpropagation Networks.*" In: Touretzky, D., Hinton, G., and Sejnowski, T. (Eds.): Proc. of the Connectionist Models Summer School 1988, Morgan Kaufman Publ., San Mateo, California, 1988.

Merzenich, M.M., Recanzone, G., Jenkins, W.M., Allard, T.T., and Nudo, R.J.: "*Cortical Representational Plasticity.*" In: Rakie, P. and Singer, W. (Eds.): Neurobiology of Neocortex. John Wiley and Sons Limited. S. Bernhard. Dahlem Konferenzen, 1988.

Mitchell, T.M., Keller, R.M., and Kedar-Cabelli, S.T.: "*Explanation-Based Generalization: A Unifying View.*" Machine Learning 1, 1986, 47-80.

Morris, R.G.M. and Willshaw, D.J.: "*Must What Goes Up Come Down?*" Nature, Vol. 339, 18 May 1989, pp. 175-176.

Rumelhart, D.E. and McClelland, J.L. (Eds.): *Parallel Distributed Processing. Vol 1.: Foundations.* The MIT Press, Cambridge, Mass., 1986

Shastri, L.: *Semantic Networks: An Evidential Formalization and its Connectionist Realization. Research Notes in Artificial Intelligence*, Morgan Kaufman Publ. Inc., San Mateo, California ,1988.

Stanton, P.K. and Sejnowski, T.J.: "*Associative Long-Term Depression in the Hippocampus Induced by Hebbian Covariance.*" Nature, Vol. 339, 18 May 1989, pp. 215-218.

Vemuri, V. (Ed.): *Artificial Neural Networks: Theoretical Concepts.* IEEE Computer Society Press, Los Alamitos, California, 1988.

von der Malsburg, Ch.: "Goal and Architecture of Neural Computers." In: Eckmiller, R. and von der Malsburg, Ch. (Eds.): *Neural Computers.* Springer Verlag, Berlin, West Germany, 1988.

Connectionist Learning Procedures

Geoffrey E. Hinton

Computer Science Department, University of Toronto,
10 King's College Road, Toronto, Ontario, Canada M5S 1A4

ABSTRACT

A major goal of research on networks of neuron-like processing units is to discover efficient learning procedures that allow these networks to construct complex internal representations of their environment. The learning procedures must be capable of modifying the connection strengths in such a way that internal units which are not part of the input or output come to represent important features of the task domain. Several interesting gradient-descent procedures have recently been discovered. Each connection computes the derivative, with respect to the connection strength, of a global measure of the error in the performance of the network. The strength is then adjusted in the direction that decreases the error. These relatively simple, gradient-descent learning procedures work well for small tasks and the new challenge is to find ways of improving their convergence rate and their generalization abilities so that they can be applied to larger, more realistic tasks.

1. Introduction

Recent technological advances in VLSI and computer aided design mean that it is now much easier to build massively parallel machines. This has contributed to a new wave of interest in models of computation that are inspired by neural nets rather than the formal manipulation of symbolic expressions. To understand human abilities like perceptual interpretation, content-addressable memory, commonsense reasoning, and learning it may be necessary to understand how computation is organized in systems like the brain which consist of massive numbers of richly interconnected but rather slow processing elements.

This paper focuses on the question of how internal representations can be learned in "connectionist" networks. These are a recent subclass of neural net models that emphasize computational power rather than biological fidelity. They grew out of work on early visual processing and associative memories [28, 40, 79]. The paper starts by reviewing the main research issues for connectionist models and then describes some of the earlier work on learning procedures for associative memories and simple pattern recognition devices. These learning procedures cannot generate internal representations: They are limited to forming simple associations between representations that are specified externally. Recent research has led to a variety of more powerful connectionist learning procedures that can discover good internal representations and most of the paper is devoted to a survey of these procedures.

2. Connectionist Models

Connectionist models typically consist of many simple, neuron-like processing elements called "units" that interact using weighted connections. Each unit has a "state" or "activity level" that is determined by the input received from other units in the network. There are many possible variations within this general framework. One common, simplifying assumption is that the combined effects of the rest of the network on the jth unit are mediated by a single scalar quantity, x_j. The quantity, which is called the "total input" of unit j, is usually taken to be a *linear* function of the activity levels of the units that provide input to j:

$$x_j = -\theta_j + \sum_i y_i w_{ji} , \tag{1}$$

where y_i is the state of the ith unit, w_{ji} is the weight on the connection from the ith to the jth unit and θ_j is the threshold of the jth unit. The threshold term can be eliminated by giving every unit an extra input connection whose activity level is fixed at 1. The weight on this special connection is the negative of the threshold. It is called the "bias" and it can be learned in just the same way as the other weights. This method of implementing thresholds will generally be assumed in the rest of this paper. An external input vector can be supplied to the network by clamping the states of some units or by adding an input term, I_j, that contributes to the total input of some of the units. The state of a unit is typically defined to be a nonlinear function of its total input. For units with discrete states, this function typically has value 1 if the total input is positive and value 0 (or -1) otherwise. For units with continuous states one typical nonlinear input-output function is the logistic function (shown in Fig. 1):

$$y_j = \frac{1}{1 + e^{-x_j}} .$$
(2

All the long-term knowledge in a connectionist network is encoded by wher the connections are or by their weights, so learning consists of changing th weights or adding or removing connections. The short-term knowledge of th network is normally encoded by the states of the units, but some models als have fast-changing temporary weights or thresholds that can be used to encod temporary contexts or bindings [44, 96].

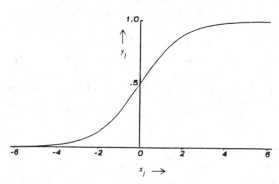

Fig. 1. The logistic input-output function defined by equation (2). It is a smoothed version of a step function.

There are two main reasons for investigating connectionist networks. First, these networks resemble the brain much more closely than conventional computers. Even though there are many detailed differences between connectionist units and real neurons, a deeper understanding of the computational properties of connectionist networks may reveal principles that apply to a whole class of devices of this kind, including the brain. Second, connectionist networks are massively parallel, so any computations that can be performed efficiently with these networks can make good use of parallel hardware.

3. Connectionist Research Issues

There are three main areas of research on connectionist networks: Search, representation, and learning. This paper focuses on learning, but a very brief introduction to search and representation is necessary in order to understand what learning is intended to produce.

3.1. Search

The task of interpreting the perceptual input, or constructing a plan, or accessing an item in memory from a partial description can be viewed as a constraint satisfaction search in which information about the current case (i.e. the perceptual input or the partial description) must be combined with knowledge of the domain to produce a solution that fits both these sources of constraint as well as possible [12]. If each unit represents a piece of a possible solution, the weights on the connections between units can encode the degree of consistency between various pieces. In interpreting an image, for example, a unit might stand for a piece of surface at a particular depth and surface orientation. Knowledge that surfaces usually vary smoothly in depth and orientation can be encoded by using positive weights between units that represent nearby pieces of surface at similar depths and similar surface orientations, and negative weights between nearby pieces of surface at very different depths or orientations. The network can perform a search for the most plausible interpretation of the input by iteratively updating the states of the units until they reach a stable state in which the pieces of the solution fit well with each other and with the input. Any one constraint can typically be overridden by combinations of other constraints and this makes the search procedure robust in the presence of noisy data, noisy hardware, or minor inconsistencies in the knowledge.

There are, of course, many complexities: Under what conditions will the network settle to a stable solution? Will this solution be the optimal one? How long will it take to settle? What is the precise relationship between weights and probabilities? These issues are examined in detail by Hummel and Zucker [52], Hinton and Sejnowski [45], Geman and Geman [31], Hopfield and Tank [51] and Marroquin [65].

3.2. Representation

For tasks like low-level vision, it is usually fairly simple to decide how to use the units to represent the important features of the task domain. Even so, there are some important choices about whether to represent a physical quantity (like the depth at a point in the image) by the state of a single continuous unit, or by the activities in a set of units each of which indicates its confidence that the depth lies within a certain interval [10].

The issues become much more complicated when we consider how a complex, articulated structure like a plan or the meaning of a sentence might be represented in a network of simple units. Some preliminary work has been done by Minsky [67] and Hinton [37] on the representation of inheritance hierarchies and the representation of frame-like structures in which a whole object is composed of a number of parts each of which plays a different role within the whole. A recurring issue is the distinction between local and distributed representations. In a local representation, each concept is represented by a single unit [13, 27]. In a distributed representation, the kinds of concepts that we have words for are represented by patterns of activity distributed over many units, and each unit takes part in many such patterns [42]. Distributed representations are usually more efficient than local ones in addition to being more damage-resistant. Also, if the distributed representation allows the weights to capture important underlying regularities in the task domain, it can lead to much better generalization than a local representation [78, 80]. However, distributed representations can make it difficult to represent several different things at the same time and so to use them effectively for representing structures that have many parts playing different roles it may be necessary to have a separate group of units for each role so that the assignment of a filler to a role is represented by a distributed pattern of activity over a group of "role-specific" units.

13

Much confusion has been caused by the failure to realize that the words "local" and "distributed" refer to the *relationship* between the terms of some descriptive language and a connectionist implementation. If an entity that is described by a single term in the language is represented by a pattern of activity over many units in the connectionist system, and if each of these units is involved in representing other entities, then the representation is distributed. But it is always possible to invent a new descriptive language such that, relative to this language, the very same connectionist system is using local representations.

3.3. Learning

In a network that uses local representations it may be feasible to set all the weights by hand because each weight typically corresponds to a meaningful relationship between entities in the domain. If, however, the network uses distributed representations it may be very hard to program by hand and so a learning procedure may be essential. Some learning procedures, like the perceptron convergence procedure [77], are only applicable if the desired states of all the units in the network are already specified. This makes the learning task relatively easy. Other, more recent, learning procedures operate in networks that contain "hidden" units [46] whose desired states are not specified (either directly or indirectly) by the input or the desired output of the network. This makes learning much harder because the learning procedure must (implicitly) decide what the hidden units should represent. The learning procedure is therefore constructing new representations and the results of learning can be viewed as a numerical solution to the problem of whether to use local or distributed representations.

Connectionist learning procedures can be divided into three broad classes: Supervised procedures which require a teacher to specify the desired output vector, reinforcement procedures which only require a single scalar evaluation of the output, and unsupervised procedures which construct internal models that capture regularities in their input vectors without receiving any additional information. As we shall see, there are often ways of converting one kind of learning procedure into another.

4. Associative Memories without Hidden Units

Several simple kinds of connectionist learning have been used extensively for storing knowledge in simple associative networks which consist of a set of input units that are directly connected to a set of output units. Since these networks do not contain any hidden units, the difficult problem of deciding what the hidden units should represent does not arise. The aim is simply to store a set of associations between input vectors and output vectors by modifying the weights on the connections. The representation of each association is typically distributed over many connections and each connection is involved in storing many associations. This makes the network robust against minor physical damage and it also means that weights tend to capture regularities in the set of input-output pairings, so the network tends to generalize these regularities to new input vectors that it has not been trained on [6].

4.1. Linear associators

In a linear associator, the state of an output unit is a linear function of the total input that it receives from the input units (see (1)). A simple, Hebbian procedure for storing a new association (or "case") is to increment each weight, w_{ji}, between the ith input unit and the jth output unit by the product of the states of the units

$$\Delta w_{ji} = y_i y_j \,, \tag{3}$$

where y_i and y_j are the activities of an input and an output unit. After a set of associations have been stored, the weights encode the cross-correlation matrix between the input and output vectors. If the input vectors are orthogonal and have length 1, the associative memory will exhibit perfect recall. Even though each weight is involved in storing many different associations, each input vector will produce exactly the correct output vector [56].

If the input vectors are not orthogonal, the simple Hebbian storage procedure is not optimal. For a given network and a given set of associations, it may be impossible to store all the associations perfectly, but we would still like the storage procedure to produce a set of weights that minimizes some sensible measure of the differences between the desired output vectors and the vectors actually produced by the network. This "error measure" can be defined as

$$E = \tfrac{1}{2} \sum_{j,c} (y_{j,c} - d_{j,c})^2 ,$$

where $y_{j,c}$ is the actual state of output unit j in input-output case c, and $d_{j,c}$ is its desired state. Kohonen [56] shows that the weight matrix that minimizes this error measure can be computed by an iterative storage procedure that repeatedly sweeps through the whole set of associations and modifies each weight by a small amount in the direction that reduces the error measure. This is a version of the least squares learning procedure described in Section 5. The cost of finding an optimal set of weights (in the least squares sense of optimal) is that storage ceases to be a simple "one-shot" process. To store one new association it is necessary to sweep through the whole set of associations many times.

4.2. Nonlinear associative nets

If we wish to store a small set of associations which have nonorthogonal input vectors, there is no simple, one-shot storage procedure for linear associative nets that guarantees perfect recall. In these circumstances, a nonlinear associative net can perform better. Willshaw [102] describes an associative net in which both the units and the weights have just two states: 1 and 0. The weights all start at 0, and associations are stored by setting a weight to 1 if ever its input and output units are both on in any association (see Fig. 2). To recall an association, each output unit must have its threshold dynamically set to be just less than m, the number of active input units. If the output unit should be on, the m weights coming from the active input units will have been set to 1 during storage, so the output unit is guaranteed to come on. If the output unit should be off, the probability of erroneously coming on is given by the probability that all m of the relevant weights will have been set to 1 when storing other associations. Willshaw showed that associative nets can make efficient use of the information capacity of the weights. If the number of active input units is the log of the total number of input units, the probability of incorrectly activating an output unit can be made very low even when the network is storing close to 0.69 of its information-theoretic capacity.

An associative net in which the input units are identical with the output units can be used to associate vectors with themselves. This allows the network to complete a partially specified input vector. If the input vector is a very degraded version of one of the stored vectors, it may be necessary to use an iterative retrieval process. The initial states of the units represent the partially specified vector, and the states of the units are then updated many times until they settle on one of the stored vectors. Theoretically, the network could oscillate, but Hinton [37] and Anderson and Mozer [7] showed that iterative retrieval normally works well. Hopfield [49] showed that if the weights are symmetrical and the units are updated one at a time the iterative retrieval process can be viewed as a form of gradient descent in an "energy function".

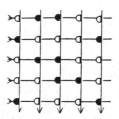

Fig. 2. An associative net (Willshaw [102]). The input vector comes in at the left and the output vector comes out at the bottom (after thresholding). The solid weights have value 1 and the open weights have value 0. The network is shown after it has stored the associations 01001 → 10001, 10100 → 01100, 00010 → 00110.

Hopfield nets store vectors whose components are all +1 or −1 using the simple storage procedure described in equation (3). To retrieve a stored vector from a partial description (which is a vector containing some 0 components), we start the network at the state specified by the partial description and then repeatedly update the states of units one at a time. The units can be chosen in random order or in any other order provided no unit is ever ignored for more than a finite time. Hopfield [49] observed that the behavior of the network is governed by the global energy function[1]

$$E = -\sum_{i<j} s_i s_j w_{ij} + \sum_j s_j \theta_j , \qquad (4)$$

where s_i and s_j are the states of two units. Each time a unit updates its state, it adopts the state that minimizes this energy function because the decision rule used to update a unit is simply the derivative of the energy function. The unit adopts the state +1 if its "energy gap" is positive and the state −1 otherwise, where the energy gap of the jth unit, ΔE_j, is the increase in the global energy caused by changing the unit from state +1 to state −1.

$$\Delta E_j = E(s_j = -1) - E(s_j = +1) = -2\theta_j + 2\sum_i s_i w_{ij} . \qquad (5)$$

So the energy must decrease until the network settles into a local minimum of the energy function. We can therefore view the retrieval process in the following way: The weights define an "energy landscape" over global states of the network and the stored vectors are local minima in this landscape. The retrieval process consists of moving downhill from a starting point to a nearby local minimum.

If too many vectors are stored, there may be spurious local minima caused by interactions between the stored vectors. Also, the basins of attraction around the correct minima may be long and narrow instead of round, so a downhill path from a random starting point may not lead to the nearest local minimum. These problems can be alleviated by using a process called "unlearning" [20, 50].

A Hopfield net with N totally interconnected units can store about $0.15N$ random vectors.[2] This means that it is storing about 0.15 bits per weight, even though the weights are integers with $m + 1$ different values, where m is the number of vectors stored. The capacity can be increased considerably by

---

[1] The energy function should not be confused with the error function described earlier. Gradient descent in the energy function is performed by changing the *states* of the units, not the *weights*.

[2] There is some confusion in the literature due to different ways of measuring storage capacity. If we insist on a fixed probability of getting *each* component of *each* vector correct, the number of vectors that can be stored is $O(N)$. If we insist on a fixed probability of getting *all* components of *all* vectors correct, the number of vectors that can be stored is $O(N/\log N)$.

abandoning the one-shot storage procedure and explicitly training the network on typical noisy retrieval tasks using the threshold least squares or perceptron convergence procedures described below.

4.3. The deficiencies of associators without hidden units

If the input vectors are orthogonal, or if they are made to be close to orthogonal by using high-dimensional random vectors (as is typically done in a Hopfield net), associators with no hidden units perform well using a simple Hebbian storage procedure. If the set of input vectors satisfy the much weaker condition of being linearly independent, associators with no hidden units can learn to give the correct outputs provided an iterative learning procedure is used. Unfortunately, linear independence does not hold for most tasks that can be characterized as mapping input vectors to output vectors because the number of relevant input vectors is typically much larger than the number of components in each input vector. The required mapping typically has a complicated structure that can only be expressed using multiple layers of hidden units.[3] Consider, for example, the task of identifying an object when the input vector is an intensity array and the output vector has a separate component for each possible name. If a given type of object can be either black or white, the intensity of an individual pixel (which is what an input unit encodes) cannot provide any direct evidence for the presence or absence of an object of that type. So the object cannot be identified by using weights on direct connections from input to output units. Obviously, it is necessary to explictly extract relationships among intensity values (such as edges) before trying to identify the object. Actually, extracting edges is just a small part of the problem. If recognition is to have the generative capacity to handle novel images of familiar objects the network must somehow encode the systematic effects of variations in lighting and viewpoint, partial occlusion by other objects, and deformations of the object itself. There is a tremendous gap between these complex regularities and the regularities that can be captured by an associative net that lacks hidden units.

5. Simple Supervised Learning Procedures

Consider a network that has input units which are directly connected to output units whose states (i.e. activity levels) are a continuous smooth function of their total input. Suppose that we want to train the network to produce particular "desired" states of the output units for each member of a set of input vectors. A measure of how poorly the network is performing with its current set of weights is:

$$E = \tfrac{1}{2} \sum_{j,c} (y_{j,c} - d_{j,c})^2 , \qquad (6)$$

where $y_{j,c}$ is the actual state of output unit j in input-output case c, and $d_{j,c}$ is its desired state.

We can minimize the error measure given in (6) by starting with any set of weights and repeatedly changing each weight by an amount proportional to $\partial E / \partial w$.

$$\Delta w_{ji} = - \varepsilon \, \frac{\partial E}{\partial w_{ji}} . \qquad (7)$$

In the limit, as ε tends to 0 and the number of updates tends to infinity, this learning procedure is guaranteed to find the set of weights that gives the least squared error. The value of $\partial E / \partial w$ is obtained by differentiating (6) and (1).

---

[3] It is always possible to redefine the units and the connectivity so that multiple layers of simple units become a single layer of much more complicated units. But this redefinition does not make the problem go away.

$$\frac{\partial E}{\partial w_{ji}} = \sum_{cases} \frac{\partial E}{\partial y_j} \frac{dy_j}{dx_j} \frac{\partial x_j}{\partial w_{ji}} = \sum_{cases} (y_j - d_j) \frac{dy_j}{dx_j} y_i \,. \tag{8}$$

If the output units are linear, the term dy_j/dx_j is a constant.

The least squares learning procedure has a simple geometric interpretation. We construct a multi-dimensional "weight space" that has an axis for each weight and one extra axis (called "height") that corresponds to the error measure. For each combination of weights, the network will have a certain error which can be represented by the height of a point in weight space. These points form a surface called the "error surface". For networks with linear output units and no hidden units, the error surface always forms a bowl whose horizontal cross-sections are ellipses and whose vertical cross-sections are parabolas. Since the bowl only has one minimum,[4] gradient descent on the error surface is guaranteed to find it.

The error surface is actually the sum of a number of parabolic troughs, one for each training case. If the output units have a nonlinear but monotonic input-output function, each trough is deformed but no new minima are created in any one trough because the monotonic nonlinearity cannot reverse the sign of the gradient of the trough in any direction. When many troughs are added together, however, it is possible to create local minima because it is possible to change the sign of the total gradient without changing the signs of any of the conflicting case-wise gradients of which it is composed. But local minima cannot be created in this way if there is a set of weights that gives zero error for all training cases. If we consider moving away from this perfect point, the error must increase (or remain constant) for each individual case and so it must increase (or remain constant) for the sum of all these cases. So gradient descent is still guaranteed to work for monotonic nonlinear input-output functions provided a perfect solution exists. However, it will be very slow at points in weight space where the gradient of the input-output function approaches zero for the output units that are in error.

The "batch" version of the least squares procedure sweeps through all the cases accumulating $\partial E/\partial w$ before changing the weights, and so it is guaranteed to move in the direction of steepest descent. The "online" version, which requires less memory, updates the weights after each input-output case [99].[5] This may sometimes increase the total error, E, but by making the weight changes sufficiently small the total change in the weights after a complete sweep through all the cases can be made to approximate steepest descent arbitrarily closely.

5.1. A least squares procedure for binary threshold units

Binary threshold units use a step function, so the term dy_j/dx_j is infinite at the threshold and zero elsewhere and the least squares procedure must be modified to be applicable to these units. In the following discussion we assume that the threshold is implemented by a "bias" weight on a permanently active input line, so the unit turns on if its total input exceeds zero. The basic idea is to define an error function that is large if the total input is far from zero and the unit is in the wrong state and is 0 when the unit is in the right state. The simplest version of this idea is to define the error of an output unit, j for a given input case to be

$$E_{j,c}^* = \begin{cases} 0\,, & \text{if output unit has the right state}\,, \\ \frac{1}{2}x_{j,c}^2\,, & \text{if output unit has the wrong state}\,. \end{cases}$$

---

[4] This minimum may be a whole subspace.

[5] The online version is usually called the "least mean squares" or "LMS" procedure.

Unfortunately, this measure can be minimized by setting all weights and biases to zero so that units are always exactly at their threshold (Yann Le Cun, personal communication). To avoid this problem we can introduce a margin, m, and insist that for units which should be *on* the total input is at least m and for units that should be *off* the total input is at most $-m$. The new error measure is then

$$E_{j,c}^* = \begin{cases} 0, & \text{if output unit has the right state by at least } m, \\ \frac{1}{2}(m - x_{j,c})^2, & \text{if output unit should be on but has } x_{j,c} < m, \\ \frac{1}{2}(m + x_{j,c})^2, & \text{if output unit should be off but has } x_{j,c} > -m. \end{cases}$$

The derivative of this error measure with respect to $x_{j,c}$ is

$$\frac{\partial E_{j,c}^*}{\partial x_{j,c}} = \begin{cases} 0, & \text{if output unit has the right state by at least } m, \\ x_{j,c} - m, & \text{if output unit should be on but has } x_{j,c} < m, \\ x_{j,c} + m; & \text{if output unit should be off but has } x_{j,c} > -m. \end{cases}$$

So the "threshold least squares procedure" becomes:

$$\Delta w_{ji} = -\varepsilon \sum_c \frac{\partial E_{j,c}^*}{\partial x_{j,c}} y_{i,c}.$$

5.2. The perceptron convergence procedure

One version of the perceptron convergence procedure is related to the online version of the threshold least squares procedure in the following way: The magnitude of $\partial E_{j,c}^* / \partial x_{j,c}$ is ignored and only its sign is taken into consideration. So the weight changes are:

$$\Delta w_{ji,c} = \begin{cases} 0, & \text{if output unit behaves correctly by at least } m, \\ +\varepsilon y_{i,c}, & \text{if output unit should be on but has } x_{j,c} < m, \\ -\varepsilon y_{i,c}, & \text{if output unit should be off but has } x_{j,c} > -m. \end{cases}$$

Because it ignores the magnitude of the error, this procedure changes weights by at least ε even when the error is very small. The finite size of the weight steps eliminates the need for a margin so the standard version of the perceptron convergence procedure does not use one.

Because it ignores the magnitude of the error this procedure does not even stochastically approximate steepest descent in E, the sum squared error. Even with very small ε, it is quite possible for E to rise after a complete sweep through all the cases. However, each time the weights are updated, the perceptron convergence procedure is guaranteed to reduce the value of a different cost measure that is defined solely in terms of weights.

To picture the least squares procedure we introduced a space with one dimension for each weight and one extra dimension for the sum squared error in the output vectors. To picture the perceptron convergence procedure, we do not need the extra dimension for the error. For simplicity we shall consider a network with only one output unit. Each case corresponds to a constraint hyperplane in weight space. If the weights are on one side of this hyperplane, the output unit will behave correctly and if they are on the other side it will behave incorrectly (see Fig. 3). To behave correctly for all cases, the weights

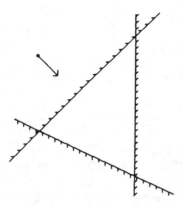

Fig. 3. Some hyperplanes in weight space. Each plane represents the constraint on the weights caused by a particular input-output case. If the weights lie on the correct (unshaded) side of the plane, the output unit will have the correct state for that case. Provided the weight changes are proportional to the activities of the input lines, the perceptron convergence procedure moves the weights perpendicularly towards a violated constraint plane.

must lie on the correct side of all the hyperplanes, so the combinations of weights that give perfect performance form a convex set. *Any* set of weights in this set will be called "ideal."

The perceptron convergence procedure considers the constraint planes one at a time, and whenever the current combination of weights is on the wrong side, it moves it perpendicularly towards the plane. This reduces the distance between the current combination of weights and *any* of the ideal combinations. So provided the weights move by less than twice the distance to the violated constraint plane, a weight update is guaranteed to reduce the measure

$$\sum_i \left(w_{i,\text{actual}} - w_{i,\text{ideal}} \right)^2 .$$

The perceptron convergence procedure has many nice properties, but it also has some serious problems. Unlike the threshold least squares procedure, it does not necessarily settle down to a reasonable compromise when there is no set of weights that will do the job perfectly. Also, there are obvious problems in trying to generalize to more complex, multi-layered nets in which the ideal combinations of weights do not form a single convex set, because the idea of moving towards *the* ideal region of weight space breaks down. It is therefore not surprising that the more sophisticated procedures required for multi-layer nets are generalizations of the least squares procedure rather than the perceptron convergence procedure: They learn by decreasing a squared performance error, not a distance in weight space.

5.3. The deficiencies of simple learning procedures

The major deficiency of both the least squares and perceptron convergence procedures is that most "interesting" mappings between input and output vectors cannot be captured by any combination of weights in such simple networks, so the guarantee that the learning procedure will find the best possible combination of weights is of little value. Consider, for example, a network composed of two input units and one output unit. There is no way of setting the two weights and one threshold to solve the very simple task of producing an output of 1 when the input vector is $(1, 1)$ or $(0, 0)$ and an output of 0 when the input vector is $(1, 0)$ or $(0, 1)$. Minsky and Papert [68] give a clear analysis of the limitations on what mappings can be computed by three-layered nets. They focus on the question of what preprocessing must be done by the units in the intermediate layer to allow a task to be solved. They generally assume that the preprocessing is fixed, and so they avoid the problem of how to make the units in the intermediate layer learn useful predicates. So, from the learning perspective, their intermediate units are not true hidden units.

Another deficiency of the least squares and perceptron learning procedures is that gradient descent may be very slow if the elliptical cross-section of the error surface is very elongated so that the surface forms a long ravine with steep sides and a very low gradient along the ravine. In this case, the gradient at most points in the space is almost perpendicular to the direction towards the minimum. If the coefficient ε in (7) is large, there are divergent oscillations across the ravine, and if it is small the progress along the ravine is very slow. A standard method for speeding the convergence in such cases is recursive least squares [100]. Various other methods have also been suggested [5, 71, 75].

We now consider learning in more complex networks that contain hidden units. The next five sections describe a variety of supervised, unsupervised, and reinforcement learning procedures for these nets.

6. Backpropagation: A Multi-layer Least Squares Procedure

The "backpropagation" learning procedure [80, 81] is a generalization of the least squares procedure that works for networks which have layers of hidden units between the input and output units. These multi-layer networks can compute much more complicated functions than networks that lack hidden units, but the learning is generally much slower because it must explore the space of possible ways of using the hidden units. There are now many examples in which backpropagation constructs interesting internal representations in the hidden units, and these representations allow the network to generalize in sensible ways. Variants of the procedure were discovered independently by Werbos [98], Le Cun [59] and Parker [70].

In a multi-layer network it is possible, using (8), to compute $\partial E/\partial w_{ji}$ for *all* the weights in the network provided we can compute $\partial E/\partial y_j$ for all the units that have modifiable incoming weights. In a system that has no hidden units, this is easy because the only relevant units are the output units, and for them $\partial E/\partial y_j$ is found by differentiating the error function in (6). But for hidden units, $\partial E/\partial y_j$ is harder to compute. The central idea of backpropagation is that these derivatives can be computed efficiently by starting with the output layer and working backwards through the layers. For each input-output case, c, we first use a forward pass, starting at the input units, to compute the activity levels of all the units in the network. Then we use a backward pass, starting at the output units, to compute $\partial E/\partial y_j$ for all the hidden units. For a hidden unit, j, in layer J the only way it can affect the error is via its effects on the units, k, in the next layer, K (assuming units in one layer only send their outputs to units in the layer above). So we have

$$\frac{\partial E}{\partial y_j} = \sum_k \frac{\partial E}{\partial y_k} \frac{\mathrm{d}y_k}{\mathrm{d}x_k} \frac{\mathrm{d}x_k}{\mathrm{d}y_j} = \sum_k \frac{\partial E}{\partial y_k} \frac{\mathrm{d}y_k}{\mathrm{d}x_k} w_{kj}, \tag{9}$$

where the index c has been suppressed for clarity. So if $\partial E/\partial y_k$ is already known for all units in layer K, it is easy to compute the same quantity for units in layer J. Notice that the computation performed during the backward pass is very similar in form to the computation performed during the forward pass (though it propagates error derivatives instead of activity levels, and it is entirely linear in the error derivatives).

6.1. The shape of the error surface

In networks without hidden units, the error surface only has one minimum (provided a perfect solution exists and the units use smooth monotonic input-output functions). With hidden units, the error surface may contain many local minima, so it is possible that steepest descent in weight space will get stuck at poor local minima. In practice, this does not seem to be a serious problem. Backpropagation has been tried for a wide variety of tasks and poor local minima are rarely encountered, provided the network contains a few more units and connections than are required for the task. One reason for this is that there are typically a very large number of qualitatively different perfect solutions, so we avoid the typical combinatorial optimization task in which one minimum is slightly better than a large number of other, widely separated minima.

In practice, the most serious problem is the speed of convergence, not the presence of nonglobal minima. This is discussed further in Section 12.

6.2. Backpropagation for discovering semantic features

To demonstrate the ability of backpropagation to discover important underlying features of a domain, Hinton [38] used a multi-layer network to learn the

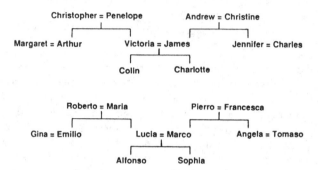

Fig. 4. Two isomorphic family trees.

family relationships between 24 different people (see Fig. 4). The information in a family tree can be represented as a set of triples of the form ($\langle$person1$\rangle$, $\langle$relationship$\rangle$, $\langle$person2$\rangle$), and a network can be said to "know" these triples if it can produce the third term of any triple when given the first two terms as input. Figure 5 shows the architecture of the network that was used to learn the triples. The input vector is divided into two parts, one of which specifies a person and the other a relationship (e.g. has-father). The network is trained to produce the related person as output. The input and output encoding use a different unit to represent each person and relationship, so all pairs of people are equally similar in the input and output encoding: The encodings do not give any clues about what the important features are. The architecture is designed so that all the information about an input person must be squeezed through a narrow bottleneck of 6 units in the first hidden layer. This forces the network

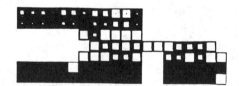

Fig. 5. The activity levels in a five-layer network after it has learned. The bottom layer has 24 input units on the left for representing person1 and 12 units on the right for representing the relationship. The white squares inside these two groups show the activity levels of the units. There is one active unit in the first group (representing Colin) and one in the second group (representing has-aunt). Each of the two groups of input units is totally connected to its own group of 6 units in the second layer. These two groups of 6 must learn to encode the input terms as distributed patterns of activity. The second layer is totally connected to the central layer of 12 units, and this layer is connected to the penultimate layer of 6 units. The activity in the penultimate layer must activate the correct output units, each of which stands for a particular person2. In this case, there are two correct answers (marked by black dots) because Colin has two aunts. Both the input and output units are laid out spatially with the English people in one row and the isomorphic Italians immediately below.

to represent people using distributed patterns of activity in this layer. The aim of the simulation is to see if the components of these distributed patterns correspond to the important underlying features of the domain.

After prolonged training on 100 of the 104 possible relationships, the network was tested on the remaining 4. It generalized correctly because during the training it learned to represent each of the people in terms of important features such as age, nationality, and the branch of the family tree that they belonged to (see Fig. 6), even though these "semantic" features were not at all explicit in the input or output vectors. Using these underlying features, much of the information about family relationships can be captured by a fairly small number of "micro-inferences" between features. For example, the father of a middle-aged person is an old person, and the father of an Italian person is an Italian person. So the features of the output person can be derived from the features of the input person and of the relationship. The learning procedure can only discover these features by searching for a set of features that make it easy to express the associations. Once these features have been discovered, the *internal* representation of each person (in the first hidden layer) is a distributed pattern of activity and similar people are represented by similar patterns. Thus the network constructs its own internal similarity metric. This is a significant advance over simulations in which good generalization is achieved because the experimenter chooses representations that already have an appropriate similarity metric.

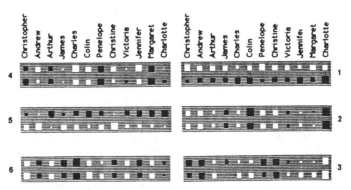

Fig. 6. The weights from the 24 input units that represent people to the 6 units in the second layer that learn distributed representations of people. White rectangles stand for excitatory weights, black for inhibitory weights, and the area of the rectangle encodes the magnitude of the weight. The weights from the 12 English people are in the top row of each unit. Beneath each of these weights is the weight from the isomorphic Italian. Unit 1 learns to encode nationality, unit 2 encodes generation (using three values), and unit 4 encodes the branch of the family tree to which a person belongs. During the learning, each weight was given a tendency to decay towards zero. This tendency is balanced by the error gradient, so the final magnitude of a weight indicates how useful it is in reducing the error.

6.3. Backpropagation for mapping text to speech

Backpropagation is an effective learning technique when the mapping from input vectors to output vectors contains both regularities and exceptions. For example, in mapping from a string of English letters to a string of English phonemes there are many regularities but there are also exceptions such as the word "women." Sejnowski and Rosenberg [84] have shown that a network with one hidden layer can be trained to pronounce letters surprisingly well. The input layer encodes the identity of the letter to be pronounced using a different unit for each possible letter. The input also encodes the local context which consists of the three previous letters and three following letters in the text (space and punctuation are treated as special kinds of letters). This seven-letter window is moved over the text, so the mapping from text to speech is performed sequentially, one letter at a time. The output layer encodes a phoneme using 21 articulatory features and 5 features for stress and syllable boundaries. There are 80 hidden units each of which receives connections from all the input units and sends connections to all the output units (see Fig. 7). After extensive training, the network generalizes well to new examples which demonstrates that it captures the regularities of the mapping. Its performance on new words is comparable to a conventional computer program which uses a large number of hand-crafted rules.

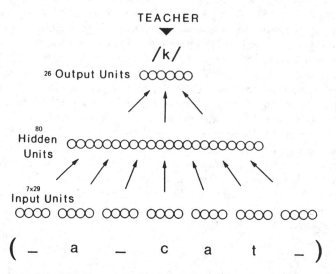

Fig. 7. The network has 309 units and 18,629 connections. A window seven letters wide is moved over the text, and the network pronounces the middle letter. It assumes a preprocessor to identify characters, and a postprocessor to turn phonemes into sounds.

6.4. Backpropagation for phoneme recognition

Speech recognition is a task that can be used to assess the usefulness of backpropagation for real-world signal-processing applications. The best existing techniques, such as hidden Markov models [9], are significantly worse than people, and an improvement in the quality of recognition would be of great practical significance.

A subtask which is well-suited to backpropagation is the bottom-up recognition of highly confusable consonants. One obvious approach is to convert the sound into a spectrogram which is then presented as the input vector to a multi-layer network whose output units represent different consonants. Unfortunately, this approach has two serious drawbacks. First, the spectrogram must have many "pixels" to give reasonable resolution in time and frequency, so each hidden unit has many incoming weights. This means that a very large number of training examples are needed to provide enough data to estimate the weights. Second, it is hard to achieve precise time alignment of the input data, so the spatial pattern that represents a given phoneme may occur at many different positions in the spectrogram. To learn that these shifts in position do not change the identity of the phoneme requires an immense amount of training data. We already know that the task has a certain symmetry—the same sounds occurring at different times mean the same phoneme. To speed learning and improve generalization we should build this a priori knowledge into the network and let it use the information in the training data to discover structure that we do not already understand.

An interesting way to build in the time symmetry is to use a multi-layer, feed-forward network that has connections with time delays [88]. The input units represent a single time frame from the spectrogram and the whole spectrogram is represented by stepping it through the input units. Each hidden unit is connected to each unit in the layer below by several different connections with different time delays and different weights. So it has a limited temporal window within which it can detect temporal patterns in the activities of the units in the layer below. Since a hidden unit applies the same set of weights at different times, it inevitably produces similar responses to similar patterns that are shifted in time (see Fig. 8).

Kevin Lang [58] has shown that a time delay net that is trained using a generalization of the backpropagation procedure compares favorably with hidden Markov models at the task of distinguishing the words "bee", "dee", "ee", and "vee" spoken by many different male speakers in a very noisy environment. Waibel et al. [97] have shown that the same network can achieve excellent speaker-dependent discrimination of the phonemes "b", "d", and "g" in varying phonetic contexts.

An interesting technical problem arises in computing the error derivatives for the output units of the time delay network. The adaptive part of the

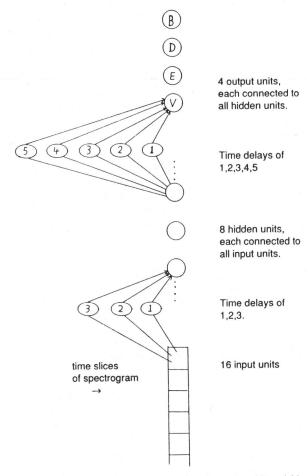

4 output units, each connected to all hidden units.

Time delays of 1,2,3,4,5

8 hidden units, each connected to all input units.

Time delays of 1,2,3.

16 input units

time slices of spectrogram →

Fig. 8. Part of the time delay network used to recognize phonemes with variable onset times. A unit in one layer is connected to a unit in the layer below by several different connections which have different time delays and learn to have different weights.

network contains one output unit for each possible phoneme and these units respond to the input by producing a sequence of activations. If the training data is labeled with the exact time of occurrence of each phoneme, it is possible to specify the exact time at which an output unit should be active. But in the absence of precisely time-aligned training data, it is necessary to compute error derivatives for a sequence of activations without knowing when the phoneme occurred. This can be done by using a fixed postprocessing layer to integrate the activity of each output unit over time. We interpret the instantaneous activity of an output unit as a representation of the probability that the phoneme occurred at exactly that time. So, for the phoneme that really occurred, we know that the time integral of its activity should be 1 and for the other phonemes it should be 0. So at each time, the error derivative is simply the difference between the desired and the actual integral. After training, the network localizes phonemes in time, even though the training data contains no information about time alignment.

6.5. Postprocessing the output of a backpropagation net

Many people have suggested transforming the raw input vector with a module that uses unsupervised learning before presenting it to a module that uses supervised learning. It is less obvious that a supervised module can also benefit from a nonadaptive postprocessing module. A very simple example of this kind of postprocessing occurs in the time delay phoneme recognition network described in Section 6.4.

David Rumelhart has shown that the idea of a postprocessing module can be applied even in cases where the postprocessing function is initially unknown. In trying to imitate a sound, for example, a network might produce an output vector which specifies how to move the speech articulators. This output vector needs to be postprocessed to turn it into a sound, but the postprocessing is normally done by physics. Suppose that the network does not receive any direct information about what it should do with its articulators but it does "know" the desired sound and the actual sound, which is the transformed "image" of the output vector. If we had a postprocessing module which transformed the activations of the speech articulators into sounds, we could backpropagate through this module to compute error derivatives for the articulator activations.

Rumelhart uses an additional network (which he calls a mental model) that first learns to perform the postprocessing (i.e. it learns to map from output vectors to their transformed images). Once this mapping has been learned, backpropagation through the mental model can convert error derivatives for the "images" into error derivatives for the output vectors of the basic network.

6.6. A reinforcement version of backpropagation

Munro [69] has shown that the idea of using a mental model can be applied even when the image of an output vector is simply a single scalar value—the reinforcement. First, the mental model learns to predict expected reinforcement from the combination of the input vector and the output vector. Then the derivative of the expected reinforcement can be backpropagated through the mental model to get the reinforcement derivatives for each component of the output vector of the basic network.

6.7. Iterative backpropagation

Rumelhart, Hinton, and Williams [80] show how the backpropagation procedure can be applied to iterative networks in which there are no limitations on the connectivity. A network in which the states of the units at time t determine the states of the units at time $t + 1$ is equivalent to a net which has one layer for each time slice. Each weight in the iterative network is implemented by a whole set of identical weights in the corresponding layered net, one for each time slice (see Fig. 9). In the iterative net, the error is typically the difference between the actual and desired final states of the network, and to compute the error derivatives it is necessary to backpropagate through time, so the history of states of each unit must be stored. Each weight will have many different error derivatives, one for each time step, and the sum of all these derivatives is used to determine the weight change.

Backpropagation in iterative nets can be used to train a network to generate sequences or to recognize sequences or to complete sequences. Examples are given by Rumelhart, Hinton and Williams [81]. Alternatively, it can be used to store a set of patterns by constructing a point attractor for each pattern. Unlike the simple storage procedure used in a Hopfield net, or the more sophisticated storage procedure used in a Boltzmann machine (see Section 7), backpropagation takes into account the path used to reach a point attractor. So it will not construct attractors that cannot be reached from the normal range of starting points on which it is trained.[6]

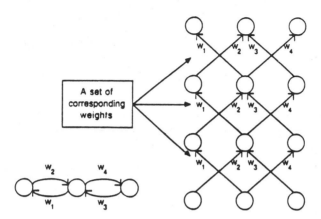

Fig. 9. On the left is a simple iterative network that is run synchronously for three iterations. On the right is the equivalent layered network.

6.8. Backpropagation as a maximum likelihood procedure

If we interpret each output vector as a specification of a conditional probability distribution over a set of output vectors given an input vector, we can interpret the backpropagation learning procedure as a method of finding weights that maximize the likelihood of generating the desired conditional probability distributions. Two examples of this kind of interpretation will be described.

Suppose we only attach meaning to binary output vectors and we treat a real-valued output vector as a way of specifying a probability distribution over binary vectors.[7] We imagine that a real-valued output vector is stochastically converted into a binary vector by treating the real values as the probabilities that individual components have value 1, and assuming independence between components. For simplicity, we can assume that the desired vectors used during training are binary vectors, though this is not necessary. Given a set of training cases, it can be shown that the likelihood of producing *exactly* the desired vectors is maximized when we minimize the cross-entropy, C, between the desired and actual conditional probability distributions:

$$C = -\sum_{j,c} d_{j,c} \log_2(y_{j,c}) + (1 - d_{j,c}) \log_2(1 - y_{j,c}) \, ,$$

where $d_{j,c}$ is the desired probability of output unit j in case c and $y_{j,c}$ is its actual probability.

So, under this interpretation of the output vectors, we should use the cross-entropy function rather than the squared difference as our cost measure. In practice, this helps to avoid a problem caused by output units which are firmly off when they should be on (or vice versa). These units have a very small value of $\partial y/\partial x$ so they need a large value of $\partial E/\partial y$ in order to change their incoming weights by a reasonable amount. When an output unit that should have an activity level of 1 changes from a level of 0.0001 to level of 0.001, the

---

[6] A backpropagation net that uses asymmetric connections (and synchronous updating) is not guaranteed to settle to a single stable state. To encourage it to construct a point attractor, rather than a limit cycle, the point attractor can be made the desired state for the last few iterations.
[7] Both the examples of backpropagation described above fit this interpretation.

squared difference from 1 only changes slightly, but the cross-entropy decreases a lot. In fact, when the derivative of the cross-entropy is multiplied by the derivative of the logistic activation function, the product is simply the difference between the desired and the actual outputs, so $\partial C_{j,c} / \partial x_{j,c}$ is just the same as for a linear output unit (Steven Nowlan, personal communication).

This way of interpreting backpropagation raises the issue of whether, under some other interpretation of the output vectors, the squared error might not be the correct measure for performing maximum likelihood estimation. In fact, Richard Golden [32] has shown that minimizing the squared error is equivalent to maximum likelihood estimation if both the actual and the desired output vectors are treated as the centers of Gaussian probability density functions over the space of all real vectors. So the "correct" choice of cost function depends on the way the output vectors are most naturally interpreted.

6.9. Self-supervised backpropagation

One drawback of the standard form of backpropagation is that it requires an external supervisor to specify the desired states of the output units (or a transformed "image" of the desired states). It can be converted into an unsupervised procedure by using the input itself to do the supervision, using a multi-layer "encoder" network [2] in which the desired output vector is identical with the input vector. The network must learn to compute an approximation to the identity mapping for all the input vectors in its training set, and if the middle layer of the network contains fewer units than the input layer, the learning procedure must construct a compact, invertible code for each input vector. This code can then be used as the input to later stages of processing.

The use of self-supervised backpropagation to construct compact codes resembles the use of principal components analysis to perform dimensionality reduction, but it has the advantage that it allows the code to be a nonlinear transform of the input vector. This form of backpropagation has been used successfully to compress images [19] and to compress speech waves [25]. A variation of it has been used to extract the underlying degrees of freedom of simple shapes [83].

It is also possible to use backpropagation to predict one part of the perceptual input from other parts. For example, in predicting one patch of an image from neighboring patches it is probably helpful to use hidden units that explicitly extract edges, so this might be an unsupervised way of discovering edge detectors. In domains with sequential structure, one portion of a sequence can be used as input and the next term in the sequence can be the desired output. This forces the network to extract features that are good predictors. If this is applied to the speech wave, the states of the hidden units will form a nonlinear predictive code. It is not yet known whether such codes are more helpful for speech recognition than linear predictive coefficients.

A different variation of self-supervised backpropagation is to insist that all or part of the code in the middle layer change as slowly as possible with time. This can be done by making the desired state of each of the middle units be the state it actually adopted for the previous input vector. This forces the network to use similar codes for input vectors that occur at neighboring times, which is a sensible principle if the input vectors are generated by a process whose underlying parameters change more slowly than the input vectors themselves.

6.10. The deficiencies of backpropagation

Despite its impressive performance on relatively small problems, and its promise as a widely applicable mechanism for extracting the underlying structure of a domain, backpropagation is inadequate, in its current form, for larger tasks because the learning time scales poorly. Empirically, the learning time on a serial machine is very approximately $O(N^3)$ where N is the number of weights in the network. The time for one forward and one backward pass is $O(N)$. The number of training examples is typically $O(N)$, assuming the amount of information per output vector is held constant and enough training cases are used to strain the storage capacity of the network (which is about 2 bits per weight). The number of times the weights must be updated is also approximately $O(N)$. This is an empirical observation and depends on the nature of the task.[8] On a parallel machine that used a separate processor for each connection, the time would be reduced to approximately $O(N^2)$. Back-propagation can probably be improved by using the gradient information in more sophisticated ways, but much bigger improvements are likely to result from making better use of modularity (see Section 12.4).

As a biological model, backpropagation is implausible. There is no evidence that synapses can be used in the reverse direction, or that neurons can propagate error derivatives backwards (using a linear input-output function) as well as propagating activity levels forwards using a nonlinear input-output function. One approach is to try to backpropagate the derivatives using separate circuitry that *learns* to have the same weights as the forward circuitry [70]. A second approach, which seems to be feasible for self-supervised backpropagation, is to use a method called "recirculation" that approximates gradient descent and is more biologically plausible [41]. At present, backpropagation should be treated as a mechanism for demonstrating the kind of learning that can be done using gradient descent, without implying that the brain does gradient descent in the same way.

7. Boltzmann Machines

A Boltzmann machine [2, 46] is a generalization of a Hopfield net (see Section 4.2) in which the units update their states according to a *stochastic* decision rule. The units have states of 1 or 0,[9] and the probability that unit j adopts the state 1 is given by

$$p_j = \frac{1}{1 + e^{-\Delta E_j / T}}, \tag{10}$$

where $\Delta E_j = x_j$ is the total input received by the jth unit and T is the "temperature." It can be shown that if this rule is applied repeatedly to the units, the network will reach "thermal equilibrium." At thermal equilibrium the units still change state, but the *probability* of finding the network in any global state remains constant and obeys a Boltzmann distribution in which the probability ratio of any two global states depends solely on their energy difference:

$$\frac{P_A}{P_B} = e^{-(E_A - E_B)/T}$$

At high temperature, the network approaches equilibrium rapidly but low energy states are not much more probable than high energy states. At low temperature the network approaches equilibrium more slowly, but low energy states are much more probable than high energy states. The fastest way to approach low temperature equilibrium is generally to start at a high temperature and to gradually reduce the temperature. This is called "simulated annealing" [55]. Simulated annealing allows Boltzmann machines to find low energy states with high probability. If some units are clamped to represent an input vector, and if the weights in the network represent the constraints of the task domain, the network can settle on a very plausible output vector given the current weights and the current input vector.

[8] Tesauro [90] reports a case in which the number of weight updates is roughly proportional to the number of training cases (it is actually a 4/3 power law). Judd shows that in the worst case it is exponential [53].

[9] A network that uses states of 1 and 0 can always be converted into an equivalent network that uses states of $+1$ and -1 provided the thresholds are altered appropriately.

For complex tasks there is generally no way of expressing the constraints by using weights on pairwise connections between the input and output units. It is necessary to use hidden units that represent higher-order features of the domain. This creates a problem: Given a limited number of hidden units, what higher-order features should they represent in order to approximate the required input-output mapping as closely as possible? The beauty of Boltzmann machines is that the simplicity of the Boltzmann distribution leads to a very simple learning procedure which adjusts the weights so as to use the hidden units in an optimal way.

The network is "shown" the mapping that it is required to perform by clamping an input vector on the input units and clamping the required output vector on the output units. If there are several possible output vectors for a given input vector, each of the possibilities is clamped on the output units with the appropriate frequency. The network is then annealed until it approaches thermal equilibrium at a temperature of 1. It then runs for a fixed time at equilibrium and each connection measures the fraction of the time during which both the units it connects are active. This is repeated for all the various input-output pairs so that each connection can measure $\langle s_i s_j \rangle^+$, the expected probability, averaged over all cases, that unit i and unit j are simultaneously active at thermal equilibrium when the input and output vectors are both clamped.

The network must also be run in just the same way but without clamping the output units. Again, it reaches thermal equilibrium with each input vector clamped and then runs for a fixed additional time to measure $\langle s_i s_j \rangle^-$, the expected probability that both units are active at thermal equilibrium when the output vector is determined by the network. Each weight is then updated by an amount proportional to the difference between these two quantities

$$\Delta w_{ij} = \varepsilon (\langle s_i s_j \rangle^+ - \langle s_i s_j \rangle^-) .$$

It has been shown [2] that if ε is sufficiently small this performs gradient descent in an information-theoretic measure, G, of the difference between the behavior of the output units when they are clamped and their behavior when they are not clamped.

$$G = \sum_{\alpha, \beta} P^+(I_\alpha, O_\beta) \log \frac{P^+(O_\beta | I_\alpha)}{P^-(O_\beta | I_\alpha)} , \qquad (11)$$

where I_α is a state vector over the input units, O_β is a state vector over the output units, P^+ is a probability measured when both the input and output units are clamped, and P^- is a probability measured at thermal equilibrium when only the input units are clamped.

G is called the "asymmetric divergence" or "Kullback information," and its gradient has the same form for connections between input and hidden units, connections between pairs of hidden units, connections between hidden and output units, and connections between pairs of output units. G can be viewed as the difference of two terms. One term is the cross-entropy between the "desired" conditional probability distribution that is clamped on the output units and the "actual" conditional distribution exhibited by the output units when they are not clamped. The other term is the entropy of the "desired" conditional distribution. This entropy cannot be changed by altering the weights, so minimizing G is equivalent to minimizing the cross-entropy term, which means that Boltzmann machines use the same cost function as one form of backpropagation (see Section 6.8).

A special case of the learning procedure is when there are no input units. It can then be viewed as an unsupervised learning procedure which learns to model a probability distribution that is specified by clamping vectors on the output units with the appropriate probabilities. The advantage of modeling a distribution in this way is that the network can then perform completion. When a partial vector is clamped over a subset of the output units, the network produces completions on the remaining output units. If the network has learned the training distribution perfectly, its probability of producing each completion is guaranteed to match the environmental conditional probability of this completion given the clamped partial vector.

The learning procedure can easily be generalized to networks where each term in the energy function is the product of a weight, $w_{i,j,k,...}$ and an arbitrary function, $f(i, j, k, ...)$, of the states of a subset of the units. The network must be run so that it achieves a Boltzmann distribution in the energy function, so each unit must be able to compute how the global energy would change if it were to change state. The generalized learning procedure is simply to change the weight by an amount proportional to the difference between $\langle f(i, j, k, ...)\rangle^+$ and $\langle f(i, j, k, ...)\rangle^-$.

The learning procedure using simple pairwise connections has been shown to produce appropriate representations in the hidden units [2] and it has also been used for speech recognition [76]. However, it is considerably slower than backpropagation because of the time required to reach equilibrium in large networks. Also, the process of estimating the gradient introduces several practical problems. If the network does not reach equilibrium the estimated gradient has a systematic error, and if too few samples are taken to estimate $\langle s_i s_j\rangle^+$ and $\langle s_i s_j\rangle^-$ accurately the estimated gradient will be extremely noisy because it is the difference of two noisy estimates. Even when the noise in the estimate of the difference has zero mean, its variance is a function of $\langle s_i s_j\rangle^+$ and $\langle s_i s_j\rangle^-$. When these quantities are near zero or one, their estimates will have much lower variance than when they are near 0.5. This nonuniformity in the variance gives the hidden units a surprisingly strong tendency to develop weights that cause them to be on all the time or off all the time. A familiar version of the same effect can be seen if sand is sprinkled on a vibrating sheet of tin. Nearly all the sand clusters at the points that vibrate the least, even though there is no bias in the direction of motion of an individual grain of sand.

One interesting feature of the Boltzmann machine is that it is relatively easy to put it directly onto a chip which has dedicated hardware for each connection and performs the annealing extremely rapidly using analog circuitry that computes the energy gap of a unit by simply allowing the incoming charge to add itself up, and makes stochastic decisions by using physical noise. Alspector and Allen [3] are fabricating a chip which will run about 1 million times as fast as a simulation on a VAX. Such chips may make it possible to apply connectionist learning procedures to practical problems, especially if they are used in conjunction with modular approaches that allow the learning time to scale better with the size of the task.

There is another promising method that reduces the time required to compute the equilibrium distribution and eliminates the noise caused by the sampling errors in $\langle s_i s_j\rangle^+$ and $\langle s_i s_j\rangle^-$. Instead of directly simulating the stochastic network it is possible to estimate its mean behavior using "mean field theory" which replaces each stochastic binary variable by a deterministic real value that represents the expected value of the stochastic variable. Simulated annealing can then be replaced by a deterministic relaxation procedure that operates on the real-valued parameters [51] and settles to a single state that gives a crude representation of the whole equilibrium distribution. The product of the "activity levels" of two units in this settled state can be used as an approximation of $\langle s_i s_j\rangle$ so a version of the Boltzmann machine learning procedure can be applied. Peterson and Anderson [74] have shown that this works quite well.

7.1. Maximizing reinforcement and entropy in a Boltzmann machine

The Boltzmann machine learning procedure is based on the simplicity of the expression for the derivative of the asymmetric divergence between the conditional probability distribution exhibited by the output units of a Boltzmann machine and a desired conditional probability distribution. The derivatives of certain other important measures are also very simple if the network is allowed to reach thermal equilibrium. For example, the entropy of the states of the machine is given by

$$H = -\sum_{\alpha} P_{\alpha} \log_e P_{\alpha} \, ,$$

where P_{α} is the probability of a global configuration, and H is measured in units of $\log_2 e$ bits. Its derivative is

$$\frac{\partial H}{\partial w_{ij}} = \frac{1}{T} \left(\langle E s_i s_j \rangle - \langle E \rangle \langle s_i s_j \rangle \right) . \tag{12}$$

So if each weight has access to the global energy, E, it is easy to manipulate the entropy.

It is also easy to perform gradient ascent in expected reinforcement if the network is given a global reinforcement signal, R, that depends on its state. The derivative of the expected reinforcement with respect to each weight is

$$\frac{\partial R}{\partial w_{ij}} = \frac{1}{T} \left(\langle R s_i s_j \rangle - \langle R \rangle \langle s_i s_j \rangle \right) . \tag{13}$$

A recurrent issue in reinforcement learning procedures is how to trade off short-term optimization of expected reinforcement against the diversity required to discover actions that have a higher reinforcement than the network's current estimate. If we use entropy as a measure of diversity, and we assume that the system tries to optimize some linear combination of the expected reinforcement and the entropy of its actions, it can be shown that its optimal strategy is to pick actions according to a Boltzmann distribution, where the expected reinforcement of a state is the analog of negative energy and the parameter that determines the relative importance of expected reinforcement and diversity is the analog of temperature. This result follows from the fact that the Boltzmann distribution is the one which maximizes entropy (i.e. diversity) for a given expected energy (i.e. reinforcement).

This suggests a learning procedure in which the system represents the expected value of an action by its negative energy, and picks actions by allowing a Boltzmann machine to reach thermal equilibrium. If the weights are updated using equations (12) and (13) the negative energies of states will tend to become proportional to their expected reinforcements, since this is the way to make the derivative of H balance the derivative of R. Once the system has learned to represent the reinforcements correctly, variations in the temperature can be used to make it more or less conservative in its choice of actions whilst always making the optimal tradeoff between diversity and expected reinforcement. Unfortunately, this learning procedure does not make use of the most important property of Boltzmann machines which is their ability to compute the quantity $\langle s_i s_j \rangle$ *given* some specified state of the output units. Also, it is much harder to compute the derivative of the entropy if we are only interested in the entropy of the state vectors over the output units.

8. Maximizing Mutual Information: A Semisupervised Learning Procedure

One "semisupervised" method of training a unit is to provide it with information about what category the input vector came from, but to refrain from specifying the state that the unit ought to adopt. Instead, its incoming weights are modified so as to maximize the information that the state of the unit provides about the category of the input vector. The derivative of the mutual information is relatively easy to compute and so it can be maximized by gradient ascent [73]. For difficult discriminations that cannot be performed in a single step this is a good way of producing encodings of the input vector that allow the discrimination to be made more easily. Figure 10 shows an example of a difficult two-way discrimination and illustrates the kinds of discriminant function that maximize the information provided by the state of the unit.

If each unit within a layer independently maximizes the mutual information between its state and the category of the input vector, many units are likely to discover similar, highly correlated features. One way to force the units to diversify is to make each unit receive its inputs from a different subset of the units in the layer below. A second method is to ignore cases in which the input vector is correctly classified by the final output units and to maximize the

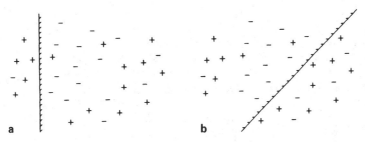

Fig. 10. (a) There is high mutual information between the state of a binary threshold unit that uses the hyperplane shown and the distribution (+ or −) that the input vector came from. (b) The probability, given that the unit is on, that the input came from the "+" distribution is not as high using the diagonal hyperplane. However, the unit is on more often. Other things being equal, a unit conveys most mutual information if it is on half the time.

mutual information between the state of each intermediate unit and the category of the input *given that the input is incorrectly classified*.[10]

If the two input distributions that must be discriminated consist of examples taken from some structured domain and examples generated at random (but with the same first-order statistics as the structured domain), this semisupervised procedure will discover higher-order features that characterize the structured domain and so it can be made to act like the type of unsupervised learning procedure described in Section 9.

9. Unsupervised Hebbian Learning

A unit can develop selectivity to certain kinds of features in its ensemble of input vectors by using a simple weight modification procedure that depends on the correlation between the activity of the unit and the activity on each of it input lines. This is called a "Hebbian" learning rule because the weight modification depends on both presynaptic and postsynaptic activity [36]. Typical examples of this kind of learning are described by Cooper, Liberman and Oja [18] and by Bienenstock, Cooper, and Munro [16]. A criticism of early versions of this approach, from a computational point of view, was that the researchers often postulated a simple synaptic modification rule and then explored its consequences rather than rigorously specifying the computational goal and then deriving the appropriate synaptic modification rule. However, an important recent development unifies these two approaches by showing that a relatively simple Hebbian rule can be viewed as the gradient of an interesting function. The function can therefore be viewed as a specification of what the learning is trying to achieve.

9.1. A recent development of unsupervised Hebbian learning

In a recent series of papers Linsker has shown that with proper normalization of the weight changes, an unsupervised Hebbian learning procedure in which the weight change depends on the correlation of presynaptic and postsynaptic activity can produce a surprising number of the known properties of the receptive fields of neurons in visual cortex, including center-surround fields [61], orientation-tuned fields [62] and orientation columns [63]. The procedure operates in a multi-layer network in which there is innate spatial structure so that the inputs to a unit in one layer tend to come from nearby locations in the layer below. Linsker demonstrates that the emergence of biologically suggestive receptive fields depends on the relative values of a few generic parameters. He also shows that for each unit, the learning procedure is performing gradient ascent in a measure whose main term is the ensemble average (across all the

[10] This method of weighting the statistics by some measure of the overall error or importance of a case can often be used to allow global measures of the performance of the whole network to influence local, unsupervised learning procedures.

various patterns of activity in the layer below) of

$$\sum_{i,j} w_i s_i w_j s_j \, ,$$

where w_i and w_j are the weights on the ith and jth input lines of a unit and s_i and s_j are the activities on those input lines.

It is not initially obvious why maximizing the pairwise covariances of the weighted activities produces receptive fields that are useful for visual information processing. Linsker does not discuss this question in his original three papers. However, he has now shown [64] that the learning procedure maximizes the variance in the activity of the postsynaptic unit subject to a "resource" constraint on overall synaptic strength. This is almost equivalent to maximizing the ratio of the postsynaptic variance to the sum of the squares of the weights, which is guaranteed to extract the first principal component (provided the units are linear). This component is the one that would minimize the sum-squared reconstruction error if we tried to reconstruct the activity vector of the presynaptic units from the activity level of the postsynaptic unit. Thus we can view Linsker's learning procedure as a way of ensuring that the activity of a unit conveys as much information as possible about its presynaptic input vector. A similar analysis can be applied to competitive learning (see Section 10).

10. Competitive Learning

Competitive learning is an unsupervised procedure that divides a set of input vectors into a number of disjoint clusters in such a way that the input vectors within each cluster are all similar to one another. It is called competitive learning because there is a set of hidden units which compete with one another to become active. There are many variations of the same basic idea, and only the simplest version is described here. When an input vector is presented to the network, the hidden unit which receives the greatest total input wins the competition and turns on with an activity level of 1. All the other hidden units turn off. The winning unit then adds a small fraction of the current input vector to its weight vector. So, in future, it will receive even more total input from this input vector. To prevent the same hidden unit from being the most active in all cases, it is necessary to impose a constraint on each weight vector that keeps the sum of the weights (or the sum of their squares) constant. So when a hidden unit becomes more sensitive to one input vector it becomes less sensitive to other input vectors.

Rumelhart and Zipser [82] present a simple geometrical model of competitive learning. If each input vector has three components and is of unit length it can be represented by a point on the surface of the unit sphere. If the weight vectors of the hidden units are also constrained to be of unit length, they too can be represented by points on the unit sphere as shown in Fig. 11. The

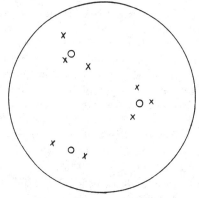

Fig. 11. The input vectors are represented by points marked "×" on the surface of a sphere. The weight vectors of the hidden units are represented by points marked "○." After competitive learning, each weight vector will be close to the center of gravity of a cluster of input vectors.

learning procedure is equivalent to finding the weight vector that is closest to the current input vector, and moving it closer still by an amount that is proportional to the distance. If the weight changes are sufficiently small, this process will stabilize when each weight vector is at the center of gravity of a cluster of input vectors.

We can think of the network as performing the following task: Represent the current input vector, y_c, as accurately as possible by using a single active hidden unit. The representation is simply the weight vector, w_c, of the hidden unit which is active in case c. If the weight changes are sufficiently small, this version of competitive learning performs steepest descent in a measure of the sum-squared inaccuracy of the representation. The solutions it finds are minima of the function

$$E = \tfrac{1}{2} \sum_c (w_c - y_c)^2 \, .$$

Although they use the geometrical analogy described above, Rumelhart and Zipser actually use a slightly different learning rule which cannot be interpreted as performing steepest descent in such a simple error function.

There are many variations of competitive learning in the literature [4, 29, 33, 95] and there is not space here to review them all. A model with similarities to competitive learning has been used by Willshaw and von der Malsburg [103] to explain the formation of topographic maps between the retina and the tectum. Recently, it has been shown that a variation of this model can be interpreted as performing steepest descent in an error function and can be applied to a range of optimization problems that involve topographic mappings between geometrical structures [23].

One major theme has been to show that competitive learning can produce topographic maps [57]. The hidden units are laid out in a spatial structure (usually two-dimensional) and instead of just updating the weight vector of the hidden unit that receives the greatest total input, the procedure also updates the weight vectors of adjacent hidden units. This encourages adjacent units to respond to similar input vectors, and it can be viewed as a way of performing gradient descent in a cost function that has two terms. The first term measures how inaccurately the weight vector of the most active hidden unit represents the input vector. The second term measures the dissimilarity between the input vectors that are represented by adjacent hidden units. Kohonen has shown that this version of competitive learning performs dimensionality reduction, so that surplus degrees of freedom are removed from the input vector and it is represented accurately by a point in a lower-dimensional space [57]. It is not clear how this compares in efficiency with self-supervised backpropagation (see Section 6.9) for dimensionality reduction.

Fukushima and Miyake [30] have demonstrated that a version of competitive learning can be used to allow a multi-layer network to recognize simple two-dimensional shapes in a number of different positions. After learning, the network can recognize a familiar shape in a novel position. The ability to generalize across position depends on using a network in which the layers of units that learn are interleaved with layers of nonlearning units which are prewired to generalize across position. Thus, the network does not truly learn translation invariance. By contrast, it is possible to design a backpropagation network that starts with no knowledge of the effects of translation and no knowledge of which input units are adjacent in the image. After sufficient experience, the network can correctly identify familiar, simple shapes in novel positions [39].

10.1. The relationship between competitive learning and backpropagation

Because it is performing gradient descent in a measure of how accurately the input vector could be reconstructed, competitive learning has a close relationship to self-supervised backpropagation. Consider a three-layer encoder network in which the desired states of the output units are the same as the actual states of the input units. Suppose that each weight from an input unit to a hidden unit is constrained to be identical to the weight from that hidden unit to the corresponding output unit. Suppose, also, that the output units are linear and the hidden units, instead of using the usual nonlinear input-output function, use the same "winner-take-all" nonlinearity as is used in competitive learning. So only one hidden unit will be active at a time, and the actual states of the output units will equal the weights of the active hidden unit. This makes it easy to compute the error derivatives of the weights from the hidden units to the output units. For weights from the active hidden unit the derivatives are simply proportional to the difference between the actual and desired outputs (which equals the difference between the weight and the corresponding component of the input vector). For weights from inactive hidden units the error derivatives are all zero. So gradient descent can be performed by making the weights of the active hidden unit regress towards the input vector, which is precisely what the competitive learning rule does.

Normally, backpropagation is needed in order to compute the error derivatives of the weights from the input units to the hidden units, but the winner-take-all nonlinearity makes backpropagation unnecessary in this network because all these derivatives are equal to zero. So long as the same hidden unit wins the competition, its activity level is not changed by changing its input weights. At the point where a small change in the weights would change the winner from one hidden unit to another, both hidden units fit the input vector equally well, so changing winners does not alter the total error in the output (even though it may change the output vector a lot). Because the error derivatives are so simple, we can still do the learning if we omit the output units altogether. This removes the output weights, and so we no longer need to constrain the input and output weights of a hidden unit to be identical. Thus the simplified version of competitive learning is a degenerate case of self-supervised backpropagation.

It would be interesting if a mechanism as simple as competitive learning could be used to implement gradient descent in networks that allow the m most activated hidden units to become fully active (where $m > 1$). This would allow the network to create more complex, distributed representations of the input vectors. Unfortunately the implementation is not nearly as simple because it is no longer possible to omit the output layer. The output units are needed to combine the effects of all the active hidden units and compare the combined effect with the input vector in order to compute the error derivatives of the output weights. Also, at the point at which one hidden unit ceases to be active and another becomes active, there may be a large change in the total error, so at this point there are infinite error derivatives for the weights from the input to the hidden units. It thus appears that the simplicity of the mechanism required for competitive learning is crucially dependent on the fact that only one hidden unit within a group is active.

11. Reinforcement Learning Procedures

There is a large and complex literature on reinforcement learning procedures which is beyond the scope of this paper. The main aim of this section is to give an informal description of a few of the recent ideas in the field that reveals their relationship to other types of connectionist learning.

A central idea in many reinforcement learning procedures is that we can assign credit to a local decision by *measuring* how it correlates with the global reinforcement signal. Various different values are tried for each local variable (such as a weight or a state), and these variations are correlated with variations in the global reinforcement signal. Normally, the local variations are the result of independent stochastic processes, so if enough samples are taken each local variable can average away the noise caused by the variation in the other variables to reveal its own effect on the global reinforcement signal (given the current average behavior of the other variables). The network can then perform gradient ascent in the expected reinforcement by altering the probability distribution of the value of each local variable in the direction that increases the expected reinforcement. If the probability distributions are altered after each trial, the network performs a stochastic version of gradient ascent.

The main advantage of reinforcement learning is that it is easy to implement because, unlike backpropagation which *computes* the effect of changing a local variable, the "credit assignment" does not require any special apparatus for *computing* derivatives. So reinforcement learning can be used in complex systems in which it would be very hard to analytically compute reinforcement derivatives. The main disadvantage of reinforcement learning is that it is very inefficient when there are more than a few local variables. Even in the trivial case when all the local variables contribute independently to the global reinforcement signal, $O(NM)$ trials are required to allow the measured effects of each of the M possible values of a variable to achieve a reasonable signal-to-noise ratio by averaging away the noise caused by the N other variables. So reinforcement learning is very inefficient for large systems unless they are divided into smaller modules. It is as if each person in the United States tried to decide whether he or she had done a useful day's work by observing the gross national product on a day-by-day basis.

A second disadvantage is that gradient ascent may get stuck in local optima. As a network concentrates more and more of its trials on combinations of values that give the highest expected reinforcement, it gets less and less information about the reinforcements caused by other combinations of values.

11.1. Delayed reinforcement

In many real systems, there is a delay between an action and the resultant reinforcement, so in addition to the normal problem of deciding how to assign credit to decisions about hidden variables, there is a temporal credit assignment problem [86]. If, for example, a person wants to know how their behavior affects the gross national product, they need to know whether to correlate today's GNP with what they did yesterday or with what they did five years ago. In the iterative version of backpropagation (Section 6.7), temporal credit assignment is performed by explicitly computing the effect of each activity level on the eventual outcome. In reinforcement learning procedures, temporal credit assignment is typically performed by learning to associate "secondary" reinforcement values with the states that are intermediate in time between the action and the external reinforcement. One important idea is to make the reinforcement value of an intermediate state regress towards the weighted average of the reinforcement values of its successors, where the weightings reflect the conditional probabilities of the successors. In the limit, this causes the reinforcement value of each state to be equal to the expected reinforcement of its successor, and hence equal to the expected final reinforcement.[11] Sutton [87] explains why, in a stochastic system, it is typically more efficient to regress towards the reinforcement value of the next state rather than the reinforcement value of the final outcome. Barto, Sutton and Anderson [15] have demonstrated the usefulness of this type of procedure for learning with delayed reinforcement.

11.2. The A_{R-P} procedure

One obvious way of mapping results from learning automata theory onto connectionist networks is to treat each unit as an automaton and to treat the states it adopts as its actions. Barto and Anandan [14] describe a learning procedure of this kind called "associative reward-penalty" or A_{R-P} which uses stochastic units like those in a Boltzmann machine (see (10)). They prove that if the input vectors are linearly independent and the network only contains one

---

[11] There may also be a "tax" imposed for failing to achieve the external reinforcement quickly. This can be implemented by reducing the reinforcement value each time it is regressed to an earlier state.

unit, A_{R-P} finds the optimal values of the weights. They also show empirically that if the same procedure is applied in a network of such units, the hidden units develop useful representations. Williams [101] has shown that a limiting case of the A_{R-P} procedure performs stochastic gradient ascent in expected reinforcement.

11.3. Achieving global optimality by reinforcement learning

Thatachar and Sastry [91] use a different mapping between automata and connectionist networks. Each *connection* is treated as an automaton and the weight values that it takes on are its actions. On each trial, each connection chooses a weight (from a discrete set of alternatives) and then the network maps an input vector into an output vector and receives positive reinforcement if the output is correct. They present a learning procedure for updating the probabilities of choosing particular weight values. If the probabilities are changed slowly enough, the procedure is guaranteed to converge on the globally optimal combination of weights, even if the network has hidden layers. Unfortunately their procedure requires exponential space because it involves storing and updating a table of estimated expected reinforcements that contains one entry for every combination of weights.

11.4. The relative payoff procedure

If we are content to reach a local optimum, it is possible to use a very simple learning procedure that uses yet another way of mapping automata onto connectionist networks. Each connection is treated as a stochastic switch that has a certain probability of being closed at any moment [66]. If the switch is open, the "postsynaptic" unit receives an input of 0 along that connection, but if the switch is closed it transmits the state of the "presynaptic" unit. A real synapse can be modeled as a set of these stochastic switches arranged in parallel. Each unit computes some fixed function of the vector of inputs that it receives on its incoming connections. Learning involves altering the switch probabilities to maximize the expected reinforcement signal.

A learning procedure called L_{R-I} can be applied in such networks. It is only guaranteed to find a local optimum of the expected reinforcement, but it is very simple to implement. A "trial" consists of four stages:

(1) Set the switch configuration. For each switch in the network, decide whether it is open or closed on this trial using the current switch probability. The decisions are made independently for all the switches.

(2) Run the network with this switch configuration. There are no constraints on the connectivity so cycles are allowed, and the units can also receive external inputs at any time. The constraint on the external inputs is that the probability distribution over patterns of external input must be stationary.

(3) Compute the reinforcement signal. This can be any nonnegative, stationary function of the behavior of the network and of the external input it received during the trial.

(4) Update the switch probabilities. For each switch that was closed during the trial, we increment its probability by $\varepsilon R(1-p)$, where R is the reinforcement produced by the trial, p is the switch probability and ε is a small coefficient. For each switch that was open, we decrement its probability by $\varepsilon R p$.

If ε is sufficiently small this procedure stochastically approximates hill climbing in expected reinforcement. The "batch" version of the procedure involves observing the reinforcement signal over a large number of trials before updating the switch probabilities. If a sufficient number of trials are observed, the following "relative payoff" update procedure always increases expected reinforcement (or leaves it unchanged): Change the switch probability to be equal to the fraction of the total reinforcement received when the switch was closed. This can cause large changes in the probabilities, and I know of no proof that it hill-climbs in expected reinforcement, but in practice it always works. The direction of the jump in switch probability space caused by the batch version of the procedure is the same as the expected direction of the small change in switch probabilities caused by the "online" version.

A variation of the relative payoff procedure can be used if the goal is to make the "responses" of a network match some desired probability distribution rather than maximize expected reinforcement. We simply define the reinforcement signal to be the desired probability of a response divided by the network's current probability of producing that response. If a sufficient number of trials are made before updating the switch probabilities, it can be shown (Larry Gillick and Jim Baker, personal communication) that this procedure is guaranteed to decrease an information-theoretic measure of the difference between the desired probability distribution over responses and the actual probability distribution. The measure is actually the G measure described in (11) and the proof is an adaptation of the proof of the EM procedure [22].

11.5. Genetic algorithms

Holland and his co-workers [21, 48] have investigated a class of learning procedures which they call "genetic algorithms" because they are explicitly inspired by an analogy with evolution. Genetic algorithms operate on a population of individuals to produce a better adapted population. In the simplest case, each individual member of the population is a binary vector, and the two possible values of each component are analogous to two alternative versions (alleles) of a gene. There is a fitness function which assigns a real-valued fitness to each individual and the aim of the "learning" is to raise the average fitness of the population. New individuals are produced by choosing two existing individuals as parents (with a bias towards individuals of higher than average fitness) and copying some component values from one parent and some from the other. Holland [48] has shown that for a large class of fitness functions, this is an effective way of discovering individuals that have high fitness.

11.6. Genetic learning and the relative payoff rule

If an entire generation of individuals is simultaneously replaced by a generation of their offspring, genetic learning has a close relationship to the batch form of the L_{R-I} procedure described in Section 11.4. This is most easily understood by starting with a particularly simple version of genetic learning in which every individual in generation $t + 1$ has many different parents in generation t. Candidate individuals for generation $t + 1$ are generated from the existing individuals in generation t in the following way: To decide the value of the ith component of a candidate, we randomly choose one of the individuals in generation t and copy the value of its ith component. So the probability that the ith component of a candidate has a particular value is simply the relative frequency of that value in generation t. A selection process then operates on the candidates: Some are kept to form generation $t + 1$ and others are discarded. The fitness of a candidate is simply the probability that it is not discarded by the selection process. Candidates that are kept can be considered to have received a reinforcement of 1 and candidates that are discarded receive a reinforcement of 0. After selection, the probability that the ith component has a particular value is equal to the fraction of the successful candidates that have that value. This is exactly the relative payoff rule described in Section 11.4. The probabilities it operates on are the relative frequencies of alleles in the population instead of switch probabilities.

If the value of every component is determined by an independently chosen parent, information about the correlations between the values of different components is lost when generation $t + 1$ is produced from generation t. If, however, we use just two parents we maximize the tendency for the pairwise and higher-order correlations to be preserved. This tendency is further increased if components whose correlations are important are near one another and the values of nearby components are normally taken from the same parent. So a population of individuals can effectively represent the probabilities of small combinations of component values as well as the probabilities of individual values. Genetic learning works well when the fitness of an individual is determined by these small combinations, which Holland calls critical schemas.

11.7. Iterated genetic hill climbing

It is possible to combine genetic learning with gradient descent (or hill climbing) to get a hybrid learning procedure called "iterated genetic hill climbing" or "IGH" that works better than either learning procedure alone [1, 17]. IGH is as a form of multiple restart hill climbing in which the starting points, instead of being chosen at random, are chosen by "mating" previously discovered local optima. Alternatively, it can be viewed as genetic learning in which each new individual is allowed to perform hill climbing in the fitness function before being evaluated and added to the population. Ackley [1] shows that a stochastic variation of IGH can be implemented in a connectionist network that is trying to learn which output vector produces a high enough payoff to satisfy some external criterion.

12. Discussion

This review has focused on a small number of recent connectionist learning procedures. There are many other interesting procedures which have been omitted [24, 26, 34, 35, 47, 54, 94]. In particular, there has been no discussion of a large class of procedures which dynamically allocate new units instead of simply adjusting the weights in a fixed architecture. Rather than attempting to cover all of these I conclude by discussing two major problems that plague most of the procedures I have described.

12.1. Generalization

A major goal of connectionist learning is to produce networks that generalize correctly to new cases after training on a sufficiently large set of typical cases from some domain. In much of the research, there is no formal definition of what it means to generalize correctly. The network is trained on examples from a domain that the experimenter understands (like the family relationships domain described in Section 6) and it is judged to generalize correctly if its generalizations agree with those of the experimenter. This is sufficient as an informal demonstration that the network can indeed perform nontrivial generalization, but it gives little insight into the reasons why the generalizations of the network and the experimenter agree, and so it does not allow predictions to be made about when networks will generalize correctly and when they will fail.

What is needed is a formal theory of what it means to generalize correctly. One approach that has been used in studying the induction of grammars is to define a hypothesis space of possible grammars, and to show that with enough training cases the system will converge on the correct grammar with probability 1 [8]. Valiant [93] has recently introduced a rather more subtle criterion of success in order to distinguish classes of boolean function that can be induced from examples in polynomial time from classes that require exponential time. He assumes that the hypothesis space is known in advance and he allows the training cases to be selected according to *any* stationary distribution but insists that the same distribution be used to generate the test cases. The induced function is considered to be good enough if it differs from the true function on less than a small fraction, $1/h$, of the test cases. A class of boolean functions is considered to be learnable in polynomial time if, for any choice of h, there is a probability of at least $(1 - 1/h)$ that the induced function is good enough after a number of training examples that is polynomial in both h and the number of arguments of the boolean function. Using this definition, Valiant has succeeded in showing that several interesting subclasses of boolean function are learnable in polynomial time. Our understanding of other connectionist learning procedures would be considerably improved if we could derive similar results that were as robust against variations in the distribution of the training examples.

The work on inducing grammars or boolean functions may not provide an appropriate framework for studying systems that learn inherently stochastic functions, but the general idea of starting with a hypothesis space of possible functions carries over. A widely used statistical approach involves maximizing the a posteriori likelihood of the model (i.e. the function) given the data. If the data really is generated by a function in the hypothesis space and if the amount of information in the training data greatly exceeds the amount of information required to specify a point in the hypothesis space, the maximum likelihood function is very probably the correct one, so the network will then generalize correctly. Some connectionist learning schemes (e.g. the Boltzmann machine learning procedure) can be made to fit this approach exactly. If a Boltzmann machine is trained with much more data than there are weights in the machine, and if it really does find the global minimum of G, and if the correct answer lies in the hypothesis space (which is defined by the architecture of the machine),[12] then there is every reason to suppose that it will generalize correctly, even if it has only been trained on a small fraction of the *possible* cases. Unfortunately, this kind of guarantee is of little use for practical problems where we usually know in advance that the "true" model does not lie in the hypothesis space of the network. What needs to be shown is that the best available point within the hypothesis space (even though it is not a perfect model) will also generalize well to test cases.

A simple thought experiment shows that the "correct" generalization from a set of training cases, however it is defined, must depend on how the input and output vectors are encoded. Consider a mapping, M_I, from entire input vectors onto entire input vectors and a mapping, M_O, from entire output vectors onto entire output vectors. If we introduce a precoding stage that uses M_I and a postcoding stage that uses M_O we can convert a network that generalizes in one way into a network that generalizes in any other way we choose simply by choosing M_I and M_O appropriately.

12.2. Practical methods of improving generalization

One very useful method of improving the generalization of many connectionist learning procedures is to introduce an extra term into the error function. This term penalizes large weights and it can be viewed as a way of building in an a priori bias is favor of simple models (i.e. models in which there are not too many strong interactions between the variables). If the extra term is the sum of the squares of the weights, its derivative corresponds to "weight decay"—each weight continually decays towards zero by an amount proportional to its magnitude. When the learning has equilibrated, the magnitude of a weight is equal to its error derivative because this error derivative balances the weight decay. This often makes it easier to interpret the weights. Weight decay tends to prevent a network from using table lookup and forces it to discover regularities in the training data. In a simple linear network without hidden units, weight decay can be used to find the weight matrix that minimizes the effect of adding zero-mean, uncorrelated noise to the input units [60].

Another useful method is to impose equality constraints between weights that encode symmetries in the task. In solving any practical problem, it is wasteful to make the network learn information that is known in advance. If possible, this information should be encoded by the architecture or the initial weights so that the training data can be used to learn aspects of the task that we do not already know how to model.

---

[12] One popular idea is that evolution implicitly chooses an appropriate hypothesis space by constraining the architecture of the network and learning then identifies the most likely hypothesis within this space. How evolution arrives at sensible hypothesis spaces in reasonable time is usually unspecified. The evolutionary search for good architectures may actually be guided by learning [43].

12.3. The speed of learning

Most existing connectionist learning procedures are slow, particularly procedures that construct complicated internal representations. One way to speed them up is to use optimization methods such as recursive least squares that converge faster. If the second derivatives can be computed or estimated they can be used to pick a direction for the weight change vector that yields faster convergence than the direction of steepest descent [71]. It remains to be seen how well such methods work for the error surfaces generated by multi-layer networks learning complex tasks.

A second method of speeding up learning is to use dedicated hardware for each connection and to map the inner-loop operations into analog instead of digital hardware. As Alspector and Allen [3] have demonstrated, the speed of one particular learning procedure can be increased by a factor of about a million if we combine these techniques. This significantly increases our ability to explore the behavior of relatively small systems, but it is not a panacea. By using silicon in a different way we typically gain a large but constant factor (optical techniques may eventually yield a *huge* constant factor), and by dedicating a processor to each of the N connections we gain at most a factor of N in time at the cost of at least a factor of N in space. For a learning procedure with a time complexity of, say, $O(N \log N)$ a speed up of N makes a very big difference. For a procedure with a complexity of, say, $O(N^3)$ alternative technologies and parallelism will help significantly for small systems, but not for large ones.[13]

12.4. Hardware modularity

One of the best and commonest ways of fighting complexity is to introduce a modular, hierarchical structure in which different modules are only loosely coupled [85]. Pearl [72] has shown that if the interactions between a set of probabilistic variables are constrained to form a tree structure, there are efficient parallel methods for estimating the interactions between "hidden" variables. The leaves of the tree are the observables and the higher-level nodes are hidden. The probability distribution for each variable is constrained by the values of its immediate parents in the tree. Pearl shows that these conditional probabilities can be recovered in time $O(N \log N)$ from the pairwise correlations between the values of the leaves of the tree. Remarkably, it is also possible to recover the tree structure itself in the same time.

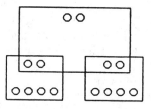

Fig. 12. The lower-level variables of a high-level module are the higher-level variables of several low-level modules.

Self-supervised backpropagation (see Section 6.9) was originally designed to allow efficient bottom-up learning in domains where there is hierarchical modular structure. Consider, for example, an ensemble of input vectors that are generated in the following modular way: Each module has a few high-level variables whose values help to constrain the values of a larger number of low-level variables. The low-level variables of each module are partitioned into several sets, and each set is identified with the high-level variables of a lower module as shown in Fig. 12.

---

[13] Tsotsos [92] makes similar arguments in a discussion of the space complexity of vision.

Now suppose that we treat the values of all the low-level variables of the leaf modules as a single input vector. Given a sufficiently large ensemble of input vectors and an "innate" knowledge of the architecture of the generator, it should be possible to recover the underlying structure by using self-supervised backpropagation to learn compact codes for the low-level variables of each leaf module. It is possible to learn codes for all the lowest-level modules in parallel. Once this has been done, the network can learn codes at the next level up the hierarchy. The time taken to learn the whole hierarchical structure (given parallel hardware) is just proportional to the depth of the tree and hence it is $O(\log N)$ where N is the size of the input vector. An improvement on this strictly bottom-up scheme is described by Ballard [11]. He shows why it is helpful to allow top-down influences from more abstract representations to less abstract ones, and presents a working simulation.

12.5. Other types of modularity

There are several other helpful types of modularity that do not necessarily map so directly onto modular hardware but are nevertheless important for fast learning and good generalization. Consider a system which solves hard problems by creating its own subgoals. Once a subgoal has been created, the system can learn how best to satisfy it and this learning can be useful (on other occasions) even if it was a mistake to create that subgoal on this particular occasion. So the assignment of credit to the decision to create a subgoal can be decoupled from the assignment of credit to the actions taken to achieve the subgoal. Since the ability to achieve the subgoals can be learned separately from the knowledge about when they are appropriate, a system can use achievable subgoals as building blocks for more complex procedures. This avoids the problem of learning the complex procedures from scratch. It may also constrain the way in which the complex procedures will be generalized to new cases, because the knowledge about how to achieve each subgoal may already include knowledge about how to cope with variations. By using subgoals we can increase modularity and improve generalization even in systems which use the very same hardware for solving the subgoal as was used for solving the higher-level goal. Using subgoals, it may even be possible to develop reasonably fast reinforcement learning procedures for large systems.

There is another type of relationship between easy and hard tasks that can facilitate learning. Sometimes a hard task can be decomposed into a set of easier constituents, but other times a hard task may just be a version of an easier task that requires finer discrimination. For example, throwing a ball in the general direction of another person is much easier than throwing it through a hoop, and a good way to train a system to throw it through a hoop is to start by training it to throw it in the right general direction. This relation between easy and hard tasks is used extensively in "shaping" the behavior of animals and should also be useful for connectionist networks (particularly those that use reinforcement learning). It resembles the use of multi-resolution techniques to speed up search in computer vision [89]. Having learned the coarse task, the weights should be close to a point in weight space where minor adjustments can tune them to perform the finer task.

One application where this technique should be helpful is in learning filters that discriminate between very similar sounds. The approximate shapes of the filters can be learned using spectrograms that have low resolution in time and frequency, and then the resolution can be increased to allow the filters to resolve fine details. By introducing a "regularization" term that penalizes filters which have very different weights for adjacent cells in the high resolution spectrogram, it may be possible to allow filters to "attend" to fine detail when necessary without incurring the cost of estimating all the weights from scratch. The regularization term encodes prior knowledge that good filters should generally be smooth and so it reduces the amount of information that must be extracted from the training data.

12.6. Conclusion

There are now many different connectionist learning procedures that can construct appropriate internal representations in small domains, and it is likely that many more variations will be discovered in the next few years. Major new advances can be expected on a number of fronts: Techniques for making the learning time scale better may be developed; attempts to apply connectionist procedures to difficult tasks like speech recognition may actually succeed; new technologies may make it possible to simulate much larger networks; and finally the computational insights gained from studying connectionist systems may prove useful in interpreting the behavior of real neural networks.

ACKNOWLEDGMENT

This research was funded by grant IS8520359 from the National Science Foundation and by contract N00014-86-K-00167 from the Office of Naval Research. I thank Dana Ballard, Andrew Barto, David Rumelhart, Terry Sejnowski, and the members of the Carnegie-Mellon Boltzmann Group for many helpful discussions. Geoffrey Hinton is a fellow of the Canadian Institute for Advanced Research.

REFERENCES

1. Ackley, D.H., Stochastic iterated genetic hill-climbing, Ph.D. Thesis, Carnegie-Mellon University, Pittsburgh, PA (1987).
2. Ackley, D.H., Hinton, G.E. and Sejnowski, T.J., A learning algorithm for Boltzmann machines, *Cognitive Sci.* **9** (1985) 147–169.
3. Alspector, J. and Allen, R.B., A neuromorphic VLSI learning system, in: P. Loseleben (Ed.), *Advanced Research in VLSI: Proceedings of the 1987 Stanford Conference* (MIT Press, Cambridge, MA, 1987).
4. Amari, S.-I., Field theory of self-organizing neural nets, *IEEE Trans. Syst. Man Cybern.* **13** (1983) 741–748.
5. Amari, S.-I., A theory of adaptive pattern classifiers, *IEEE Trans. Electron. Comput.* **16** (1967) 299–307.
6. Anderson, J.A. and Hinton, G.E., Models of information processing in the brain, in: G.E. Hinton and J.A. Anderson (Eds.), *Parallel Models of Associative Memory* (Erlbaum, Hillsdale, NJ, 1981).
7. Anderson, J.A. and Mozer, M.C., Categorization and selective neurons, in: G.E. Hinton and J.A. Anderson (Eds.), *Parallel Models of Associative Memory* (Erlbaum, Hillsdale, NJ, 1981).
8. Angluin, D. and Smith, C.H., Inductive inference: Theory and methods, *Comput. Surv.* **15** (1983) 237–269.
9. Bahl, L.R., Jelinek, F. and Mercer, R.L., A maximum likelihood approach to continuous speech recognition, *IEEE Trans. Pattern Anal. Mach. Intell.* **5** (1983) 179–190.
10. Ballard, D.H., Cortical connections and parallel processing: Structure and function, *Behav. Brain Sci.* **9** (1986) 67–120.
11. Ballard, D.H., Modular learning in neural networks, in: *Proceedings AAAI-87*, Seattle, WA (1987) 279–284.
12. Ballard, D.H., Hinton, G.E. and Sejnowski, T.J., Parallel visual computation, *Nature* **306** (1983) 21–26.
13. Barlow, H.B., Single units and sensation: A neuron doctrine for perceptual psychology? *Perception* **1** (1972) 371–394.
14. Barto, A.G. and Anandan, P., Pattern recognizing stochastic learning automata, *IEEE Trans. Syst. Man Cybern.* **15** (1985) 360–375.
15. Barto, A.G., Sutton, R.S. and Anderson, C.W., Neuronlike elements that solve difficult learning control problems, *IEEE Trans. Syst. Man Cybern.* **13** (1983).
16. Bienenstock, E.L., Cooper, L.N. and Munro, P.W., Theory for the development of neuron selectivity: Orientation specificity and binocular interaction in visual cortex, *J. Neurosci.* **2** (1982) 32–48.
17. Brady, R.M., Optimization strategies gleaned from biological evolution, *Nature* **317** (1985) 804–806.
18. Cooper, L.N., Liberman, F. and Oja, E., A theory for the acquisition and loss of neuron specificity in visual cortex, *Biol. Cybern.* **33** (1979) 9–28.
19. Cottrell, G.W., Munro, P. and Zipser, D., Learning internal representations from gray-scale images: An example of extensional programming, in: *Proceedings Ninth Annual Conference of the Cognitive Science Society* Seattle, WA (1987) 461–473.
20. Crick, F. and Mitchison, G., The function of dream sleep, *Nature* **304** (1983) 111–114.
21. Davis, L. (Ed.), *Genetic Algorithms and Simulated Annealing* (Pitman, London, 1987).
22. Dempster, A.P., Laird, N.M. and Rubin, D.B., Maximum likelihood from incomplete data via the EM algorithm, *Proc. Roy. Stat. Soc.* (1976) 1–38.
23. Durbin, R. and Willshaw, D., The elastic net method: An analogue approach to the travelling salesman problem, *Nature* **326** (1987) 689–691.

24. Edelman, G.M. and Reeke, G.N., Selective networks capable of representative transformations, limited generalizations, and associative memory, *Proc. Nat. Acad. Sci. USA* **79** (1982) 2091–2095.

25. Elman, J.L. and Zipser, D., Discovering the hidden structure of speech, Tech. Rept. No. 8701, Institute for Cognitive Science, University of California, San Diego, CA (1987).

26. Feldman, J.A., Dynamic connections in neural networks, *Biol. Cybern.* **46** (1982) 27–39.

27. Feldman, J.A., Neural representation of conceptual knowledge, Tech. Rept. TR189, Department of Computer Science, University of Rochester, Rochester, NY (1986).

28. Feldman, J.A. and Ballard, D.H., Connectionist models and their properties, *Cognitive Sci.* **6** (1982) 205–254.

29. Fukushima, K., Cognitron: A self-organizing multilayered neural network, *Biol. Cybern.* **20** (1975) 121–136.

30. Fukushima, K. and Miyake, S., Neocognitron: A new algorithm for pattern recognition tolerant of deformations and shifts in position, *Pattern Recogn.* **15** (1982) 455–469.

31. Geman, S. and Geman, D., Stochastic relaxation, Gibbs distributions, and the Bayesian restoration of images, *IEEE Trans. Pattern Anal. Mach. Intell.* **6** (1984) 721–741.

32. Golden, R.M., A unified framework for connectionist systems, Manuscript, Learning Research and Development Center, University of Pittsburgh, Pittsburgh, PA (1987).

33. Grossberg, S., Adaptive pattern classification and universal recoding, I: Parallel development and coding of neural feature detectors, *Biol. Cybern.* **23** (1976) 121–134.

34. Grossberg, S., How does the brain build a cognitive code? *Psychol. Rev.* **87** (1980) 1–51.

35. Hampson, S.E. and Volper, D.J., Disjunctive models of boolean category learning, *Biol. Cybern.* **55** (1987) 1–17.

36. Hebb, D.O., *The Organization of Behavior* (Wiley, New York, 1949).

37. Hinton, G.E., Implementing semantic networks in parallel hardware, in: G.E. Hinton and J.A. Anderson (Eds.), *Parallel Models of Associative Memory* (Erlbaum, Hillsdale, NJ, 1981).

38. Hinton, G.E., Learning distributed representations of concepts, in: *Proceedings Eighth Annual Conference of the Cognitive Science Society*, Amherst, MA (1986).

39. Hinton, G.E., Learning translation invariant recognition in a massively parallel network, in: *PARLE: Parallel Architectures and Languages Europe* **1** (Springer, Berlin, 1987) 1–14.

40. Hinton, G.E. and Anderson J.A., (Eds.), *Parallel Models of Associative Memory* (Erlbaum, Hillsdale, NJ, 1981).

41. Hinton, G.E. and McClelland, J.L., Learning representations by recirculation, in: D.Z. Anderson (Ed.), *Neural Information Processing Systems* (American Institute of Physics, New York, 1988).

42. Hinton, G.E., McClelland, J.L. and Rumelhart, D.E., Distributed representations, in: D.E. Rumelhart, J.L. McClelland and the PDP Research Group (Eds.), *Parallel Distributed Processing: Explorations in the Microstructure of Cognition*, I: *Foundations* (MIT Press, Cambridge, MA, 1986).

43. Hinton, G.E. and Nowlan, S.J., How learning can guide evolution, *Complex Syst.* **1** (1987) 495–502.

44. Hinton, G.E. and Plaut, D.C., Using fast weights to deblur old memories, in: *Proceedings Ninth Annual Conference of the Cognitive Science Society*, Seattle, WA (1987).

45. Hinton, G.E. and Sejnowski, T.J., Optimal perceptual inference, in: *Proceedings IEEE Conference on Computer Vision and Pattern Recognition*, Washington, DC (1983) 448–453.

46. Hinton, G.E. and Sejnowski, T.J., Learning and relearning in Boltzmann machines, in: D.E. Rumelhart, J.L. McClelland and the PDP Research Group (Eds.), *Parallel Distributed Processing: Explorations in the Microstructure of Cognition*, I: *Foundations* (MIT Press, Cambridge, MA, 1986).

47. Hogg, T. and Huberman, B.A., Understanding biological computation: Reliable learning and recognition, *Proc. Nat. Acad. Sci. USA* **81** (1984) 6871–6875.

48. Holland, J.H., *Adaptation in Natural and Artificial Systems* (University of Michigan Press, Ann Arbor, MI, 1975).

49. Hopfield, J.J., Neural networks and physical systems with emergent collective computational abilities, *Proc. Nat. Acad. Sci. USA* **79** (1982) 2554–2558.

50. Hopfield, J.J., Feinstein, D.I. and Palmer, R.G., "Unlearning" has a stabilizing effect in collective memories, *Nature* **304** (1983).

51. Hopfield, J.J. and Tank, D.W., "Neural" computation of decisions in optimization problems, *Biol. Cybern.* **52** (1985) 141–152.

52. Hummel, R.A. and Zucker, S.W., On the foundations of relaxation labeling processes, *IEEE Trans. Pattern Anal. Mach. Intell.* **5** (1983) 267–287.

53. Judd, J.S., Complexity of connectionist learning with various node functions, COINS Tech. Rept. 87-60, University of Amherst, Amherst, MA (1987).

54. Kerszberg, M. and Bergman, A., The evolution of data processing abilities in competing automata, in: *Proceedings Conference on Computer Simulation in Brain Science*, Copenhagen, Denmark (1986).

55. Kirkpatrick, S., Gelatt, C.D. and Vecchi, M.P., Optimization by simulated annealing, *Science* **220** (1983) 671–680.

56. Kohonen, T., *Associative Memory: A System-Theoretical Approach* (Springer, Berlin, 1977).

57. Kohonen, T., Clustering, taxonomy, and topological maps of patterns, in: *Proceedings Sixth International Conference on Pattern Recognition*, Munich, F.R.G. (1982).

58. Lang, K.J., Connectionist speech recognition, Thesis proposal, Carnegie-Mellon University, Pittsburgh, PA (1987).

59. Le Cun, Y., A learning scheme for asymmetric threshold networks, in: *Proceedings Cognitiva 85*, Paris, France (1985) 599–604.

60. Le Cun, Y., Modèles connexionnistes de l'apprentissage, Ph.D. Thesis, Université Pierre et Marie Curie, Paris, France (1987).

61. Linsker, R., From basic network principles to neural architecture: Emergence of spatial opponent cells, *Proc. Nat. Acad. Sci. USA* **83** (1986) 7508–7512.

62. Linsker, R., From basic network principles to neural architecture: Emergence of orientation-selective cells, *Proc. Nat. Acad. Sci. USA* **83** (1986) 8390–8394.

63. Linsker, R., From basic network principles to neural architecture: Emergence of orientation columns, *Proc. Nat. Acad. Sci. USA* **83** (1986) 8779–8783.

64. Linsker, R., Development of feature-analyzing cells and their columnar organization in a layered self-adaptive network, in: R. Cotterill (Ed.), *Computer Simulation in Brain Science* (Cambridge University Press, Cambridge, 1987).

65. Marroquin, J.L., Probabilistic solution of inverse problems, Ph.D. Thesis, MIT, Cambridge, MA (1985).

66. Minsky, M.L., Theory of neural-analog reinforcement systems and its application to the brain-model problem, Ph.D. Dissertation, Princeton University, Princeton, NJ (1954).

67. Minsky, M.L., Plain talk about neurodevelopmental epistemology, in: *Proceedings IJCAI-77*, Cambridge, MA (1977) 1083–1092.

68. Minsky, M.L. and Papert, S., *Perceptrons* (MIT Press, Cambridge, MA, 1969).

69. Munro, P.W., A dual back-propagation scheme for scalar reinforcement learning, in: *Proceedings Ninth Annual Conference of the Cognitive Science Society*, Seattle, WA (1987).

70. Parker, D.B., Learning-logic, Tech. Rept. TR-47, Sloan School of Management, MIT, Cambridge, MA (1985).

71. Parker, D.B., Second order back-propagation: An optimal adaptive algorithm for any adaptive network, Unpublished manuscript (1987).

72. Pearl, J., Fusion, propagation, and structuring in belief networks, *Artificial Intelligence* **29** (1986) 241–288.

73. Pearlmutter, B.A. and Hinton, G.E., G-maximization: An unsupervised learning procedure for discovering regularities, in: J.S. Denker (Ed.), *Neural Networks for Computing: American Institute of Physics Conference Proceedings* **151** (American Institute of Physics, New York, 1986) 333–338.

74. Peterson, C. and Anderson, J.R., A mean field theory learning algorithm for neural networks, MCC Tech. Rept. EI-259-87, Microelectronics and Computer Technology Corporation, Austin, TX (1987).

75. Plaut, D.C. and Hinton, G.E., Learning sets of filters using back-propagation, *Comput. Speech Lang.* **2** (1987) 36–61.

76. Prager, R., Harrison, T.D. and Fallside, F., Boltzmann machines for speech recognition, *Comput. Speech Lang*, **1** (1986) 1–20.

77. Rosenblatt, F., *Principles of Neurodynamics* (Spartan Books, New York, 1962).

78. Rumelhart, D.E. and McClelland, J.L., On the acquisition of the past tense in English, in: J.L. McClelland, D.E. Rumelhart and the PDP Research Group (Eds.), *Parallel Distributed Processing: Explorations in the Microstructure of Cognition*, II: *Applications* (MIT Press, Cambridge, MA, 1986).

79. Rumelhart, D.E., McClelland, J.L. and the PDP Research Group (Eds.), *Parallel Distributed Processing: Explorations in the Microstructure of Cognition*, I: *Foundations* (MIT Press, Cambridge, MA, 1986).

80. Rumelhart, D.E., Hinton, G.E. and Williams, R.J., Learning internal representations by back-propagating errors, *Nature* **323** (1986) 533–536.

81. Rumelhart, D.E., Hinton, G.E. and Williams, R.J., Learning internal representations by error propagation, in: D.E. Rumelhart, J.L. McClelland and the PDP Research Group (Eds.), *Parallel Distributed Processing: Explorations in the Microstructure of Cognition*, I: *Foundations* (MIT Press, Cambridge, MA, 1986).

82. Rumelhart, D.E. and Zipser, D., Competitive learning, *Cognitive Sci.* **9** (1985) 75–112.

83. Saund, E., Abstraction and representation of continuous variables in connectionist networks, in: *Proceedings AAAI-86*, Philadelphia, PA (1986) 638–644.

84. Sejnowski, T.J. and Rosenberg, C.R., Parallel networks that learn to pronounce English text, *Complex Syst.* **1** (1987) 145–168.

85. Simon, H.A., *The Sciences of the Artificial* (MIT Press, Cambridge, MA, 1969).

86. Sutton, R.S., Temporal credit assignment in reinforcement learning, Ph.D. Thesis, COINS Tech. Rept. 84-02, University of Massachusetts, Amherst, MA (1984).

87. Sutton, R.S., Learning to predict by the method of temporal differences, Tech. Rept. TR87-509.1, GTE Laboratories, Waltham, MA (1987).

88. Tank, D.W. and Hopfield, J.J., Neural computation by concentrating information in time, *Proc. Nat. Acad. Sci. USA* **84** (1987) 1896–1900.

89. Terzopoulos, D., Multiresolution computation of visible surface representations., Ph.D. Dissertation, Department of Electrical Engineering and Computer Science, MIT, Cambridge MA (1984).

90. Tesauro, G., Scaling relationships in back-propagation learning: Dependence on training set size, *Complex Syst.* **2** (1987) 367–372.

91. Thatachar, M.A.L. and Sastry, P.S., Learning optimal discriminant functions through a cooperative game of automata, Tech. Rept. EE/64/1985, Department of Electrical Engineering, Indian Institute of Science, Bangalore, India (1985).

92. Tsotsos, J.K., A "complexity level" analysis of vision, in: *Proceedings First International Conference on Computer Vision*, London (1987) 346–355.

93. Valiant, L.G., A theory of the learnable, *Commun. ACM* **27** (1984) 1134–1142.

94. Volper, D.J. and Hampson, S.E., Connectionist models of boolean category representation, *Biol. Cybern.* **54** (1986) 393–406.

95. von der Malsburg, C., Self-organization of orientation sensitive cells in striate cortex, *Kybernetik* **14** (1973) 85–100.

96. von der Malsburg, C., The correlation theory of brain function. Internal Rept. 81-2, Department of Neurobiology, Max-Plank Institute for Biophysical Chemistry, Göttingen, F.R.G. (1981).

97. Waibel, A., Hanazawa, T., Hinton, G., Shikano, K. and Lang, K., Phoneme recognition using time-delay neural networks, Tech. Rept. TR-1-0006, ATR Interpreting Telephony Research Laboratories, Japan (1987).

98. Werbos, P.J., Beyond regression: New tools for prediction and analysis in the behavioral sciences, Ph.D. Thesis, Harvard University, Cambridge, MA (1974).

99. Widrow, B. and Hoff, M.E., Adaptive switching circuits, in: *IRE WESCON Conv. Record* **4** (1960) 96–104.

100. Widrow, B. and Stearns, S.D., *Adaptive Signal Processing* (Prentice-Hall, Englewood Cliffs, NJ, 1985).

101. Williams, R.J., Reinforcement learning in connectionist networks: A mathematical analysis, Tech. Rept., Institute for Cognitive Science, University of California San Diego, La Jolla, CA (1986).

102. Willshaw, D., Holography, associative memory, and inductive generalization, in: G.E. Hinton and J.A. Anderson (Eds.), *Parallel Models of Associative Memory* (Erlbaum, Hillsdale, NJ, 1981).

103. Willshaw, D.J. and von der Malsburg, C., A marker induction mechanism for the establishment of ordered neural mapping: Its application to the retino-tectal connections, *Philos. Trans. Roy. Soc. Lond. B* **287** (1979) 203–243.

Dynamic Connections in Neural Networks

Jerome A. Feldman

Computer Science Department, University of Rochester, Rochester, USA

Abstract. Massively parallel (neural-like) networks are receiving increasing attention as a mechanism for expressing information processing models. By exploiting powerful primitive units and stability-preserving construction rules, various workers have been able to construct and test quite complex models, particularly in vision research. But all of the detailed technical work was concerned with the structure and behavior of *fixed* networks. The purpose of this paper is to extend the methodology to cover several aspects of change and memory.

1. Introduction

For a variety of reasons, there is currently a broadening of interest in massively parallel computation structures like neural networks. Technological reasons for this include the growing ability to synthesize massively parallel computers and the fact that individual circuit speeds are nearing their limit. Several workers in Psychology (Dell, 1981; McClelland and Rumelhart, 1981) and Artificial Intelligence (Marr and Poggio, 1976; Hanson and Riseman, 1978) have found parallel models that better suit their scientific goals. Computational complexity theory shows that sequential computers of neuronal speeds could not approach human reaction times. In addition, rapid progress in the neurosciences has allowed researchers in these fields to consider the system properties of the networks under investigation (Barlow, 1981; Richter and Ullman, 1982).

The most striking common features of this line of work is the attempt to match specific computational models to detailed behavioral data. Although there has been some work along these lines for years (Dev, 1975), recent efforts are much more ambitious and sophisticated. One result of these various efforts is the development of new mathematical and computational tools for dealing with neural-net like models. A crude characterization of the methodology is that it emphasizes discrete structures which can be composed rather like digital circuits. As with digital circuits, the idea is to design in such a way as to minimize instability and other non-controllable behavior. Work on specific and general problems in neural-level modeling is producing a variety of new methods for computing reliably and efficiently with massively parallel systems (Feldman and Ballard, 1982; Fahlman, 1982; Hinton and Anderson, 1981). These techniques have permitted the construction of much more complex neural-level models than was previously possible (Sabbah, 1981). Ambitious neural-level modeling efforts are underway at several laboratories, but all of the current efforts rely on networks which are totally pre-specified.

The purpose of this paper is to suggest a general way of treating immediate and long-term change in connectionist neural models. All of the specific modeling efforts mentioned above assume that the computational power of the network arises directly from its connection structure and not through complex symbollic signals or a higher-level interpreter. The connectionist assumption is the only current theory consistent with the biological, computational and behavioral constraints on the system. The classic difficulty with connectionist models is change – How could a hard-wired system directly encode rapidly changing information? We will describe some general ways of solving this "dynamic connection" problem for models that assume slow change of synaptic weights as the only plasticity in the system. The solutions incorporate both immediate and permanent change and appear to be both biologically and computationally plausible.

The dynamic connection algorithms are development in the context of a specific connectionist modeling formalism that is being used in many specific tasks. Section 2 contains a brief description of the formalism and examples of useful fixed networks. Section 3 describes in detail how a uniform interconnection structure can rapidly capture an arbitrary permutation of connections between two layers of units. Section 4 shows how one can approximate this result with random networks. An extension of the random interconnection network suggests a way in which concept learning could occur with direct connections. Section 5 indicates how conventional weight-changing algorithms could be employed to make dynamic changes permanent.

2. Definitions and Notation

2.1. Units

The first step in a careful study of parallel networks is to define an abstract computing unit. Our unit is rather more general than previous proposals and is intended to capture the current understanding of the information processing capabilities of neurons. Among the key ideas are local memory, non-homogeneous and non-linear functions, and the notions of mutual inhibition and stable coalitions.

A *unit* is a computational entity comprising

$\{q\}$ a set of *discrete states*, < 10
p a continuous value in $[-10, 10]$, called *potential* (accuracy of several digits)
v an *output value*, integers $0 \leq v \leq 9$
$\mathbf{i}$ a vector of *inputs* $i_1, \dots, i_n$

and functions from old to new values of these

$$p \leftarrow f(\mathbf{i}, p, q),$$
$$q \leftarrow g(\mathbf{i}, p, q),$$
$$v \leftarrow h(\mathbf{i}, p, q).$$

The form of the f, g, and h functions will vary, but will generally be restricted to conditionals and simple functions. Most often, the potential and output of a unit will be encoding its *confidence*, and we will sometimes use this term. The "$\leftarrow$" notation is borrowed from the assignment statement of programming languages. This notation covers both continuous and discrete time formulations and allows us to talk about some issues without any explicit mention of time.

The restriction that output take on small integer values is central to our enterprise. The firing frequencies of neurons range from a few to a few hundred impulses per second. In the 1/10 s needed for basic mental events, there can only be a limited amount of information encoded in frequencies. The ten output values are an attempt to capture this idea.

The inclusion of a discrete set $\{q\}$ of different states has both biological and computational advantages. It

allows the system to accommodate models of fatigue, peptide modulators and other qualitative state changes. Computationally it permits the use of analysis and proof techniques from computer science (Feldman and Nigam, 1980), for example in Sect. 3 of this paper.

For some applications, we will be able to use a particularly simple kind of unit (p-unit) whose output v is proportional to its potential p (rounded) when $p \geq 0$ and which has only one state. In other words

$$p \leftarrow p + \beta \sum w_k i_k \qquad\qquad [0 \leq w_k \leq 1]$$
$$v \leftarrow \text{if } v > 0 \text{ then round } (p - \theta) \text{ else } 0 \quad [v = 0 \dots 9],$$

where β, θ are constants and w_k are weights on the input values. The weights are the sole locus of change with experience in the current model. A formal specification of weight change rules for the model will be given in Sect. 5. The p-unit is somewhat like classical linear threshold elements (Minsky and Papert, 1972), but there are several differences. The potential, p, is a crude form of memory and is an abstraction of the instantaneous membrane potential that characterizes neurons; is greatly reduces the noise sensitivity of our networks.

One problem with the definition above of a p-unit is that its potential does not decay in the absence of input. This decay is both a physical property of neurons and an important computational feature for our highly parallel models. One computational trick to solve this is to have an inhibitory connection from the unit back to itself. Informally, we identify the negative self feedback with an exponential decay in potential which is mathematically equivalent. With this addition, p-units can be used for many CM tasks of intermediate difficulty. The Interactive Activation models of (McClelland and Rumelhart, 1981) can be described naturally with p-units, and some of our own work (Ballard, 1981) and that of others (Marr and Poggio, 1976) can be done with p-units. But there are a number of additional features which we have found valuable in more complex modeling tasks (Feldman and Ballard, 1982).

It is both computationally efficient and biologically realistic to allow a unit to respond to one of a number of alternative conditions. In terms of our formalism, this could be described in a variety of ways. One of the simplest is to define the potential in terms of the maximum of the separate computations, e.g.,

$$p \leftarrow p + \beta \, \text{Max}(i_1 + i_2 - \varphi, i_3 + i_4 - \varphi, i_5 + i_6 - i_7 - \varphi),$$

where β is a scale constant as in the p-unit and φ is a constant chosen (usually > 10) to suppress noise and require the presence of multiple activity inputs (Sabbah, 1981). The max-of-sum unit is the continuous analog of a logical OR-of-AND (disjunctive normal form) unit and we will sometimes use the latter as an approximate version of the former. The OR-of-AND unit corresponding to the definition above is:

$$p \leftarrow p + \alpha \, \mathrm{OR}(i_1 \& i_2, i_3 \& i_4, i_5 \& i_6 \& [\text{not } i_7]).$$

Most of the constructions in later sections will employ these "conjunctive connection" units.

2.2. Networks of Units

A very general problem that arises in any distributed computing situation is how to get the entire system to make a decision (or perform a coherent action, etc.). One way to deal with the issue of coherent decisions in a connectionist framework is to introduce winner-take-all (WTA) networks, which have the property that only the unit with the highest potential (among a set of contenders) will have output above zero after some settling time (Fig. 1). There are a number of ways to construct WTA networks from the units described above, and several of these have been discussed in (Feldman and Ballard, 1982) and elsewhere. For our purposes it is enough to consider one example of a WTA network which will operate in one time step for a set of contenders each of whom can read the potential of all of the others. Each unit in the network computes its new potential according to the rule:

$$p \leftarrow \text{if } p > \max(i_j, 1) \text{ then } p \text{ else } 0.$$

A problem with previous neural modeling attempts is that the circuits proposed were often unnaturally delicate (unstable). Small changes in parameter values would cause the networks to oscillate or converge to incorrect answers. What appears to be required are some building blocks and combination rules that preserve the desired properties. For example, the WTA subnetworks above will not oscillate in the absence of oscillating inputs. This is also true of any symmetric mutually inhibitory subnetwork (cf. Grossberg, 1980).

Another useful principle is the employment of lower-bound and upper-bound cells to keep the total activity of a network within bounds. Suppose that we add two extra units, LB and UB, to a network which has coordinated output. The LB cell compares the total (sum) activity of the units of the network with a lower bound and sends positive activation uniformly to all members if the sum is too low. The UB cell inhibits all units equally if the sum of activity is too high. Under a wide range of conditions (but not all), the LB-UB augmented network can be designed to preserve order relationships among the outputs v_j of the original network while keeping the sum between LB and UB. We will often assume that LB-UB pairs are used to keep the sum of outputs from a network within a given range. This same mechanism also goes

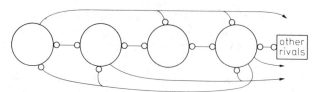

Fig. 1. Winner-take-all network. Each unit stops if it sees a higher value

far towards eliminating the twin perils of uniform saturation and uniform silence which can easily arise in mutual inhibition networks. Thus we will often be able to reason about the computation of a network assuming that it stays active and bounded.

For a massively parallel system such as the ones we are envisioning to make a decision (or do something), there will have to be states in which some activity strongly dominates. One example of this is the WTA network. But the general idea is that a very large complex subsystem must stabilize, e.g. to a fixed interpretation of visual input. The way we believe this to happen is through mutually reinforcing coalitions which dominate all rival activity for a period of time. Formally, a coalition will be called stable when the output of all its members is non-decreasing. Notice that a coalition is not a particular anatomical structure, but a temporarily mutually reinforcing set of units, in the spirit of Hebb's cell assemblies.

The mathematical analysis of CM networks and stable coalitions continues to be a problem of interest. We have achieved some understanding of special cases (Feldman and Ballard, 1982) and these results have been useful in designing CM too complex to analyze in closed form (Sabbah, 1981).

By combining the ideas of conjunctive connections, WTA and stable coalitions, we can develop networks of considerable power and flexibility. Consider the relation between depth, physical size, and retinal size of a circle. (Assume that the circle is centered on and orthogonal to the line of sight, that the focus is fixed, etc.) Then there is a fixed relation between the size of retinal image and the size of the physical circle for any given depth. That is, each depth specifies a *mapping* from retinal to physical size (see Fig. 2).

Here we suppose the scales for depth and the two sizes are chosen so that unit depth means the same numerical size. If we knew the depth of the object (by touch stereopsis, or magic) we would know its physical size. For example, physical size $=4$ and depth $=1$ make a *conjunctive connection* with retinal size $=4$. Each of the variables may also form a separate WTA network; hence rivalry for different depth values can be settled via inhibitory connections in the depth network. Notice that this network implements a function phys$=f$(ret, dep) that maps from retinal size and

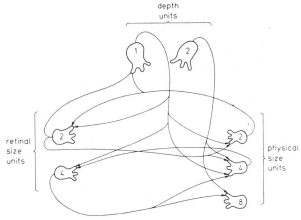

Fig. 2.

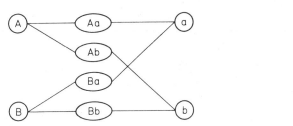

Fig. 3. Dynamic links. A must be quickly linkable to either *a* or *b*

depth to physical size, providing an example of how to implement functions with parameters. For the simple case of looking at one object perpendicular to the line of sight, there will be one consistent *coalition* of units which will be *stable*. The network does something more; the network can represent the consistency relation *R* among the three quantities: depth, retinal size, and physical size. It embodies not only the function *f*, but its two inverse functions as well [dep $=f_1$(ret, phys), and ret $=f_2$(phys, dep)]. Much of the vision work in our lap (Ballard, 1981; Feldman, 1982b) and elsewhere (Hanson and Riseman, 1978) relies on the interaction among constraint networks like those of Fig. 2.

3. Active Memory in Uniform Networks

In the previous section, we saw how fixed CM networks could be designed to compute functions and relations quite efficiently. These fixed networks could have a certain amount of built-in flexibility by explicitly incorporating *parameters*. One can view the depth networks of Fig. 2 as computing the physical size of objects from the retinal size, parameterized by depth.

But there are also a number of situations where it does not seem plausible to assume the existence of either fixed or parameterized links. An obvious, though artificial, set of examples are the paired-associate tasks with nonsense syllables used by psychologists. A closely related real task is learning someone's

name or the Hebrew word for apple. One cannot assume that all the required connections are pre-established, and it is known that they do not grow rapidly enough (in fact, very little at all) (Cotman, 1978). What does seem plausible is that there is a built-in network, something like a telephone switching network, which can be configured to capture the required link between two units. We refer to this as establishing a "dynamic connection" in the uniform network. We are assuming (as is commonly done) that the weight of synaptic connections cannot change rapidly enough to do this, so that all dynamic connections are based on changes in the potential (*p*) and state (*q*) of individual units. The other basic constraints that we impose on possible solutions are that units broadcast their outputs and that there is no central controller available to set up the dynamic connections. These assumptions differ from those in the switching literature (Pippenger, 1978), and the results there don't carry over in any obvious way. The assumption is that only one dynamic connection is made at a time, but that several (e.g. 7 ± 2) must be sustainable without cross talk. We will examine this problem in considerable detail, because it is central to the entire development.

The example task we will be considering is to make arbitrary dynamic connections between two sets of units labelled *A...Z* and *a...z*, respectively. These could be words in different languages, paired associates, words and images, and so on. The simplest case involves just 2 units on each side, but even this illustrates the basic problem. The obvious connection scheme is shown in Fig. 3.

The problem is how to establish, for example, the link $A-b$ without also linking $A-a$ since the network is originally uniform. More precisely, we require an algorithm which, given the simultaneous activation of *A* and *b*, will establish *p* and *q* values in the units of our network such that (for some time) activating *A* will stimulate *b* but not *a*. For the most part we will consider symmetric networks where the "dynamic connection" $A-b$ will also have the activation of *b* stimulate *A* and *B*. It should be clear that primitive units without any internal state (memory) will not be usable in such tasks.

One simple notion of how to solve the dynamic link problem is to use residual activation. Suppose that the intermediate units (*Ab*, *Ba*, etc.) supplied half the strength needed to activate an end unit. Then if *A* and *b* were activated, their potential would remain higher than that of their rivals. As long as the potential of *A* was greater than 1/2, activating *b* would have the following effect: the firing of *b* would cause both intermediate units *Ab* and *Bb* to be active, but *B* would get only half of its threshold while *A* would be above threshold. This appears to solve the problem, but fails totally if the network has to sustain more than one dynamic link simultaneously. For example, the links $A-b$ and $B-a$ would lead to the "crosstalk" activation of a when A was fired. It turns out that neither residual activation in the intermediate units nor lateral inhibition amongst end units are sufficient for maintaining multiple dynamic links without crosstalk. The basic solution that we will employ throughout is to assume mutual inhibition between the alternative interunits. For notational convenience, we will sometimes represent this situation as an array of units, with the understanding that the array is a winner-take-all (WTA) network. Figure 4 depicts the situation for a uniform 3-network, where only some of the connections are drawn in. If the only active link were $B-c$, then only the three starred units would be active.

The idea here is that there is a separate intermediate unit dedicated to each possible pairing. The starred unit for $B-c$ is in two WTA networks, the column which is "inputs to c" and the "outputs from B" WTA net which is drawn in explicitly. When $B-c$ is active, it blocks all others uses of both B and c, which is the desired effect. The fact that our solution requires N^2 intermediate nodes to connet $2N$ units makes it impractical for linking up sets of 10^5 units like an educated person's vocabulary. Later in this section we will show how to reduce the required number of units to a reasonable value.

The immediate problem is that we have not yet specified precisely the structure of our units and how the dynamic connections could be established (without a central controller). Figure 4 contains proposed finite-state tables for both the end units and inter-units of a uniform dynamic connection network. The states are given in the left-hand column and the possible inputs as column headings. Each box describes what the unit will do if it is in a given state (row) and gets the input of that column. Blank entries are for no change and an X entry is impossible. Entries in the "$-$" column and parenthesized entries imply a time delay. For example, if an interunit is in state "Low" and gets "Dual" input, it will go to "High" state and block its rivals.

Let us consider the operation of the network of Fig. 4 with the units in the appropriate places. We are assuming for simplicity that the links in Fig. 4 are two-way. A dynamic connection will be established by starting exactly one node in each bank "at the same time;" suppose it is $B-c$ again, Two consecutive "start" signals will cause the units B and c to enter state "High" and send activation to all inter-units connected to either B or c (5 of them in Fig. 4). Of these, four will get input from only one end and enter state "Low", but $B-c$ will get dual inputs and go to state "High" and begin blocking its four rivals. At the next step, the four

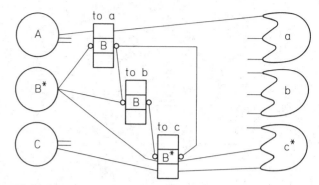

Fig. 4. State and output tables for dynamic connections

losing inter-units will be blocked, and the units B and c will get additional input from $B-c$, keeping them in "High." This forms a dynamic link $B-Bc-c$ which will stay High until it decays to state Low in all three units. The High state corresponds to the association being attended and the Low state to short-term memory but unattended.

Suppose all 3 units B, Bc, and c are in Low state and one of the ends (say c) gets another "start." Then c will go to High and increase its output to Bc, driving it to High. This will, in turn, drive B to High so that the association $B-Bc-c$ is on High. That is, as long as the dynamic link holds, it is as if B and c were physically connected – "starting" either of them activates the other (exclusively). This also keeps the rivals of Bc blocked, so the network can support additional dynamic links, e.g., Ab and Ca, without any mutual interference (crosstalk).

We can recast the same solution largely in terms of numerical potential ($-10 \leq p \leq 10$) of units rather than discrete states. It will not always be possible to express discrete state solutions in terms of the single numerical value but our units (and Natures) allow for mixed solutions. A particular numerical model of the dynamic link network is shown and a trace of its behavior given in Fig. 5.

The idea is that each unit sends positive output (here $+4$) to all its neighbors when in High state ($p \geq 7$), and inter-units also block their rivals while in this state. Forming a new dynamic link is shown in steps 1–5 of Fig. 5. Once a link is formed it will be stable until eliminated by other inputs or by decay. We assume here that a unit fatigues after reaching saturation (± 10) and decays. By step 11 the residual activation is barely enough to have a new input to B rebuild the association to c (steps 12–14). Notice that nothing much would change if the units decayed at a somewhat different rate or if small amounts of noise polluted some signals. In fact, the uniform dynamic connection network presented here is too good to be a model of active memory; such a network could encode a unique

Inter-unit		End-unit	
Idle	$P=0$	Idle	$P=0$
Low	$0<p<7$	Low	$0<p<7$
High	$7\leqq p\leqq 10$	High	$7\leqq p\leqq 10$
Blocked	$-10<p<0$		

Decay is 1 per time step, after saturation; activation strength is 4 per time step when in high; blocking strength is -10 per time step; starting signal is 4

		B	c	$B-c$	Ba	Bb	Ac	Bc
$t=$	0	0	0	0	0	0	0	0
Start B, c	1	4	4	0	0	0	0	0
	2	8	8	0	0	0	0	0
	3	8	8	8	4	4	4	4
	4	10	10	10	-6	-6	-6	-6
	5	9	9	9	-10	-10	-10	-10
	.							
	.							
	10	4	4	4	-5	-5	-5	-5
Start B	11	8	3	3	-4	-4	-4	-4
	12	8	2	7	-3	-3	-3	-3
	13	10	6	10	-2	-2	-2	-2
	14	9	10	9	-10	-10	-10	-10
	15	8	9	8	-9	-9	-9	-9

Time course of establishing a link $B-c$ and re-triggering it

Fig. 5. Numerical version of dynamic link network

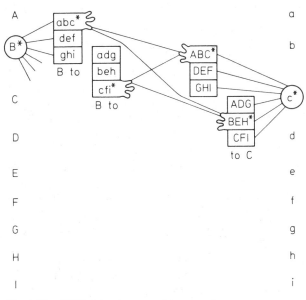

Fig. 6. The $4N^{3/2}$ dynamic connection network

link for each end unit without crosstalk for as long as the decay time. We do believe that it is essentially plausible as a model of how one can form reversible dynamic links in situations like integrating information from separate eye fixations or building up a conceptual representation of a conversation. The remainder of this section is devoted to a technical result

showing that one does not need N^2 intermediate units to capture the behavior of the uniform dynamic connection network described above. We will continue to use the unbiological assumption that links are bidirectional. Neurons clearly fire in one direction, but it is not hard to translate the networks of our examples to realistic ones. The idea is to replace each intermediate unit with a pair of units, one of which fires in each direction. The paired units need to be tightly coupled so that their potentials are at all times approximately equal, but this presents no serious problems. The assumption of symmetric links becomes more problematical in the context of random networks of the next section, and is treated in more detail there.

The two computational tricks employed in the dynamic connection networks were mutual inhibition and extra activation by simultaneous positive signals. We can use the same two ideas to reduce the number of inter-units from N^2 to $4N^{3/2}$, which does make networks for $N=10^6$ appear to be feasible.

There is a sense in which N^2 separate activation sites are strictly required for a dynamic connection network that will support N independent connections (a permutation) without crosstalk. Because we are dealing with units that broadcast, if two associates (e.g. Bc and Qa) share a unit, this unit will respond to them equally. The $4N^{3/2}$ construction exploits the fact that our units (realistically) allow several alternative sites of activation on a single unit. The "fingers" on the units in Fig. 6 depict these sites, each one of which separately computes a sum; the maximum of these is used to compute the potential of the unit. Figure 6 shows a fragment of such a network for $N=9$.

The links in the figure are again to be viewed as bidirectional, but with the property that outgoing signals are broadcast while incoming signals come just to the appropriate "finger." For example, the third finger of the $Babc$ unit will activate the unit if it receives simultaneous input from $ABCc$ and $BEHc$. These units will also send activation to $Aabc$, $Acfi$, $Cabc$, $Ccfi$, $Eabc$, $Ecfi$, and so on. The second finger of $ABCc$ collects inputs relating to Bc. The dynamic link Bc will be maintained by the activation of exactly the starred units in Fig. 6. Let us consider again the problem of potential crosstalk. We assume that end units require two simultaneous inputs from inter-units and that inter-units require one active site plus activation from its end unit. Again, the simultaneous inputs to B must come from $Babc$ and $Bcfi$ because the others are blocked. But for $Bcfi$ to fire accidentally there would have to be two simultaneous inputs to a particular (f or i) site. One input would be caused, e.g., by activating Ef, but a second input would have to come from another use of f which cannot happen under our assumption of one link per letter.

There are a few other properties of the dynamic connection network of Fig. 6 that are worth mentioning. Each end unit connects to $2\sqrt{N}$ inter-units. Each inter-unit connects to its end unit, $2\sqrt{N}$ related inter-units and $\sqrt{N-1}$ mutually inhibitory inter-units. The fact that all units have about $\sqrt{N}$ connections is consistent with neuroanatomical data as is the requirement for conjunctive connections. The exact network given in Fig. 6 is too precise to be biologically realistic but is also superhuman in its ability to support many dynamic links. One can imagine a variety of approximations to Fig. 6 which would be more realistic. The obvious alternative to these highly structured interconnection networks are random networks, the subject of the next section.

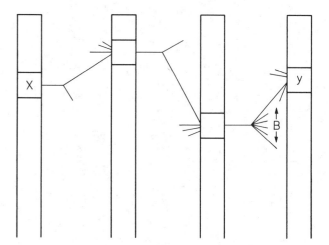

Fig. 7. Making a connection

4. Random Networks

Random Interconnection Networks

There are both anatomical (Buser, 1978) and computational reasons for looking carefully at random interconnection schemes. We will first consider the possibility of using random interconnection networks (in place of the uniform networks of the last section) to dynamically connect arbitrary pairs of units from two distinct layers. As before we will think of N units with about $\sqrt{N}$ connections each where N is in the millions. Figure 7 depicts the basic situation.

The columns on the left and the right depict "layers" of units which could represent, e.g., typed words and dictionary word-senses. As before, each unit is postulated to have (for now, bi-directional) links to some large number of intermediate units, whose role is strictly a linking one. In any random connection scheme there will be some finite probability that the required path is simply not present. The remarkable fact is that this failure probability can be made vanishingly small for networks of quite moderate size. The probability of totally failing to find a path from X to y is approximately expressed as the following double exponential relation.

$$P = (1-F)^B,$$

where B is the number of outgoing branches per unit, $F = B/N$ is the fraction of units reached from a given unit, and K is the number of intermediate layers. Although F is typically quite small, for there to be no path from X to y, all $B(\sim 1000)$ trials must fail in each intermediate level. Another way to view this is to notice that in K steps, a unit on the left has about B^{K+1} links to the right hand column. The formula is exact for one intermediate layer; for more layers there is a

small correction for the probability that two links hit the same unit in the succeeding layer. This result has been known for some time and has been used as the basis of a proposed highly parallel computer (Fahlman, 1980).

Many of the algorithms and arguments used in Sect. 3 for uniform interconnection networks carry over to random networks, but there are some important differences. The number of intermediate units required, KN, is much less than in the uniform networks. We could not expect random networks to be able to dynamically link arbitrary permutations because we are well short of the required $N \log N$ intermediate units. An important issue is crosstalk: If there are dynamic links from $X-y$ and $A-b$, how can the unwanted links $A-y$ and $X-b$ be avoided? The expected number of dynamic links maintainable in a random interconnection network will be a function of several parameters of network topology and of the algorithms for making and retaining dynamic links. We will present here only an outline of the basic considerations.

One key to understanding the crosstalk problem for random nets can be read directly from the table of Fig. 7. For the given choice of $B = 1000$, the table gives the probability and thus the expected number of paths from X to y passing through each intermediate layer. Consider the middle column, where $N = 10^7$. In the first layer there are $1000 = B$ units on paths to y (or anywhere). In the second intermediate level there are about $(1-0.9)10^7 = 10^6$ units reachable from X, ignoring multiple links to the same unit. But we can also look at the situation from the other direction, where the layers have 10^3, 10^6 links respectively from y. Since the links in the two directions are assumed to be independent, the joint probability that an intermediate unit is on the two-way path is given by

$$P(\text{int unit on path}) = (10^3/10^7)(10^6/10^7) = 10^{-5}$$

which says that about 100 units in each intermediate layer will be on a path from X to y, and the chance of crosstalk will be small. The calculations for the other two columns are slightly less favorable, but there is a wide range of feasible parameter choices.

The operational characteristics of random linking networks differ somewhat from those used for uniform networks. The major computational devices employed in Sect. 3 were coincident signals and mutual inhibition. We will not be able to rely upon mutual inhibition in random networks, because it seems unreasonable to suppose that the random pattern somehow includes inhibitory links to rival units. The coincident signal technique can be employed much as before. Recall that intermediate units in the uniform N^2 network could be driven to a HIGH state by simultaneous inputs from both ends (Fig. 4). With the $N^{3/2}$ network (Fig. 6) we required a unit to get two simultaneous inputs to one of its terminals along with an input from the other end. The assumption was that the units could be made unresponsive to one input from each side and thus avoid crosstalk. An end unit was designed to be activated by two inputs, but not by a single input. These conditions implicitly established the noise tolerance of the network.

In the random network, we will use the coincidence of many inputs as the signal to activate a unit. Consider again the example with $N = 10^7$ in Fig. 7. If a dynamic link has been activated, each end unit would be expected to get about 100 active inputs. By setting a threshold of 50 at end units, one could achieve a reasonable tradeoff between false positive and negative responses. More generally, the end units of a given random connection network can be specified to have a fixed (or variable) point on the characteristic operating curve for the system, trading false positive and negative responses. The activation condition for intermediate units again reguires input from both ends rather than a pure count.

Another difference between the current random interconnection networks and the uniform ones of the previous section is in relaxing the assumption of bi-directional links. It is well established that real synaptic links are uni-directional. Some neural networks do appear to connection structures that look like mutual connections, and these would be equivalent to bi-directional links for our purposes. In a model that assumes uniform intermediate layers (as in Sect. 3), it is no more outrageous to assume that the uniform interconnections are mutual, and we did so. This assumption (like mutual inhibition) is not consistent

with the random networks considered here. There are two plausible ways of extending the random layer interconnection networks to the case of uni-directional links.

One solution is to assume that the links from each end layer to its neighboring interconnection layer are bi-directional, but the intermediate links are not. We have already seen that links from end units must be treated specially in our random networks, and it does not seem unreasonable to suppose that the developmental linkage to interconnection units results in bi-directional links. In this case, the control for forming a dynamic link is straightforward. An intermediate unit goes to High state if it receives strong input from one end unit and from a quota of intermediate units. The quota is determined as usual from the expected number of inputs. This calculation was done previously for the case $N = 10^7$ and yielded about 100 units which would be activated (the quota was one). For any particular configuration, one can calculate the probability of crosstalk as a function of the number of links being simultaneously maintained. As long as there is any correlation between linkage patterns in the two directions, this can be exploited to provide some dynamic link and noise resistance capabilities.

It is premature to speculate on the degree to which animals are more like the uniform or random networks (if either) but we can say something about the computational advantages of each. Uniform networks appear to be most useful for maintaining many simultaneous dynamic links which are easily turned on and off. They could only be expected to occur in well-structured stable domains because of the strong consistency requirements. In general, we would like to view uniform dynamic links as a mechanism roughly equivalent to modifiable or conjunctive connections where the number of possibilities is too great to wire up directly.

Random interconnection networks are not as stable and predictable as uniform ones, but have some other advantages. The lower requirements on the number and precision of wiring of intermediate units are clearly important. But the must interesting property of the random networks is the relative ease with which they could be made permanent. Suppose that instead of rapid change we wanted relatively long term linkage of units from the two layers. Our model specifies that this must be done by changing connection weights w_j as is discussed in Sect. 5. The point to be made here is that the random networks already have some units biased towards linking any particular pair from the two layers. By selectively strengthening the active inputs (on command) of the most appropriate units, the network can relatively quickly forge a reliable link between the pair. The details of how we propose that this about are given in Sect. 5.

Random Chunking Networks

The fact that random (as opposed to uniform) interconnection networks could be readily specialized suggests that random networks may play an important role in permanent change and memory. The intermediate linking structures of Fig. 7 could be used fairly directly to model the learning of permanent connections between pairs of concepts from two domains, for example, French and English words. Any one of a wide range of weight-changing rules (cf. Sect. 5) could be used to adjust the weights (w_j) of the active inputs when a dynamic link was formed. After enough training, the originally random inter-connection network would become one in which there was essentially a hard-wired connection between particular pairs of units from the two spaces. Of course, once this has happened, the network will not be able to represent competing dynamic links, but its ability to capture new pairings will remain intact until a large fraction of the nodes are used up (cf. Fahlman, 1980).

The problem with this scheme as a proto-model of long term memory is that most of our knowledge is structured much more richly than paired associates. It is technically true that one can reduce any relational structure to one involving only pairings, and Fahlman (1980) suggests that the best current hardware approach is along these lines. But the intuitive, psychological and physiological (Wickelgren, 1979) notions of conceptual structures involve the direct use of more complex connection patterns. It turns out that the results of the previous section on random interconnection layers extend nicely to the more general case.

The basic situation is shown in Fig. 8. There are again $N(=16)$ units connected to $\sqrt{N}$ others, but without any layer structure. We are assuming that all units and connections are identical and that each unit has, at each time step

$$v \leftarrow 2p,$$

$$p \leftarrow p + 1\sum i - 2 (= \text{decay when } p \neq 0).$$

We are assuming that at each time step, the unit subtracts 2 from its current potential if not zero, and then adds the sum of its input values. The table in Fig. 8 shows successive values of p for various units, assuming that at $T=0$, units F and I have $p=10$ and are maintained for six time steps. The unit O happens to be directly connected to F and I and thus will eventually saturate (under the rules above).

After step 5, the coalition (F, O, I) is self-sustaining and would actually need to be stopped by fatigue or an

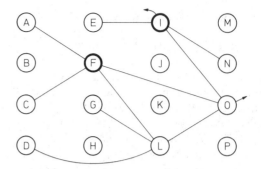

Fig. 8. Random chunking network

	$d = 2\sqrt{N}$	$d = 3\sqrt{N}$	$d = 4\sqrt{N}$
$N = 10^6$	1 − 39,042	1 − 57,953	1 − 76,467
$N = 10^6$	2 − 733	2 − 1,628	2 − 2,854
	3 − 8	3 − 29	3 − 67
	4 − 0	4 − 0	4 − 0
$N = 10^7$	1 − 144,352	1 − 215,709	1 − 286,547
	2 − 1,001	2 − 2,242	2 − 3,966
	3 − 4	3 − 14	3 − 35
	4 − 0	4 − 0	4 − 0
$N = 10^8$	1 − 518,595	1 − 776,848	1 − 10^6
	2 − 1,295	2 − 2,909	2 − 5,162
	3 − 2	3 − 7	3 − 16
	4 − 0	4 − 0	4 − 0

Each box has expected number of nodes linking to $k = (1, 2, 3, 4)$ units of random set R of size $\log_2 N \sim 20$

Fig. 9. Exputed number of links into a small random subset

external input. In some sense, we can view this coalition as having *recruited* unit O to maintain the dynamic link between F and I. The main differences from the examples given earlier is that here the linking can take place between any set of units and there is no distinction between end and intermediate units. This is a simple example of the basic mechanism which we believe to support associative learning and appears to be close to what Wickelgren (1979) had in mind. If random chunking networks can be made to support short-term associations through coalitions, the usual weight-changing algorithms would enable the associations to be made permanent.

The viability of the random chunking network concept depends on some subtle counting arguments. One requires a situation where any small set of units chosen at random can be built into a coalition which is itself stable, but which does not activate the remainder of the underlying random network. We will first analyze a closely related statistical question: given a network of size N and a small ($\sim \log N$) random subgraph R, what is the distribution over nodes of N of the number of (bi-directional) connections to R. This number will depend critically upon the branch factor, the fraction of nodes to which each unit is (randomly) connected. Again, we will assume that each unit is connected to about $\sqrt{N}$ others. As we have discussed, this appears to be quite plausible for vertebrate brains.

The results of the table in Fig. 9 suggest that the statistics do work out well for reasonable choices of the network parameters, although certainly not for all choices. The calculations of the table arise from the following analysis. Let d be the number of outgoing arcs per node ($\sim \sqrt{N}$) and $|R|$ the size of set R. The number of nodes with exactly k links into the set R is given by a formula similar to the standard binomial distribution, but differing because we assume only one link between any two nodes is possible.

$$Pr(k \text{ links}) = (\ ) \cdot [|R|/N \cdot (|R|-1)/(N-1) \ldots$$

$$\ldots (|R|-K+1)/(N-K+1)]$$

$$\cdot [(N-|R|)/N \cdot (N-|R|-1)/N \ldots$$

$$\ldots (N-|R|-(d-k-1))/N].$$

The first term is "d choose k," the number of ways that k events can occur in d trials. The second bracketed expression represents the joint probability of having k distinct links from some node of N into R, and the final term is the probability of $(d-k)$ misses. The values of this formula for several values of k, d, and N are given in Fig. 9. The most important information in the table is the expected number of units with 3 or more links into R, because these are the arcs which could be recruited to form a coalition with R.

Let us first consider the case where $N = 10^6$ and $d = 3\sqrt{N} = 3000$ links per node. If we start with a subset R having $\log N = 20$ nodes, there will be (on average) 29 additional nodes that have three links each with R and could help form a set B such that $B \cup R$ is stable. The dynamics of the situation are just as shown for $N = 16$ in Fig. 8. If all the nodes in R were simultaneously active for some time, the weights of the network could be set so that only units with three or more links to active nodes reached saturation in (say) five time steps. There would be (on average) 49 nodes in this coalition, and weight-changing rules could be used to make it more permanent. One problem is that, assuming R originally had no internal links, there is no guarantee that the new group $(B \cup R)$ is connected.

We can compute the probability that a random graph $B \cup R$ formed by the rules above will fail to be connected. We can assume (as a worst case) that there are no links from nodes in B to others in B and similarly to R. The links are all from B to R, and the first question is the probability of some node in R

getting none of the 3×29 links. This probability is given by

$$Pr(\text{miss}) = (1 - (3/|R|))^{|B|}$$

which for the case $R = 20$, $B = 29$ comes out to be about 0.01. There is an additional probability that there will be two or more disjoint sets of links from B to R, but this has a smaller probability.

A residual probability of 0.01 for the failure of a new concept coalition may appear to be too high for comfort. There are a variety of technical tricks that can be used to lower the chances of failure. The most obvious idea is to assume a higher density of connections (e.g., $4\sqrt{N}$ gives 67 nodes in B and a failure probability of about 0.00002). The difficulty with this approach is that too many nodes of the original graph begin to have single links to R. A different approach would be to recruit for B all nodes with two links to R (1628 of them in our example) which would make the failure probability negligible. There is a variant of this idea which appears to me to be the best purely technical fix. Instead of having uniform weights on input links, one could assume that the w_j were also randomly distributed in the initial network. In this case the strength of initial link from two-link nodes into R will also vary randomly. Then, depending on how important a new occurrence was deemed to be, the system could incorporate a tradeoff (threshold for recruiting) between the number of nodes recruited to B and the probability of failure to form a stable coalition.

In addition to these various mathematical tricks, there are some more substantive issues to be taken into account. We assumed here that the random set R had no internal connections. Assuming even a small number of connections among elements of R would radically lower the failure probability. For example, if there were 10 links among the 20 nodes of R in our $(10^6, 3\sqrt{N})$ example, the probability of failure drops to 0.0001. Links with R would arise because the new concept came from subconcepts that already had some relationships. It may be that our networks should not be expected to reliably learn a notion involving twenty unrelated parts.

5. Changing Weights and Long-Term Memory

There was a brief discussion of changing weights in Sect. 4 where it was suggested that random networks could easily be made to incorporate long-term change. We will examine this problem more carefully in this section, still within the constraint that all long-term change is caused by structural modification of connection weights, w_j. There is some evidence for the growth of new connections in adults (Buser, 1978), and for relatively rapid physiological change at synapses (Kandel, 1976), but neither seems to be nearly widespread or selective enough to play a dominant role in the acquisition of knowledge. The discussion in this section will be mainly technical, dealing with rules for changing weights, their properties, and some basic problems.

The standard basis of weight-changing algorithms (Sutton and Barto, 1981; Jusczyk and Klein, 1980) is reinforcement of those weights (w_j) whose inputs (i_j) correlate with desired outputs. This is almost trivially correct, but is subject to a wide range of interpretations, some of which won't work. One widely used rule is to always reinforce those w_j for which i_j was active whenever the unit fires (rapidly). This is the rule originally proposed by Hebb (Jusczyk and Klein, 1980) and has been the basis for many studies of plasticity. However, this feedback-free reinforcement rule provides no way for a system to learn from its mistakes and could not be the only rule used in nature.

In fact, while a great deal of progress has been made on weight adjustment rules, there remain at least two issues whose basic nature is problematic. The one of these that we will attack here is called in *AI* the "credit-assignment" problem – when a complex system learns that it has done something well or poorly, which of the many available adjustments should be tried (Sleeman et al., 1982). The other basic problem (which we will defer) is deferred outcomes – it may be a very long time before the outcome of particular action becomes available for feedback and other events may intervene.

Our formal definition of weight changing in the abstract units depends on a hypothesized ability for a unit to "remember" the activity state of its incoming connections for long enough to get feedback. This assumption is commonly made by modelers (e.g., see Sutton and Barto, 1981), and has some currency among neurobiologists (e.g., Doty, 1979; Stent, 1973). The idea is that the activity at a receiving site causes chemical changes that persist and remain localized for some time.

Recall that we compute the input vector **i** from received values, weights, and modifiers:

$$\forall j, \ i_j = r_j \cdot w_j \cdot m_j \qquad j = 1, \ldots, n,$$

where r_j is the *value* received from a predecessor [$r = 0 \ldots 9$]; w_j is a changeable *weight*, [$-1 \leq w_j \leq 1$]; and m_j is a synapto-synaptic *modifier* which is either 0 or 1.

Formally, the change in weights will be determined by a function of the inputs (**i**), potential (p), state (q), and outcome value (x) for each unit. The general case

includes a provision for dealing with situations where it is not possible to decide immediately whether a given network behavior should be reinforced. We introduce a "memory" vector **μ** and two functions, c which updates **μ**, and d, which (usually later) uses values of **μ** to bring about changes in the weights **w** (Feldman, 1981b). This paper will not deal with deferred outcomes, so that we can use a simplified definition with **μ** = **w** and $c = d$. The rule for weight change becomes

$$\mathbf{w} \leftarrow d(\mathbf{i}, p, q, x, \mathbf{w}).$$

As an example, let us consider augmenting the random network of Fig. 8 to enable it to selectively strengthen connections. We will assume that all of the w_j in the network are initially set to 0.5. The table in Fig. 8 is still applicable if we assume that all units have output $v = 4p$ (instead of $2p$), because the initial weights of 0.5 will even things out. We will also have to be more precise in our treatment of bidirectional links. We interpret Fig. 8 to mean that, for example, unit O has inputs from and (separately) outputs to units $F, I, L,$ and $\hat{}$ Recruiting units (O, I, F) to form a more permanent chunk would be accomplished by strengthening their mutual positive effects.

The dynamic link established in Fig. 8 provides the information necessary for a uniform updating algorithm to choose the right weights to change. For example, the system could signal updating weights at time 5 for all units with $p > 8$. The next thing that needs specifying is a particular updating rule. A typical update rule might be

$$\Delta w_j = \alpha \cdot i_j$$

which increases weights at a rate proportional to the current input level. A well known problem with this rule is that if weights only increase they will often all saturate. One standard solution (e.g., Sutton and Barto, 1981), which works well enough in this case, is to have an increase or decrease in weights which depends on the output or potential of the unit. We could do this discretely by setting a conditional $\delta = 1$ if $p > 8$ and $\delta = -1$ if $p \leq 8$. A continuous version could be $\delta = p - 8$, which would greatly penalize active inputs to dormant units. In either case,

$$\Delta w_j = \alpha \cdot i_j \cdot \delta$$

is an acceptable updating rule. Assuming that the fourth input of unit O is idle, the new values of weights on inputs to unit O would be for ($\alpha = 0.1$):

	I	F	L	?
old	0.5	0.5	0.5	0.5
continuous	0.6	0.6	0.56	0.5
discrete	0.55	0.55	0.53	0.5

Notice that the weight on the mystery input remains unchanged because $i?$ is zero. This might not be desirable if the goal were to cut off other inputs that might cause confusion with the chunk (O, I, F). In general, different structures will be better served by different updating algorithms and one should not expect to find a uniform scheme that will be applicable in all situations. Our major departure from the literature is to allow non-linear updating rules that need not treat all w_j on a given unit identically. This is a natural extension of the more flexible computational rules we have found useful in our detailed models. Many of the results (Sutton and Barto, 1981) on the convergence and stability of correlation weight changing schemes will carry over to rules of our kind.

The original driving force behind this entire line of work was an attempt to find a biologically and computationally plausible model of visual memory (Feldman, 1981). The current paper can be viewed as an attempt to make more precise and technical some notions which were found to be necessary if any connectionist model were to have a chance. The basic problems, of course, are that connections change slowly and that there are not enough of them to have all possible experiences prewired. The way around these difficulties in conventional computers and in much current theorizing about memory is to have one or more intermediate (symbolic) representations carried by states of the underlying hardware. An alternative to the approach taken here would be to try to reduce of the proposed intermediate formalisms (e. g., predicate calculus or production systems) to biologically realistic computations. Our approach is to proceed as if there were no intermediate encoding until we reach intractable problems. We are working on simulations and experiments to test particular aspects of the development, but we must rely on the kindness of strangers to point out flaws in the formulation or crucial problems that have been overlooked.

One fundamental problem that seems to have come out surprisingly well is short-term memory. The notion of stable coalition appears to capture the intuitive idea of "reverberating loops" in a way that corresponds quite well with the basic findings on attention and interference (Posner, 1978). Residual potentiation of units (which we need for other reasons anyway) appears to be plausible as a substrate for short-term memory. Enormous numbers of questions remain unanswered, but the basic notions appear to be sound and have been used repeatedly in Sects. 3 and 4 of this paper.

The critical unsolved problems are best characterized as issues in knowledge representation. The basic questions in knowledge representation have not come close to being answered in any framework, and it would be absurd to expect to suddenly do much better. What we can do is explore the range of possible ways in which knowledge can be acquired, used, and transformed within the tight constraints of connectionist models. There are several quite specific problems for which we have yet to develop even a single satisfactory model. In the remainder of this paper we will discuss how we hope to use the results of the earlier sections to attack some of these problems.

One of the most troublesome problems is the nature of the various representations of visual information. Among the phenomena to be explained are the "illusion" of a stable visual world with eye movements, object recognition and perceptual generalization, and visual imagery. The uniform connection networks of Sect. 3 were originally conceived as a solution to problems such as this one and others like the mapping of words to their conceptual roles in scripts, etc. There is serious work in our laboratory on several of these problems. The furthest developed of these efforts is a provisional model of vision and space which presents detailed proposals for the representation of visual information (Feldman, 1982).

One topic that might appear to be easy and natural for connectionism is semantic network models of conceptual structures. By identifying semantic networks with neural nets and spreading activation (Collins and Loftus, 1975) with reinforcing coalitions, one can indeed make progress. The crucial difficulty is the incorporation of new conceptual information into the network. As must be apparent, the random chunking networks of Sect. 4 are intended to provide the mechanism for the assimilation of new knowledge in semantic/neural nets. Again, it will require detailed study and modeling to determine if the ideas could work. Our current belief is that the mechanisms of Sect. 4 will be adequate, but only if much of the conceptual knowledge required for thought is already wired in.

There is one class of problems which is already known to be beyond the scope of the technical material developed so far: the reorganization of LTM. Some preliminary work has been done on this problem and the related ones of deferred outcomes and credit assignment (Sleeeman et al., 1982; Feldman, 1981b). It appears that only one additional technical tool, *simulation*, is required to tret these problems, but the work is in a very early stage. This is just one of the many beautiful technical problems that are arising in the study of massively parallel computational structures.

Acknowledgements. Sanjaya Addanki programmed and helped design algorithms for computing the numbers in Sects. 4 and 5. He, Gary Cottrell, Lydia Hrechanyk, Lokendra Shastri, and Paul Shields made important suggestions for improving the presentation.

References

Anderson, J.R., Bower, G.H.: Human associative memory. Washington, DC: V.H. Winston and Sons 1972

Ballard, D.H.: Parameter networks. TR 75, Computer Science Dept., U. Rochester, 1981; Proc. 7th IJCAI, Vancouver, B.C., August 1981

Barto, A.G., Sutton, R.S., Brouwer, P.S.: Associative search network: a reinforcement learning associative memory. Biol. Cybern. **40**, 201–211 (1981)

Buser, P.A., Roguel-Buser, A. (eds): Cerebral correlates of conscious experience. Amsterdam: North-Holland 1978

Cotman, C.W. (ed): Neuronal plasticity. New York: Raven Press 1978

Dell, G.S., Reich, P.A.: Toward a unified model of slips of the tongue. In: Errors in linguistic performance: slips of the tongue, ear, pen, and hand. Fromkin, V.A. (ed). New York: Academic Press 1980

Dev, P.: Perception of depth surfaces in random-dot stereograms: a neural model. Intl. J. Man-Machine Stud. **7**, 511–528 (1975)

Doty, R.W.: Neurons and memory: some clues. In: Brain mechanisms in memory and learning: from the single neuron to man, Brazier, M.A.B. Int. J. Brain Research Organization Monograph Series, Vol. 4. New York: Raven Press 1979

Fahlman, S.E.: The Hashnet interconnection scheme. Computer Science Dept. Carnegie-Mellon U., June 1980

Feldman, J.A.: Four frames suffice. TR 99, Computer Science Dept., U. Rochester 1982

Feldman, J.A.: A connectionist model of visual memory. In: Parallel models of associative memory. Hinton, G.E., Anderson, J.A. (eds). Hillsdale, NJ: Lawrence Erlbaum Associates, Publishers 1981a

Feldman, J.A.: Memory and change in connection networks. TR 96, Computer Science Dept., U. Rochester 1981b

Feldman, J.A., Ballard, D.H.: Connectionist models and their properties. Cogn. Sci. 1982 (to appear)

Feldman, J.A., Nigam, A.: A model and proof technique for message-based systems. SIAM J. Comput. **9**, 4 (1980)

Grossberg, S.: Biological competition: decision rules, pattern formation, and oscillations. Proc. Natl. Acad. Sci. USA **77**, 4, 2238–2342 (1980)

Hanson, A.R., Riseman, E.M. (eds): Computer vision systems. New York: Academic Press 1978

Hinton, G.E., Anderson, J.A. (eds): Parallel models of associative memory. Hillsdale, NJ: Lawrence Erlbaum Associates, Publishers 1981

Jusczyk, P.W., Klein, R.M. (eds): The nature of thought: essays in honour of D.O. Hebb. Hillsdale, NJ: Lawrence Erlbaum Associates, Publishers 1980

Kandel, E.R.: The cellular basis of behavior. San Francisco, CA: Freeman 1976

Marr, D.C.: Vision. San Francisco, CA: Freeman 1980

Marr, D.C., Poggio, T.: Cooperative computation of stereo disparitly. Science **194**, 283–287 (1976)

McClelland, J.L., Rumelhart, D.E: An interactive activation model of the effect of context in perception. Part 1. Psych. Rev. (to appear)

Minsky, M., Papert, S.: Perceptrons. Cambridge, MA: The MIT Press 1972

Pippenger, N.: On rearrangeable and non-blocking switching networks. J. Comput. Syst. Sci. **17**, 2, October (1978)

Posner, M.I.: Chronometric explorations of mind. Hillsdale, NJ: Lawrence Erlbaum Associates, Publishers 1978

Richter, J., Ullman, S.: A model for the temporal organization of X- and Y-type receptive fields in the primate retina. Biol. Cybern. **43**, 127–145 (1982)

Sabbah, D.: Design of a highly parallel visual recognition system. Proc. 7th IJCAI, Vancouver, B.C., August 1981

Sleeman, D., Langley, P., Mitchell, T.M.: Learning from solution paths: an approach to the credit assignment problem. The AI Magazine, Spring 48–52 (1982)

Stent, G.S.: A physiological mechanism for Hebb's postulate of learning. Proc. Natl. Acad. Sci. USA **70**, 4, 997–1001 (1973)

Sutton, R.S., Barto, A.G.: Toward a modern theory of adaptive networks: expectation and prediction. Psychol. Rev. **88**, 2, 135–170 (1981)

Torioka, T.: Pattern separability in a random neural net with inhibitory connections. Biol. Cybern. **34**, 53–62 (1979)

Wickelgren, W.A.: Chunking and consolidation: a theoretical synthesis of semantic networks. configuring in conditioning, *S-R* versus cognitive learning, normal forgetting, the amnesic syndrome, and the hippocampal arousal system. Psychol. Rev. **86**, 44–60 (1979)

Received: July 27, 1982

Dr. Jerome A. Feldman
Computer Science Department
University of Rochester
Mathematical Sciences Building
Rochester, NY 14627
USA

Figure 4 (p. 31), Figure 7 (p. 33), and Figure 8 (p. 35) are incomplete as published. The correct versions of these Figures appear below and overleaf. In addition there are the following typographical errors.

p. 28, second column, line 11, should read 'v ← if p > 0 ...'

p. 30, second column, line -13, should read 'stimulate *A* and *not B*.'

p. 33, line -10, formula should be $\overline{P} = (1\text{-}F)^{B^K}$.

p. 35, line -12, formula should be 'v ← .2p'

p. 36, line 16, formula should be 'Pr(k links) = $\binom{d}{k}$ ...'

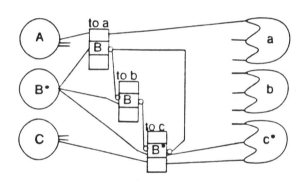

Figure 4 State and output tables for dynamic connections.

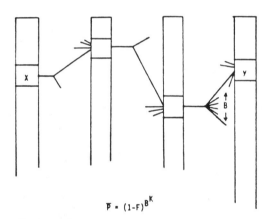

$$\overline{P} = (1\text{-}F)^{B^K}$$

$\overline{P}$ = Probability that there is <u>no</u> link from X to y
N = Number of Units in a "Layer"
B = Number of Randomly Outgoing Branches/Unit ≈ $\sqrt{N}$
F = B/N (Branching Factor)
K = Number of Intermediate Levels (2 in diagram above)

$\overline{P}$ for B = 1000; different numbers of levels and units

N= K=	10^6	10^7	10^8
0	.999	.9999	.99999
1	.367	.905	.989
2	. 10^{-440}	10^{-44}	10^{-5}

Figure 7: Making a connection.

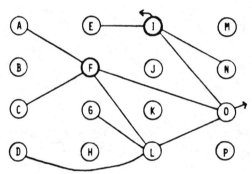

RANDOM NETWORKS:

N NODES EACH CONNECTED TO √N OTHERS

ASSUME v = .2 * POTENTIAL; DECAY IS 2

	F	I	G	L	O	A	N . . .
T = 0							
1	10	10	0	0	0	0	0
2	10	10	0	2	4	2	2
3	10	10	0	2.8	6	2	2
4	10	10	1	4	8.6	2	2
5	10	10	1	6.3	10	2	2

FIGURE 8: RANDOM CHUNKING NETWORK

Proc. of the 8th European Conference on Artificial Intelligence
(ECAI-88), Munich, 1-5 August 1988

Y. Kodratoff (Ed.), Pitman Publ., 351-356, London 1988

Connectionist Recruitment Learning

Joachim Diederich

International Computer Science Institute
1947 Center St.
Berkeley, CA 94704
USA

Abstract

Connectionist and neural network learning techniques deal with weight change rules to build internal representations for classes of functions. In contrast to these approaches, a structured connectionist learning system is introduced, which uses a built-in knowledge representation module for inferencing, and this reasoning capability for knowledge-intensive learning. The central process is the acquisition of new units and interconnection schemes of units to represent new conceptual information. The system uses a connectionist semantic network formalism as a knowledge base and requires only the presentation of a single instance to trigger learning. Free, uncommitted subnetworks are connected to the built-in knowledge network during learning in order to represent new conceptual information. The learning procedure has two steps. Connectionist inheritance methods are used to **recognize** a given example and recruitment learning is used for **constructive generalization**. Knowledge-intensive connectionist learning techniques could improve the brittleness during learning when noisy or faulty instances are given.

1. Introduction.

The realization of semantic network models for conceptual structures should be easy for connectionist systems. However, "... the crucial difficulty is the incorporation of new conceptual information into the network... Our current belief is that the mechanisms of ...[recruitment, this author] will be adequate, but only if much of the conceptual knowledge required for thought is already wired in" (Feldman 1982, p.38). This paper describes a connectionist learning approach for this task.

The proposed system uses already acquired knowledge to recognize a single example and a form of recruitment learning to build a new conceptual structure and integrate it in the existing knowledge representation system (constructive generalization). The new conceptual structure will improve the system's capability to recognize instances as described by the single example.

This paper is organized as follows. First, a brief introduction to connectionist recruitment learning is given and the architecture of the built-in knowledge base is described. Essential parts of the learning algorithm are outlined next, followed by an example of knowledge-intensive connectionist learning. Finally, experimental results for the learning algorithm are given.

2. Connectionist Recruitment Learning.

Many connectionist learning methods are extensions and generalizations of weight change rules, i.e. back-propagation learning (Rumelhart et al. 1986) and competitive learning (Rumelhart & Zipser 1985). The connectionist learning approach realized here applies not only weight change rules but also a process for the recruitment of new units and <u>interconnection schemes of units</u> to represent new conceptual information. In recruitment learning, a network consists of two classes of units:

<u>Committed Units</u>

These are units which already represent some sort of information or function, i.e. conceptual information. Committed units are connected to other committed units and their simultaneous activation must represent a meaningful state of the network. Committed units are also connected to

<u>Free Units</u>

which form a kind of "primordial network" (Shastri 1985) and are connected to other free units as well as to committed units.

Recruitment learning means to strengthen the connections between a group of committed units and one or more free units. This results in the transformation of free units into committed units. Shastri (1985) use the term "chunking" if a free node becomes committed and functions as a chunking node for the cluster [of committed units, this author] i.e., the activation of nodes in the cluster results in the activation of the chunking node and conversely, the activation of the chunking nodes activates all the nodes in the cluster". It is possible to view the subnetwork of committed units embedded in the network of free units and constructive generalization means to acquire units from the pool of free units.

3. The architecture of the knowledge base.

The knowledge base is constructed by compilation from a symbolic descriptive representation language or by previous learning. The built-in representation system used here consists of four parts: the concept space, the attribute space, the instance space and the space of the free units. The concept space contains all learned or built-in concepts. The attribute space contains the possible values of attributes. The instance space consists of single units, connected to concept units and value units in the attribute space. The free space consists of uncommitted units which are recruited during learning.

3. 1 The concept space.

The chosen representation of the concept space is similar to the one in Cottrell (1985).

The representation consists of three-unit subnetworks for the representation of each concept (called "triple subnetworks" or "3-unit networks"): the affirmative concept unit (+<unit>), the negative concept unit (-<unit>), and an additional, intermediate unit (#<unit>). The affirmative and the negative unit have excitatory links to the intermediate unit and the intermediate unit has inhibitory links to the affirmative and the negative unit. The intermediate unit guarantees that the subnetwork converges to one of three stable states (see Cottrell 1985). Either the affirmative unit or the negative unit is on, or all units are off. See Figure 1 for an explanation.

Subnetworks are connected in a hierarchy or heterarchy, reflecting the inheritance path. There are links from each affirmative unit to more general affirmative units and from each negative unit to more specific negative units.

Intermediate Unit

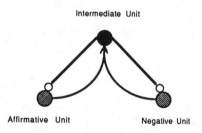

Affirmative Unit   Negative Unit

Figure 1: A triple unit subnetwork.

Units of the concept space are connected with units in the attribute space. Concepts are thereby associated with their properties. Exceptions which would realize a non-monotonic style of reasoning are built in by additional inhibitory links which modify the stimulation of concept units to connected units in the attribute space. These links modify the inheritance process. More specific units can modify the effect that links from more general concept units have on units in the attribute space. So the connection between more specific concepts and their attributes become dominant. This realizes a basic assumption of semantic networks: the more specific should dominate the more general.

3. 2 The attribute space.

The attribute space is a network, divided into subnets. Each subnet contains the possible values of an attribute. Subnets are "winner take all" (WTA) networks that use mutual inhibition (see Feldman & Ballard 1982). Currently, there is no explicit representation of an attribute itself, each subnetwork represents an attribute implicitly. Whenever a unit in a subnetwork of the attribute space is "on", the corresponding attribute is implicitly given too.

In order to maintain likelihood information, a modification of WTA networks is used which adjusts competition between units according to the total input of a WTA network. This is similar to the "network region" approach in Chun et al. (1987). Each unit in a WTA network receives the average of the total WTA network input as an inhibition signal. The network result is the restriction of the dominance of winner units. All competing units with an input above average might stay active. This kind of approach is sometimes called "winner take more" (WTM) network.

The total WTM network input is computed indirectly using the output values of all units in the WTM subnetwork. For each WTM network, an additional unit is built which receives the output of all units in the WTM net and computes the average. The additional unit, called "region unit", has inhibitory links to the units in the WTM net. The average signal is propagated to the WTM units via these inhibitory links.

3.3 The instance space.

Instances are single units connected with concept units. Activation of an instance unit is followed by activation of a concept unit and all connected value units in the attribute space. If an instance has additional properties or properties which are different from the attributes of the associated concept, explicit links to value units in the attribute space are necessary.

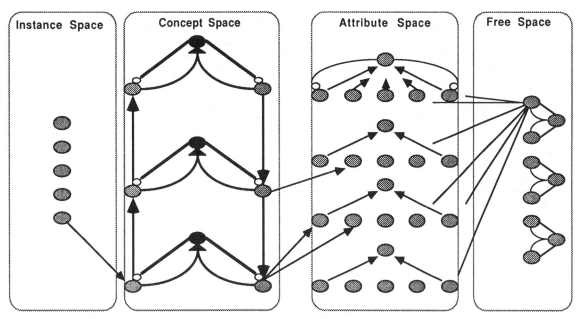

Figure 2: The architecture of the system (not all links are shown).

3.4 The free space.

The fourth space consists of free units which become committed during learning. Free units are connected like concept units (triple subnetworks). The subnetworks of the free space are connected as strict WTA networks which allow only one unit of a triple subnetwork as a winner unit (with exception of the intermediate unit) while none of the other subnetworks in free space has an active unit. Furthermore, there are bidirectional links between each value unit in the attribute space and each free unit, and each affirmative or negative concept unit with each affirmative or negative free unit. These links have zero weights and are subject to weight change during recruitment learning.

Two patterns of connectivity between free space and concept space, and free space and attribute space are explored. The first case is full connectivity. There are links between each free unit and each concept/value unit (with the exception of the intermediate units; furthermore, affirmative free units are only connected with affirmative concept units and negative free units are only connected with negative concept units).

Obviously, full connectivity has to deal with the problem of combinatorial explosion when many free units, concept units and value units are used. Therefore random connections are used as the second connectivity pattern. Twenty additional units are used as intermediate units between free space and attribute

space. There is full connectivity between random units and attribute space and there are random links between random units and free space. During network construction, there is only a 50% chance for a link between a random unit and a free unit. As in the first case, each affirmative and negative free unit has links to each value unit.

Free units receive their own output as a positive strong reinforcing signal and the output of the competing free units as negative reinforcement (inhibition). This is similar to the competitive reinforcement learning in Lynne (1987). If a new instance with unknown features is presented to system, the high activity in the attribute space will lead to a unspecific activation of the free space. The free unit with the highest potential and/or random links from the random units in the second case (random connectivity) will receive this activation (among others) and becomes a clear winner, in part through self-reinforcement. This winner unit is committed during recruitment learning.

This part of the learning process is similar to competitive learning (cf. Rumelhart & Zipser 1985) where only the winner unit gets the chance to adjust weights. However, the weight change is different in competitive learning because there is a redistribution of weights over the input lines of a winner unit. In our approach, each input link of a newly-committed unit becomes adjusted independently of other input-lines and features of the weight-vector. The weight change is based on the input-signal and the potential of the receiving unit (among other parameters).

4. Knowledge-intensive learning in a structured connectionist system.

The following sources of information are used in our system. The **domain theory** is the total knowledge base minus the free space. The **goal concept** is an affirmative concept as part of the concept space. This goal concept unit is clamped on during the learning process. The **training example** is a set of attribute/value pairs, describing an instance of the goal concept. The units in the attribute space which represent the particular value of an attribute as part of the training example are continuously activated by the corresponding instance unit. The **new concept** is defined in terms of all attribute/value pairs of the training example and attributes from the domain theory. As an additional, technical restriction we assume here that each attribute has only one individual value.

The algorithm has two parts, "RECOGNITION" and "CONSTRUCTIVE GENERALIZATION" which are **conceptual** distinctions and **not** separated during processing:

RECOGNITION:

1. Let the instance unit which represents the training example activate all connected value units in the attribute space.

2. Clamp the goal concept unit in the concept space on.

3. Run the total network until convergence.

CONSTRUCTIVE GENERALIZATION:

4. Recruit new triple structures for representing the new concept definition.

5. Connect the new triple structure with all units in the attribute space, if this has not been already done.

6. Run the total network to allow weight changes.

During recognition, an activation pattern is built which includes features of the training example necessary to describe the goal concept. In phase 3 of the algorithm above, unspecific features from more general super-concepts of the goal concept become active as well. A strong decay process is used in the concept space to restrict the influence of these unspecific features. Strong activated units represent features of the training example and the goal concept. Convergence is successful, if a) all network regions in the attribute space (all WTM networks) have clear winners, otherwise the training example does not fit the goal concept (according to our technical restriction), and b) the total network stabilizes.

The constructive generalization process is simple. The wiring between free and attribute space is already done but all weights have zero values. The weighted connections between the new concept structure and features represented by value units in the attribute space are installed by using a modified Hebb rule with slow weight change. Step 6 of the algorithm is used to allow these weight changes. *The increase of weights is restricted to the value of the received input and the potential of the receiving unit.*

In general, this method corresponds to the recruitment process in Feldman (1982), Shastri (1985) and Fanty (1988).

5. An Example.

Given:

a) The goal concept:
FAST(X) & IMPORTED(X) --> PORSCHE(X)

b) The domain theory:
PORSCHE(X) --> CAR(X),
CAR(X) --> 4-WHEELS(X) & HAS-PART(X, ENGINE) & HAS-PART(X, GEARBOX),
CAR(X) --> VEHICLE(X)

c) The training example:
FAST(OBJ1) & IMPORTED(OBJ1) & YELLOW(OBJ1) & OWNER(OBJ1, MICHAEL)

d) Criteria for the new concept: The new concept definition must be expressed in terms of structural attributes of the example, the goal-concept or super-concepts of the goal-concept.

The training example (OBJ1) can easily be recognized as a PORSCHE because of its features FAST and IMPORTED. Additional features of the training example can be inferred by the use of the domain theory after a successful classification, e.g. HAS-PART(OBJ1, ENGINE).

In full detail the method works as follows. First, the classification of the training example is done. The value units FAST and IMPORTED receive strong activation from an instance unit which causes high potentials for these units. FAST and IMPORTED have strong weights to the concept unit PORSCHE in the concept space, because the goal concept PORSCHE is defined through these two features. The affirmative concept unit PORSCHE itself stimulates the concept unit representing CAR. CAR activates other value units in the attribute space: 4-WHEELS, ENGINE and GEARBOX. The recognition is successful. We know the training example OBJ1 is a PORSCHE and therefore a CAR (and a VEHICLE) and has the features FAST, IMPORTED, 4-WHEELS, ENGINE and

GEARBOX; represented by active units in the attribute space.

The features of the training example (FAST, IM-PORTED) receive continuously activation from the instance unit representing the example. After 50 updates of the entire network, all units in the concept space are subject to a decay process. Because of this decay process, the concept units CAR and VEHICLE are loosing activation after 50 updates. Note that there is only one source of stimulation for CAR and VEHICLE, the goal concept PORSCHE. The same happens to the value units 4-WHEELS, ENGINE and GEARBOX in the attribute space, because these units receive their activation from super-concepts of the goal-concept.

After the decay process becomes effective, the second step of the method, generalization, continues with the recruitment of the new structure. As mentioned above, triples of units for the representation of concepts already exist in the free space, and the wiring between free and attribute space is already done. In the beginning, the connections have 0-valued weights; weights are restricted to integers [-1000, 1000] in general. The increase of weights between the new concept structure and features represented by active value units in the attribute space are installed by using the Hebb rule described above. The new concept (obviously a PORSCHE-914) gets therefore **strong connections** to the value units FAST and IMPORTED, and **medium- or small-weighted connections** to the value units 4-WHEELS, ENGINE and GEARBOX, as well as to YELLOW and OWNER:MICHAEL, features of the training example which received no activation from the concept space.

The learning process is finished after installation of the weighted links. The new concept definition contains features of the training example as well as inferred features from domain knowledge. The new concept definition will improve the system's ability to recognize examples similar to the training example because of the distribution of weights between PORSCHE-914 and its features in the attribute space.

6. Experimental results.

The example above was tested and implemented by use of the Rochester Connectionist Simulator (RCS; Goddard et al. 1987). In every simulation run, a solution was found in 100 update steps of the total network using fair asynchrony (units are randomly chosen for update; in our simulations, each unit was updated at least once after 243 steps).

Figure 3 shows the potentials of the free units (affirmative concept units) with full connectivity between free and attribute space during the first 5 update steps. A winner unit is available after these 5 updates. This unit becomes the new committed unit. Figure 4

...s the same process with random connectivity between free and attribute space. Note the slower increase in the potential of the winner unit.

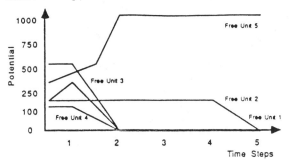

Figure 3: Processing in the free space during the first 5 update steps (full connectivity).

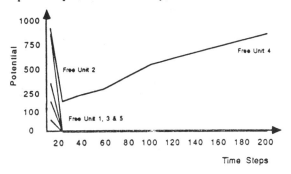

Figure 4: Processing in the free space during the first 200 update steps (random connectivity).

It is possible to distinguish three classes of units in the attribute space after the network becomes stable. The first class consists of value units which are stimulated through the instance unit **and** units in the concept space. These units receive a high potential and the **new concept unit** gets strong connections to these units. IMPORTED and FAST are members of the first class in our example. The second class of value units receives activation from the instance unit only. These have medium activation. The third class of value units receives activation from super-concepts of the goal-concept. These have low activation and the new concept unit gets links with low weights to these units (ENGINE, GEARBOX and 4-WHEELS in the example).

Figure 5 shows the weight development between the new committed unit and the value units in the attribute space when both spaces are fully connected. Figure 6 shows the same process with random connectivity. Note the decrease of some weights after 50 updates caused by the decay process in the concept space. The results for both topologies are comparable (see Figure 5 and 6), although the increase in weights is slower in case of random connectivity.

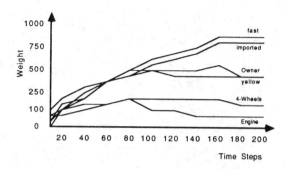

Figure 5: Weight development between the free space winner unit and value units in the attribute space (full connectivity).

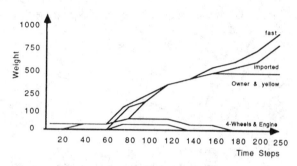

Figure 6: Weight development between the free space winner unit and value units (random connected)

7. Conclusion.

A structured connectionist learning system has been introduced, which uses a built-in knowledge representation module for performing inferences. On the implementation level, the system is an application of recruitment learning (Feldman 1982). The essential and new contribution of the approach presented here is the <u>interaction</u> between constraints on the "knowledge level" and the connectionist implementation level. On the knowledge level the approach introduces the notion of "goal concepts", restrictions for the new concept definition and the use of a single instance only. These are constraints for recruitment learning on the network level and allows for the integration of a new concept in an existing connectionist inheritance system.

8. Acknowledgement

Many thanks to Jerry Feldman, Mark Fanty and Alfred Kobsa for comments on earlier versions of this paper.

9. References.

Chun, H.W., Bookman, L.A. & Afshartous, N.: Network Regions: Alternatives to the Winner-Take-All Structure. IJCAI-87, 380-387, Milano, 1987

Cottrell, G.W.: Parallelism in Inheritance Hierarchies with Exceptions. IJCAI-85, 194-202, Los Angeles, 1985

Fanty, M.: Learning in Structured Connectionist Networks. Ph.D Thesis, CS Department, University of Rochester, 1988

Feldman, J.A.: Dynamic Connections in Neural Networks. Biol. Cybernetics, 46, 27-39, 1982

Feldman, J.A. & Ballard, D.H.: Connectionist models and their properties. Cognitive Science, 6, 205-254, 1982

Goddard, N., Lynne, K. & Mintz, T.: The Rochester Connectionist Simulator. TR233, Department of Computer Science, University of Rochester, 1987

Lynne, K.: Competitive Reinforcement Learning. Internal Paper, Department of Computer Science, University of Rochester, August 1987

Rumelhart, D.E., Hinton, G.E. & Williams, R.J.: Learning Internal Representations by Error Propagation. In: Rumelhart, D.E. & McClelland, J.L. (Eds.): Parallel Distributed Processing. Vol 1.: Foundations. The MIT Press, Cambridge, Mass. 1986

Rumelhart, D.E. & Zipser, D.: Feature Discovery by Competitive Learning. Cognitive Science 9, 75-112, 1985

Shastri, L.: Evidential reasoning in semantic networks: a formal theory and its parallel implementation. Ph.D. Thesis and TR 166, Computer Science Department, University of Rochester, September 1985

The ART of Adaptive Pattern Recognition by a Self-Organizing Neural Network

Gail A. Carpenter and Stephen Grossberg

Boston University

One of the central goals of computer science is to design intelligent machines capable of autonomous learning and skillful performance within complex environments that are not under strict external control. Many scientists have turned to a study of human capabilities as a source of new ideas for designing such machines. When a scientist undertakes such a study, he or she encounters a number of basic issues, of which we are all aware through our own personal experiences:

Why do we pay attention? Why do we learn expectations about the world? In particular, how do we cope so well with unexpected events? And, how do we manage to do as well as we do when we are on our own and do not have a teacher as a guide? How do we learn what combinations of facts are useful for dealing with a given situation, and what combinations of facts are irrelevant? How do we recognize familiar facts so quickly even though we have stored many other pieces of information? How do we combine knowledge about the external world with information about our internal needs to quickly make decisions that have a good chance of satisfying those needs? Finally, what do all of these properties have in common?

> **The adaptive resonance theory suggests a solution to the stability-plasticity dilemma facing designers of learning systems.**

The stability-plasticity dilemma and ART

Researchers have found one answer to these questions through the attempt to solve a basic design problem, called the stability-plasticity dilemma, faced by all intelligent systems capable of autonomously adapting in real time to unexpected changes in their world. A developing the-ory called adaptive resonance theory, or ART, suggests a solution to this problem.

The stability-plasticity dilemma asks: How can a learning system be designed to remain plastic, or adaptive, in response to significant events and yet remain stable in response to irrelevant events? How does the system know how to switch between its stable and its plastic modes to achieve stability without rigidity and plasticity without chaos? In particular, how can it preserve its previously learned knowledge while continuing to learn new things? And, what prevents the new learning from washing away the memories of prior learning?

We can easily dramatize the ubiquity of this problem: Imagine that you grew up in Boston before moving to Los Angeles, but periodically return to Boston to visit your parents. Although you may need to learn many new things to enjoy life in Los Angeles, these new learning experiences do not prevent you from remembering how to find your parent's house or otherwise get around Boston. A multitude of similar examples illustrate our ability to successfully adapt to environments where rules may change—without necessarily forgetting our old skills. Moreover, we are capable of successfully adapting to environments where rules may change

Reprinted from *IEEE Computer*, Volume 21, Number 3, March 1988, pages 77-88. Copyright ©1988 by The Institute of Electrical and Electronics Engineers, Inc. All rights reserved.

unpredictably, and we can do so even if no one tells us that the environment has changed. We can adapt, in short, without a teacher, through direct confrontation with our experiences. Such adaptation is called *self-organization* in the network modeling literature.

One of the key computational ideas rigorously demonstrated within the adaptive resonance theory is that top-down learned expectations focus attention upon bottom-up information in a way that protects previously learned memories from being washed away by new learning, and enables new learning to be automatically incorporated into the total knowledge base of the system in a globally self-consistent way.

The ART architectures discussed here are neural networks that self-organize stable recognition codes in real time in response to arbitrary sequences of input patterns. Within such an ART architecture, the process of adaptive pattern recognition is a special case of the more general cognitive process of hypothesis discovery, testing, search, classification, and learning. This property opens up the possibility of applying ART systems to more general problems of adaptively processing large abstract information sources and databases. This article outlines the main computational properties of these ART architectures, while comparing and contrasting these properties with those of alternative learning and recognition systems. Technical details are described in greater detail elsewhere,[1,2] and several books collect articles in which the theory was developed through the analysis and prediction of interdisciplinary data about the brain and behavior.[3,4]

Competitive learning models

ART models grew out of an analysis of a simpler type of adaptive pattern recognition network, often called a *competitive learning* model. Competitive learning models developed in the early 1970s through contributions of Christoph von der Malsburg[5] and Stephen Grossberg, leading to the description of these models in 1976 in several forms in which they are used today.[6] Authors such as Shun-ichi Amari,[7] Leon Cooper,[8] and Teuvo Kohonen[9] have further developed these models. Kohonen[9] has made particularly strong use of competitive learning in his work on self-organizing maps. Grossberg[4] has provided a historical discussion of the development of competitive learning models.

In a competitive learning model (see Figure 1), a stream of input patterns to a network F_1 can train the adaptive weights, or long-term memory (LTM) traces, that multiply the signals in the pathways from F_1 to a coding level F_2. In the simplest such model, input patterns to F_1 are normalized before passing through the adaptive filter defined by the pathways from F_1 to F_2. Level F_2 is designed as a competitive network capable of choosing the node which receives the largest total input ("winner-take-all"). The winning population then triggers associative pattern learning within the vector of LTM traces which sent its inputs through the adaptive filter.

For example, as in Figure 1, let I_i denote the input to the ith node v_i of F_1, $i = 1,2,...,M$; let x_i denote the activity, or short-term memory (STM) trace, of v_i; let x_j denote the activity, or STM trace, of the jth node v_j of F_2, $j = M + 1,...,N$; and let z_{ij} denote the adaptive weight, or long-term memory (LTM) trace, of the pathway from v_i to v_j. Then let

$$x_i = \frac{I_i}{\sum_{k=1}^{M} I_k} \qquad (1)$$

be the normalized activity of v_i in response to the input pattern $I = (I_1, I_2,...,I_M)$. For simplicity, let the output signal S_i of v_i equal x_i. Let

$$T_j = \sum_{i=1}^{M} x_i z_{ij} \qquad (2)$$

be the total signal received at v_j from F_1, let

$$x_j = \begin{cases} 1 & \text{if } T_j > \max(T_k : k \neq j) \\ 0 & \text{if } T_j < \max(T_k : k \neq j) \end{cases} \qquad (3)$$

summarize the fact that the node x_j in F_2 which receives the largest signal is chosen for short-term memory storage, and let a differential equation

$$\frac{d}{dt} z_{ij} = \epsilon x_j(- z_{ij} + x_i) \qquad (4)$$

specify that only the vector $Z_j = (z_{1j}, z_{2j},...,z_{Mj})$ of adaptive weights which abut the winning node v_j is changed due to learning. Vector Z_j learns by reducing the error between itself and the normalized vector $X = (x_1, x_2,...,x_M)$ in the direction of steepest descent.

Several equivalent ways describe how such a system recognizes input patterns I presented to F_1. The winning node v_j in F_2 is said to code, classify, cluster, partition, compress, or orthogonalize these input patterns. In engineering, such a scheme is said to perform adaptive vector quantization. In cognitive psychology, it is said to perform categorical perception.[3]

In categorical perception, input patterns are classified into mutually exclusive recognition categories separated by sharp categorical boundaries. A sudden switch in pattern classification can occur if an input pattern is deformed so much that it crosses one of these boundaries and thereby causes a different node v_j to win the competition within F_2. Categorical perception, in the strict sense of the word, occurs only if F_2 makes a choice. In more general competitive learning models, compressed but distributed recognition codes are generated by the model's coding level or levels.[3,4,9]

In response to certain input environments, a competitive learning model possesses very appealing properties. It has been mathematically proved[6] that, if not too many input patterns are presented to F_1, or if the input patterns form not too many clusters, relative to the number of coding nodes in F_2, then learning of the recognition code eventually stabilizes and the learning process elicits the best distribution of LTM traces consistent with the structure of the input environment.

Despite the demonstration of input environments that can be stably coded, it has also been shown, through explicit counterexamples,[1,2,6] that a competitive learning model does not always learn a temporally stable code in response to an arbitrary input environment. In these counterexamples, as a list of input patterns perturbs level F_1 through time, the response of level F_2 to the *same* input pattern can differ on each successive presentation of that input pattern. Moreover, the F_2 response to a given input pattern might never settle down as learning proceeds.

Such unstable learning in response to a prescribed input is due to the learning that occurs in response to the other intervening inputs. In other words, the network's adaptability, or plasticity, enables prior learning to be washed away by more recent learning in response to a wide variety of input environments. In fact, infinitely many input environments exist in which periodic presentation of just four input patterns can cause temporally unstable learning.[1,2]

Learning can also become unstable due to simple changes in an input environment. Changes in the probabilities of inputs, or in the deterministic sequencing of inputs, can readily wash away prior learning. Moreover, this instability problem is not peculiar to competitive learning models. The problem is a basic one because it arises from a combination of the very features of an adaptive coding model that, on the surface, seem so desirable: its ability to learn from experience and its ability to code, compress, or categorize many patterns into a compact internal representation. Due to these properties, when a new input pattern I retrains a vector Z_j of LTM traces, the set of all input patterns coded by v_j also changes because a change in Z_j in Equation 2 can reverse the inequalities in Equation 3 in response to many of the input patterns previously coded by v_j.

Learning systems that can become unstable in response to many input environments cannot safely be used in autonomous machines that might be unexpectedly confronted by one of these environments on the job. Adaptive resonance theory was introduced in 1976 to show how to embed a competitive learning model into a *self-regulating control structure* whose autonomous learning and recognition proceed stably and efficiently in response to an arbitrary sequence of input patterns.

Self-stabilized learning in an arbitrary input environment

Figure 2 schematizes a typical example from a class of architectures called ART 1. It has been mathematically proved[1] that an ART 1 architecture is capable of stably learning a recognition code in response to an arbitrary sequence of binary input patterns until it utilizes its full memory capacity. Moreover, the adaptive weights, or LTM traces, of an ART 1 system oscillate at most once during learning in response to an arbitrary binary input sequence, yet do not get trapped in spurious memory states or local minima. After learning self-stabilizes, the input patterns directly activate the F_2 codes that best represent them.

As in a competitive learning model, an ART architecture encodes a new input pat-

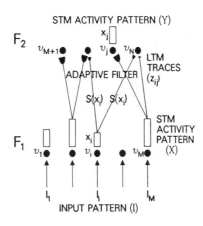

Figure 1. Stages of bottom-up activation: The input pattern I generates a pattern of STM activation $X = (x_1, x_2, ..., x_M)$ across F_1. Sufficiently active F_1 nodes emit bottom-up signals to F_2. This signal pattern S is multiplied, or gated, by long-term memory (LTM) traces z_{ij} within the $F_1 \rightarrow F_2$ pathways. The LTM-gated signals are summed before activating their target nodes in F_2. This LTM-gated and summed signal pattern T, where $T_j = \Sigma_i S_i z_{ji}$, generates a pattern of STM activation $Y = (x_{M+1}, ..., x_N)$ across F_2.

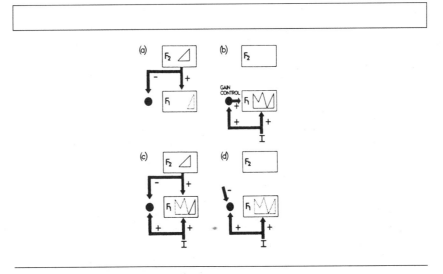

Figure 2. Matching by the 2/3 Rule: In (a), a top-down expectation from F_2 inhibits the attentional gain control source as it subliminally primes target F_1 cells. Dotted outline depicts primed activation pattern. In (b), only F_1 cells that receive bottom-up inputs and gain control signals can become supraliminally active. In (c), when a bottom-up input pattern and a top-down template are simultaneously active, only those F_1 cells that receive inputs from both sources can become supraliminally active. In (d), intermodality inhibition can shut off the F_1 gain control source and thereby prevent a bottom-up input from supraliminally activating F_1, as when attention shifts to a different input channel. Similarly, disinhibition of the F_1 gain control source in (a) may cause a top-down prime to become supraliminal, as during an internally willed fantasy.

tern, in part, by changing the adaptive weights, or LTM traces, of a bottom-up adaptive filter. This filter is contained in the pathways leading from a feature representation field F_1 to a category representation field F_2. In an ART network, however, a second, top-down adaptive filter, contained in the pathways from F_2 to F_1, leads to the crucial property of code self-stabilization. Such top-down adaptive signals play the role of learned expectations in an ART system. Before considering details about how the ART control structure automatically stabilizes the learning process, we will sketch how self-stabilization occurs in intuitive terms.

Suppose that an input pattern I activates F_1. Let F_1 in turn activate the code, or hypothesis, symbolized by the node v_{j1} at F_2 which receives the largest total signal from F_1. Then, F_2 quickly reads out its learned top-down expectation to F_1, whereupon the bottom-up input pattern and top-down learned expectation are matched across F_1. If these patterns are badly matched, then a mismatch event takes place at F_1 which triggers a reset burst to F_2. This reset burst shuts off node v_{j1} for the remainder of the coding cycle, and thereby deactivates the top-down expectation controlled by v_{j1}. Then, F_1 quickly reactivates essentially the same bottom-up signal pattern to F_2 as before. Level F_2 reinterprets this signal pattern, conditioned on the hypothesis that the earlier choice v_{j1} was incorrect, and another node v_{j2} is automatically chosen.

The parallel search, or hypothesis testing, cycle of bottom-up adaptive filtering from F_1 to F_2, code (or hypothesis) selection at F_2, read-out of a top-down learned expectation from F_2 to F_1, matching at F_1, and code reset at F_2 now repeats itself automatically at a very fast rate until one of three possibilities occurs: (1) a node v_{jm} is chosen whose top-down expectation approximately matches input I; (2) a previously uncommitted F_2 node is selected; or (3) the full capacity of the system is used and cannot accommodate input I. Until one of these outcomes prevails, essentially no learning occurs, because all the STM computations of the hypothesis testing cycle proceed so quickly that the more slowly varying LTM traces in the bottom-up and top-down adaptive filters cannot change in response to them. Significant learning occurs in response to an input pattern only after the hypothesis testing cycle that it generates comes to an end.

If the hypothesis testing cycle ends in an approximate match, then the bottom-up

---

ART architectures differ from other popular neural network learning schemes in a number of basic ways.

---

input pattern and the top-down expectation quickly deform the activity pattern $X = (x_1, x_2, \ldots, x_M)$ across F_1 into a net pattern that computes a fusion, or consensus, between the bottom-up and top-down information. This fused pattern represents the attentional focus of the system. When fusion occurs, the bottom-up and top-down signal patterns mutually reinforce each other via feedback and the system gets locked into a resonant state of STM activation. Only then can the LTM traces learn. What they learn is any new information about the input pattern represented within the fused activation pattern across F_1. The fact that learning occurs only in the resonant state suggested the name "adaptive resonance theory." Thus, the system allows alteration of one of its prior learned codes only if an input pattern is sufficiently similar to what it already knows to risk a further refinement of its knowledge.

If the hypothesis testing cycle ends by selecting an uncommitted node at F_2, then the bottom-up and top-down adaptive filters linked to this node learn the F_1 activation pattern generated directly by the input. No top-down alteration of the F_1 activation pattern occurs in this case. If the full capacity has been exhausted and no adequate match exists, learning is automatically inhibited.

In summary, an ART network refines its already learned codes based upon new information that can be safely accommodated into them via approximate matches, selects new nodes for initiating learning of novel recognition categories, or defends its fully committed memory capacity against being washed away by the incessant flux of new input events.

Alternative learning schemes

Many computational details have been worked out to make this scheme work well in an autonomous setting.[1,2] Before we describe some of these details, we should note that ART architectures differ from other popular neural network learning schemes, such as autoassociators, the Boltzmann machine, and back propagation[9-11] in a number of basic ways. These differences are schematized in Table 1.

The most robust difference is that an ART architecture is designed to learn quickly and stably in real time in response to a possibly nonstationary world with an unlimited number of inputs until it utilizes its full memory capacity. Many alternative learning schemes become unstable unless they learn slowly in a controlled stationary environment with a carefully selected total number of inputs and do not use their full memory capacity.[12] For example, a learning system that is not self-stabilizing experiences a capacity catastrophe in response to an unlimited number of inputs: New learning washes away memories of prior learning if too many inputs perturb the system. To prevent this from happening, either the total number of input patterns that perturbs the system needs to be restricted, or the learning process itself must be shut off before the capacity catastrophe occurs.

Shutting off the world is not possible in many real-time applications. In particular, how can such a system allow a familiar input to be processed and recognized, but block the processing of a novel input pattern before the pattern destabilizes its prior learning? In the absence of a self-stabilization mechanism, an external teacher must act as the system's front end to independently recognize the inputs and make the decision. Shutting off learning at just the right time to prevent either a capacity catastrophe or a premature termination of learning would also require an external teacher. In either case, the external teacher must be able to carry out the recognition tasks that the learning system was supposed to carry out. Hence, non-self-stabilizing learning systems are not capable of functioning autonomously in ill-controlled environments.

In learning systems that need an external teacher to supply the correct representation to be learned, the learning process is often driven by mismatch between desired and actual outputs.[10,11] Such schemes must learn slowly, and in a stationary environment, or risk unstable oscillations in response to the mismatches. They can also be destabilized if the external teaching signal is noisy, because such noise creates spurious mismatches.

These learning models also tend to get trapped in local minima, or globally incorrect solutions. Models such as simulated annealing and the Boltzmann machine[10] use internal system noise to escape local minima and approach a more global minimum. An externally controlled (temperature) parameter regulates this process by making it converge ever more slowly to a critical value.

In contrast, approximate matches, rather than mismatches, drive the learning process in ART. Learning in the approximate-match mode enables rapid and stable learning to occur while buffering the system's memory against external noise. The hypothesis testing cycle replaces internal system noise as a scheme for discovering a globally correct solution. It does not use an externally controlled temperature parameter or teacher.

Matching by the 2/3 rule

One of the key constraints on the design of the ART 1 architecture is its rule for matching a bottom-up input pattern with a top-down expectation at F_1. This rule, called the 2/3 Rule,[1] is necessary to regulate both the hypothesis testing cycle and the self-stabilization of learning in an ART 1 system.

The 2/3 Rule reconciles two properties whose simplicity tends to conceal their fundamental nature: In response to an arbitrary bottom-up input pattern, F_1 nodes can be *supraliminally* activated; that is, activated enough to generate output signals to other parts of the network and thereby to initiate the hypothesis testing cycle. In response to an arbitrary top-down expectation, however, F_1 nodes are only *subliminally* activated; they sensitize, prepare, or attentionally *prime* F_1 for future input patterns that may or may not generate an approximate match with this expectation, but do not, in themselves, generate output signals. Such a subliminal reaction enables an ART system to anticipate future events and thus to function as an "intentional" machine. In particular, if an attentional prime is locked into place by a high-gain top-down signal source, then an ART system can automatically

Table 1. ART architectures compared to other learning schemes.

ART architecture	Alternative learning properties
Real-time (on-line) learning	Lab-time (off-line) learning
Nonstationary world	Stationary world
Self-organizing (unsupervised)	Teacher supplies correct answer (supervised)
Memory self-stabilizes in response to arbitrarily many inputs	Capacity catastrophe in response to arbitrarily many inputs
Effective use of full memory capacity	Can only use partial memory capacity
Maintain plasticity in an unexpected world	Externally shut off plasticity to prevent capacity catastrophe
Learn internal top-down expectations	Externally impose costs
Active attentional focus regulates learning	Passive learning
Slow or fast learning	Slow learning or oscillation catastrophe
Learn in approximate-match phase	Learn in mismatch phase
Use self-regulating hypothesis testing to globally reorganize the energy landscape	Use noise to perturb system out of local minima in a fixed energy landscape
Fast adaptive search for best match	Search tree
Rapid direct access to codes of familiar events	Recognition time increases with code complexity
Variable error criterion (vigilance parameter) sets coarseness of recognition code in response to environmental feedback	Fixed error criterion in response to environmental feedback
All properties scale to arbitrarily large system capacities	Key properties deteriorate as system capacity increased

suppress all inputs that do not fall into a sought-after recognition category, yet amplify and hasten the processing of all inputs that do.[3]

To implement the 2/3 Rule, we need to assure that F_1 can distinguish between bottom-up and top-down signals, so that it can supraliminally react to the former and subliminally react to the latter. In ART 1, this distinction is determined by a third F_1 input source, called an *attentional gain control* channel, that responds differently to bottom-up and top-down signals.

Figure 2 describes how this gain control source works. When activated, it excites each F_1 node equally. The 2/3 Rule says that at least two out of three input sources are needed to supraliminally activate an

F_1 node; the three are a bottom-up input, a top-down input, and a gain control input. In the top-down processing mode (see Figure 2a), each F_1 node receives a signal from at most one input source and, hence, is only subliminally activated. In the bottom-up processing mode (Figure 2b), each active bottom-up pathway can turn on the gain control node, whose output, once on, is independent of the total number of active bottom-up pathways. Then, all F_1 nodes receive at least a gain control input, but only those nodes that also receive a bottom-up input are supraliminally activated.

When both bottom-up and top-down inputs reach F_1 (see Figure 2c), the gain control source is shut off, so that only those F_1 nodes which receive top-down

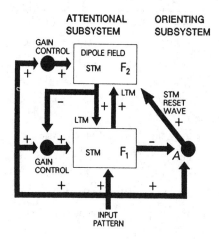

ATTENTIONAL
SUBSYSTEM

ORIENTING
SUBSYSTEM

GAIN
CONTROL

DIPOLE FIELD

STM F_2

LTM

STM
RESET
WAVE

LTM

STM F_1

A

GAIN
CONTROL

INPUT
PATTERN

Figure 3. ART 1 system: Two successive stages, F_1 and F_2, of the attentional subsystem encode patterns of activation in short-term memory (STM). Bottom-up and top-down pathways between F_1 and F_2 contain adaptive long-term memory (LTM) traces which multiply the signals in these pathways. The remainder of the circuit modulates these STM and LTM processes. Modulation by gain control enables F_1 to distinguish between bottom-up input patterns and top-down priming, or expectation, patterns, and to match these bottom-up and top-down patterns by the 2/3 Rule. Gain control signals also enable F_2 to react supraliminally to signals from F_1 while an input pattern is on. The orienting subsystem generates a reset wave to F_2 when sufficiently large mismatches between bottom-up and top-down patterns occur at F_1. This reset wave selectively and enduringly inhibits previously active F_2 cells until the input is shut off.

Figure 4. Alphabet learning: Code learning by ART 1 in response to the first presentation of the first 20 letters of the alphabet is shown. Two different vigilance levels were used, $\varrho = .5$ and $\varrho = .8$. Each row represents the total code learned after the letter at the left-hand column of the row is presented at F_1. Each column represents the learning, through time, of the top-down LTM vector, or expectation, corresponding to the F_2 node whose index is listed at the top of the column. These LTM vectors do not, in general, equal the input patterns which change them through learning. Instead, each expectation acts like a novel type of prototype for the entire set of practiced input patterns coded by that node, as well as for unfamiliar input patterns that share invariant properties with this set. The simulation illustrates the "fast learning" case, in which the altered LTM traces reach a new equilibrium in response to each new stimulus. Slow learning is more gradual than this.

confirmation of the bottom-up input are supraliminally activated. In this case, the 2/3 Rule maintains supraliminal activity only within the spatial intersection of the bottom-up input pattern and the top-down expectation. Consequently, if a bottom-up input pattern, as in Figure 2b, causes the read-out of a badly matched top-down expectation, as in Figure 2c, then the total number of supraliminally active F_1 nodes can suddenly decrease, thereby causing a decrease in the total output signal emitted by F_1. This property is used heavily in controlling the hypothesis testing and self-stabilization processes, as we will show next.

Automatic control of hypothesis testing

An ART architecture automates its hypothesis testing cycle through interactions between an attentional subsystem and an orienting subsystem. These subsystems in the ART 1 architecture are schematized in Figure 3.

The orienting subsystem A generates an output signal only when a mismatch occurs between a bottom-up input pattern and top-down expectation at level F_1 of the attentional subsystem. Thus, A functions like a novelty detector. The output signal from A is called an *STM reset wave* because it selectively inhibits the active node(s) at level F_2 of the attentional subsystem. The novelty detector A thereby disconfirms the F_2 hypothesis that led to the F_1 mismatch.

The 2/3 Rule controls the reset wave emitted by A as follows: When a bottom-up input pattern is presented, each of the active input pathways to F_1 also sends a signal to the orienting subsystem A, where all of these signals are added up. When the input pattern activates F_1, each of the activated F_1 nodes sends an inhibitory signal to A. The system is designed so that the total inhibitory signal is larger than the total excitatory signal. Thus, in the bottom-up mode, the balance between active F_1 nodes and active input lines prevents a reset wave from being triggered. (Note that level F_1 in ART 1 is not normalized as it was in Equation 1 of the competitive learning model and in the ART 2 systems discussed below. The decision of whether and how to normalize depends upon the design of the whole system.)

This balance is upset when a top-down expectation is read out that mismatches the bottom-up input pattern at F_1. As in Figure 2c, the total output from F_1 then decreases by an amount that grows with the severity of the mismatch. If the attenuation is sufficiently great, then inhibition from F_1 to A can no longer prevent A from emitting a reset wave. A parameter ϱ called the *vigilance parameter* determines how large a mismatch will be tolerated before A emits a reset wave. High vigilance forces the system to search for new categories in response to small differences between input and expectation. Then, the system learns to classify input patterns into a large number of fine categories. Low vigilance enables the system to tolerate large mismatches and thus group together input patterns according to a coarse measure of mutual similarity. The vigilance parameter may be placed under external control, being increased, for example, when the network is "punished" for failing to distinguish two inputs that give rise to different consequences.[1,3]

Figure 4 schematizes learning in response to the first 20 input presentations of a computer simulation of alphabet learning. After presenting the 20th input, nine recognition categories have formed when $\varrho = .8$, but only four categories have been formed when $\varrho = .5$. In this computer experiment, learning self-stabilized after at most three presentations of the 26 letters at any level of vigilance, and the learned LTM codes were more abstract—that is, less letter-like—at lower levels of vigilance.

Figure 5 illustrates how these properties of the interaction between levels F_1, F_2, and A regulate the hypothesis testing cycle of the ART 1 system. In Figure 5a, an input pattern I generates an STM activity pattern X across F_1. The input pattern I also excites the orienting subsystem A, but pattern X at F_1 inhibits A before it can generate an output signal. Activity pattern X also elicits an output pattern S which activates the bottom-up adaptive filter $T = ZS$, where Z is the matrix of bottom-up LTM traces. As a result, an STM pattern Y becomes active at F_2. In Figure 5b, pattern Y generates a top-down output U through the adaptive filter $V = \hat{Z}U$, where $\hat{Z}$ is the matrix of top-down LTM traces. Vector V is the top-down expectation read into F_1. Expectation V mismatches input I, significantly inhibiting STM activity across F_1. The amount by which activity in X is attenuated to generate the activity pattern X^* depends upon how much of the input pattern I is encoded within the expectation V, via the 2/3 Rule.

When a mismatch attenuates STM

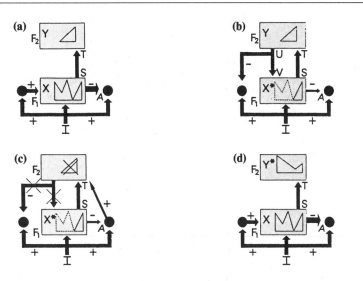

Figure 5. ART 1 hypothesis testing cycle: In (a), the input pattern I generates the STM activity pattern X at F_1 as it activates A. Pattern X both inhibits A and generates the bottom-up signal pattern S. Signal pattern S is transformed via the adaptive filter into the input pattern $T = ZS$, which activates the compressed STM pattern Y across F_2. In (b), pattern Y generates the top-down signal pattern U which is transformed by the top-down adaptive filter $V = \hat{Z}U$ into the expectation pattern V. If V mismatches I at F_1, then a new STM activity pattern X^* is generated at F_1. The reduction in total STM activity that occurs when X is transformed into X^* causes a decrease in the total inhibition from F_1 to A. In (c), then, the input-driven activation of A can release a nonspecific arousal wave to F_2, which resets the STM pattern Y at F_2. In (d), after Y is inhibited, its top-down expectation is eliminated, and X can be reinstated at F_1. Now X once again generates input pattern T to F_2, but since Y remains inhibited T can activate a different STM pattern Y^* at F_2. If the top-down expectation due to Y^* also mismatches I at F_1, then the rapid search for an appropriate F_2 code continues.

activity across F_1, the total size of the inhibitory signal from F_1 to A is also attenuated. If the attenuation is sufficiently great, inhibition from F_1 to A can no longer prevent the arousal source A from firing. Figure 5c depicts how disinhibition of A releases an arousal burst to F_2 which equally, or nonspecifically, excites all the F_2 cells. The cell populations of F_2 react to such an arousal signal in a state-dependent fashion. In the special case that F_2 chooses a single population for STM storage, the arousal burst selectively inhibits, or resets, the active population in F_2. This inhibition is long-lasting.

In Figure 5c, inhibition of Y leads to removal of the top-down expectation V, and thereby terminates the mismatch between I and V. Input pattern I can thus reinstate the original activity pattern X across F_1, which again generates the output pattern S from F_1 and the input pattern T to F_2. Due to the enduring inhibition at F_2, the input pattern T can no longer activate the original pattern Y at F_2. Level F_2 has been conditioned by the disconfirmation of the original hypothesis. A new pattern Y^* is thus generated at F_2 by I (see Figure 5d).

The new activity pattern Y^* reads out a new top-down expectation V^*. If a mismatch again occurs at F_1, the orienting subsystem is again engaged, leading to another arousal-mediated reset of STM at F_2. In this way, a rapid series of STM matching and reset events may occur. Such an STM matching and reset series controls

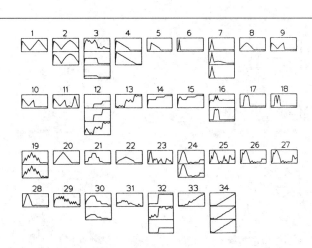

Figure 6. Category grouping by ART 2 of 50 analog input patterns into 34 recognition categories. Each input pattern *I* is depicted by a graph as a function of abscissa values i (i = 1...M), with successive ordinate I_i values connected by straight lines. The category structure established upon one complete presentation of the 50 inputs thereafter remains stable if the same inputs are presented again.

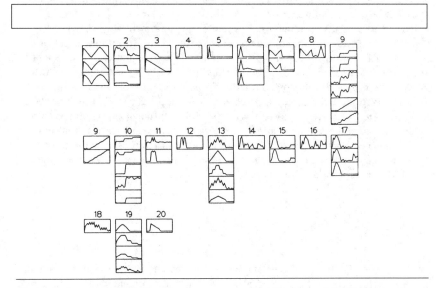

Figure 7. Lower vigilance implies coarser grouping. The same ART 2 system as used in Figure 6 has here grouped the same 50 inputs into 20 recognition categories. Note, for example, that Categories 1 and 2 of Figure 6 are joined in Category 1; Categories 14, 15, and 32 are joined in Category 10; and Categories 19-22 are joined in Category 13.

the system's hypothesis testing and search of LTM by sequentially engaging the novelty-sensitive orienting subsystem.

Although STM is reset sequentially in time by this mismatch-mediated, self-terminating LTM search process, the mechanisms that control the LTM search are all parallel network interactions, rather than serial algorithms. Such a parallel search scheme continuously adjusts itself to the system's evolving LTM codes. The

LTM code depends on both the system's initial configuration and its unique learning history, and hence cannot be predicted by a prewired search algorithm. Instead, the mismatch-mediated engagement of the orienting subsystem triggers a process of parallel self-adjusting search that tests only the hypotheses most likely to succeed, given the system's unique learning history.

The mismatch-mediated search of LTM ends when an STM pattern across F_2

reads out a top-down expectation that approximately matches *I* (to the degree of accuracy required by the level of attentional vigilance) or that has not yet undergone any prior learning. In the former case, the accessed recognition code is refined based on any novel information contained in the input *I*; that is, based upon the activity pattern resonating at F_1 that fuses together bottom-up and top-down information according to the 2/3 Rule. In the latter case, a new recognition category is established as a new bottom-up code and top-down template are learned.

ART 2: Learning to recognize an analog world

Although self-organized recognition of binary patterns is useful in many applications, such as recognition of printed or written text, as in Figure 4, many other applications require the ability to categorize arbitrary sequences of analog (including binary) input patterns. A class of architectures, generically called ART 2, has been developed for this purpose.[2]

Given the enhanced capabilities of ART 2 architectures, a sequence of arbitrary input patterns can be fed through an arbitrary preprocessor before the output patterns of the preprocessor are fed as inputs into an ART 2 system for automatic classification. Figure 6 illustrates how an ART 2 architecture has quickly learned to stably classify 50 analog input patterns, chosen to challenge the architecture in multiple ways, into 34 recognition categories after a single learning trial. Figure 7 illustrates how the same 50 input patterns have been quickly classified into 20 coarser categories after a single learning trial, using a smaller setting of the vigilance parameter.

ART 2 architectures can autonomously classify arbitrary sequences of analog input patterns into categories of arbitrary coarseness while suppressing arbitrary levels of noise. They accomplish this by modifying the ART 1 architecture to incorporate solutions of several additional design problems into their circuitry. In particular, level F_1 is split into separate sublevels for receiving bottom-up input patterns, for receiving top-down expectations, and for matching the bottom-up and top-down data, as in Figure 8.

Three versions of the ART 2 architecture are now being applied to problems such as visual pattern recognition, speech perception, and radar classification. In addition to research on ART undertaken at several universities, applications are also being developed at government laboratories and industrial firms including the MIT Lincoln Laboratory; Booz-Allen and Hamilton, Inc.; Hecht-Nielsen Neurocomputer Corp.; Science Applications International Corp.; the U.S. Army Research Center at Redstone Arsenal; and Wright-Patterson Air Force Base.

Invariant visual pattern recognition

Researchers from Boston University and the MIT Lincoln Laboratory are collaborating to carry out an application to invariant visual pattern recognition. This application uses a three-stage preprocessor, summarized in Figure 9.

First, the image figure to be recognized is detached from the image background using laser radar sensors. This can be accomplished by intersecting the images formed by two laser sensors: the image formed by a range detector focused at the distance of the figure and the image formed by another laser detector capable of differentiating figure from background, such as a doppler image when the figure is moving or the intensity of laser return when the figure is stationary.[13]

The second stage of the preprocessor contains a neural network, called a boundary contour system,[3,4] that detects, sharpens, regularizes, and completes the boundaries within noisy images.

The third stage of the preprocessor contains a Fourier-Mellin filter, whose output spectra are invariant under such image transformations as 2D spatial translation, dilation, and rotation.[14]

Thus, the input patterns to ART 2 are the invariant spectra of completed boundary segmentations of laser radar sensors. By setting ART 2 parameters to suppress (up to) a prescribed level of input noise and to tolerate (up to) a prescribed level of input deformation, this system defines a compact circuit capable of autonomously learning to recognize visual targets that are deformed, rotated, dilated, and shifted. Although this preprocessor does not purport to provide a biological solution to the problem of invariant visual object recognition, we know that the mammalian visual cortex does carry out computations analogous to aspects of the second and third stages of this preprocessor.[3,4,15]

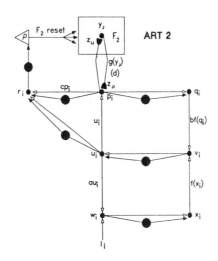

Figure 8. A typical ART 2 architecture. Open arrows indicate specific patterned inputs to target nodes. Filled arrows indicate nonspecific gain control inputs. The gain control nuclei (large filled circles) nonspecifically inhibit target nodes in proportion to the L_2-norm of STM activity in their source fields. As in ART 1, gain control (not shown) coordinates STM processing with input presentation rate.

The three R's: Recognition, reinforcement, and recall

Recognition is only one of several processes whereby an intelligent system can learn a correct solution to a problem. Reinforcement and recall are no less important in designing an autonomous intelligent system.

Reinforcement, notably reward and punishment, provides additional information in the form of environmental feedback based on the success or failure of actions triggered by a recognition event. Reward and punishment calibrate whether the action has or has not satisfied internal needs, which in the biological case include hunger, thirst, sex, and pain reduction, but may in machine applications include a wide variety of internal cost functions. Reinforcement can modify the formation of recognition codes and can shift attention to focus upon those codes whose activation promises to satisfy internal needs based on past experience. For example, both green and yellow bananas may be recognized as part of a single recognition category until reinforcement signals, contingent upon eating the

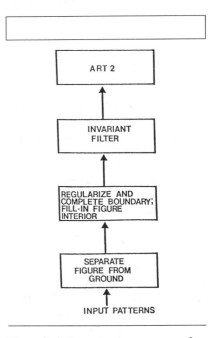

Figure 9. A three-stage preprocessor for the ART 2 system enables input patterns that are deformed, shifted, dilated, and rotated to be recognized as exemplars of the same category. The preprocessor passes laser radar images that separate figure from background through a boundary segmentation network and then through a Fourier-Mellin transform. The Fourier-Mellin spectra are the inputs to ART 2.

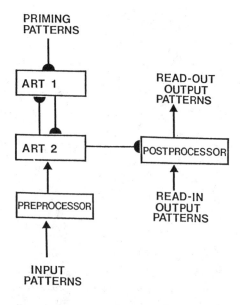

PRIMING PATTERNS

ART 1

READ-OUT OUTPUT PATTERNS

ART 2 — POSTPROCESSOR

PREPROCESSOR

READ-IN OUTPUT PATTERNS

INPUT PATTERNS

Figure 10. A self-organizing architecture for invariant pattern recognition and recall that can be expanded, as noted in the text, to include reinforcement mechanisms capable of focusing attention upon internally desired classes of external events.

bananas, differentiate them into separate categories.

Recall can generate equivalent responses or actions to input events classified by different recognition codes. For example, printed and script letters might generate distinct recognition codes, yet can also elicit identical learned naming responses.

Our own research program during the past two decades at Boston University has been devoted to discovering and implementing models of self-organizing biological systems wherein all the ingredients of recognition, reinforcement, and recall join together in a single integrated circuit.[3,4] The system depicted in Figure 10 provides a framework for implementing some of these circuit designs. In particular, as ART 2 self-organizes recognition categories in response to the preprocessed inputs, its categorical choices at the F_2 classifying level self-stabilize through time. In examples wherein F_2 makes a choice, ART 2 can be used as the first level of an ART 1 architecture, or yet another ART 2 architecture. Let us call the classifying level of this latter architecture

F_3. Level F_3 can be used as a source of pre-wired priming inputs to F_2.

Alternatively, as in Figure 10, self-stabilizing choices by F_3 can quickly be learned in response to the choices made at F_2. Then, F_3 can be used as a source of self-organized priming inputs to F_2, and a source of priming patterns can be associated with each of the F_3 choices via mechanisms of associative pattern learning.[3] After learning of these primes, turning on a particular prime can activate a learned $F_3 \rightarrow F_2$ top-down expectation. Then F_2 can be supraliminally activated only by an input exemplar which is a member of the recognition category of the primed F_2 node.

The architecture ignores all but the primed set of input patterns. In other words, the prime causes the architecture to pay attention only to expected sources of input information. Due to the spatial invariance properties of the preprocessor, the expected input patterns can be translated, dilated, or rotated in 2D without damaging recognition. Due to the similarity grouping properties of ART 2 at a fixed

level of vigilance, suitable deformations of these input patterns, including deformations due to no more than anticipated levels of noise, can also be recognized.

The output pathways from level F_2 of ART 2 to the postprocessor can learn to recall any spatial pattern or spatiotemporal pattern of outputs by applying theorems about associative learning in a type of circuit called an *avalanche*.[3] In particular, distinct recognition categories can learn to generate identical recall responses. Thus, the architecture as a whole can stably self-organize an invariant recognition code and an associative map to an arbitrary format of output patterns.

The interactions (priming → ART) and (ART → postprocessor) in Figure 10 can be modified so that output patterns are read out only if the input patterns have yielded rewards in the past and if the machine's internal needs for these rewards have not yet been satisfied.[3,4] In this variation of the architecture, the priming patterns supply motivational signals for releasing outputs only if an input exemplar from an internally desired recognition category is detected. The total circuit forms a neural network architecture which can

• stably self-organize an invariant pattern recognition code in response to a sequence of analog or binary input patterns

• be attentionally primed to ignore all but a designated category of input patterns

• automatically shift its prime as it satisfies internal criteria in response to actions based upon the recognition of a previously primed category of input patterns and

• learn to generate an arbitrary spatiotemporal output pattern in response to any input pattern exemplar of an activated recognition category.

Such circuits, and their real-time adaptive autonomous descendents, may prove useful in some of the many applications where preprogrammed rule-based systems, and systems requiring external teachers not naturally found in the applications environments, fear to tread.

Self-stabilization of speech perception and production

The insights gleaned from the design of ART 2 have also begun to clarify how we can design hierarchical learning systems with multiple ART levels. Figure 11 shows a hierarchical ART system for learning to recognize and produce speech. The system self-stabilizes its learning in real time without using a teacher. This ART architecture is being developed at Boston University by Michael Cohen, Stephen Grossberg, and David Stork. Top-down ART expectation mechanisms at several levels of the architecture help to self-stabilize learned codes and to self-organize the selection of invariant recognition properties. Of particular interest in this speech architecture is the role of top-down expectation signals from the architecture's articulatory, or motor, system to its auditory, or perception, system. These expectations help to explain classical results from motor theory, which state that speech is perceived in terms of how it would have been produced, even during passive listening.

The key insights of the motor theory take on new meaning through the self-stabilizing properties of top-down articulatory-to-auditory expectations. These expectations self-stabilize the learned imitative associative map that transforms the perceptual codes which represent heard speech into motor codes for generating spoken speech. In so doing, the articulatory-to-auditory expectations deform the bottom-up auditory STM patterns via 2/3 Rule-like matching into activation patterns consistent with invariant properties of the motor commands. These motorically modified STM codes are then encoded in long-term memory in a bottom-up adaptive filter within the auditory system itself. This bottom-up adaptive filter activates a partially compressed speech code at the auditory system's next processing level. The motorically modified speech code is thus activated during passive listening as well as during active imitation.

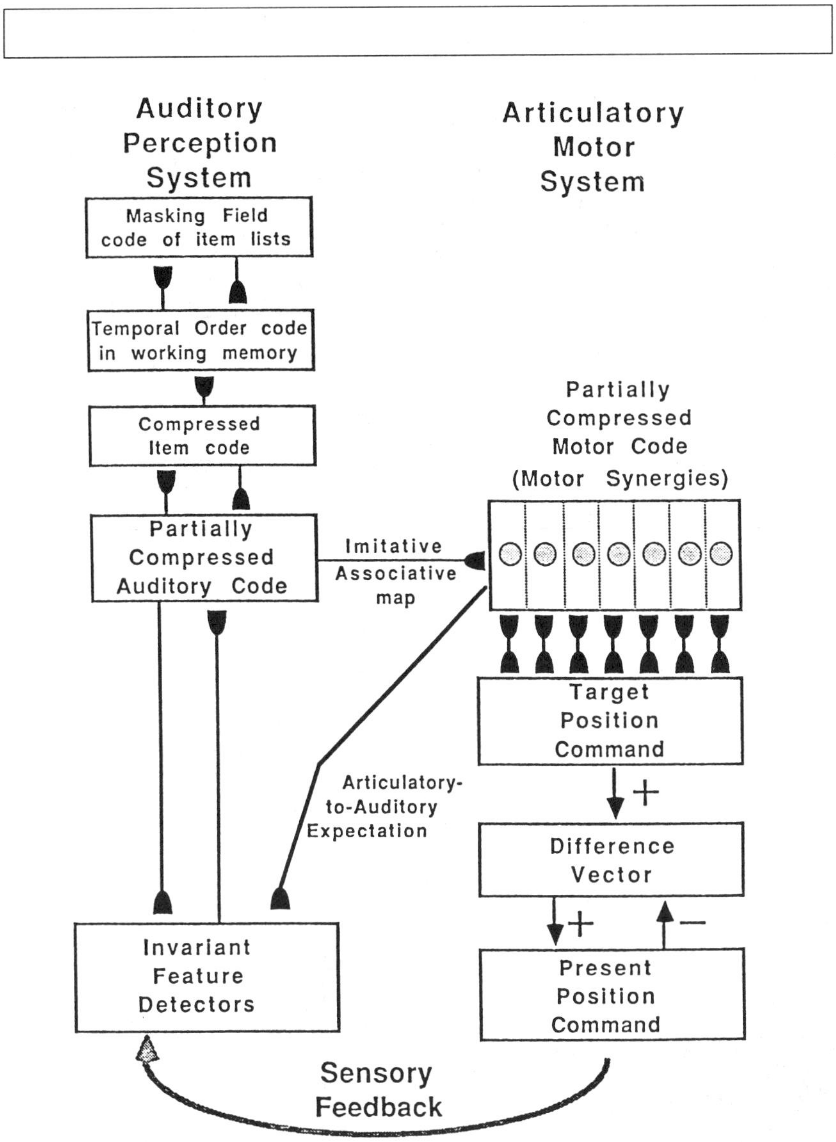

Psychophysiological and neurophysiological predictions of ART

Although applications of ART to computer science depend upon the computational power of these systems for solving real-world problems, ART systems are also models of the biological processes whose analysis led to their discovery. In fact, in addition to suggesting mechanistic explanations of many interdisciplinary data about the mind and brain, the theory has also made a number of predictions

Figure 11. Schematic of some processing stages in an architecture for a self-organizing speech perception and production system. The left-hand side of the figure depicts five stages of the auditory model; the right-hand side depicts four stages of the motor model. The pathways from the partially compressed auditory code to the motor system learn an imitative associative map which joins auditory feedback patterns to the motor commands that generated them. These motor commands are compressed via bottom-up and top-down adaptive filters within the motor system into motor synergies. The synergies read out top-down learned articulatory-to-auditory expectations, which select the motorically consistent auditory data for incorporation into the learned speech codes of the auditory system.

partially supported by experiments. For example, in 1976, it was predicted that both norepinephrine (NE) mechanisms and attentional mechanisms modulate the adaptive development of thalamocortical visual feature detectors. In 1976 and 1978, Kasamatsu and Pettigrew described NE modulation of feature detector development, and Wolf Singer reported attentional modulation in 1982. In 1978, a word length effect in word recognition paradigms was predicted. In 1982 and 1983, Samuel, van Santen, and Johnston reported a word length effect in word superiority experiments. In 1978 and 1980, a hippocampal generator of the P300 event-related potential was predicted. In 1980, Halgren and his colleagues reported the existence of a hippocampal P300 generator in humans. The existence and correlations between other event-related potentials, such as processing negativity (PN), early positive wave (P120), and N200 were also predicted in these theoretical articles. These predictions and supportive data are described in several recent books.[3,4]

Thus, ART systems provide a fertile ground for gaining a new understanding of biological intelligence. They also suggest novel computational theories and real-time adaptive neural network architectures with promising properties for tackling some of the outstanding problems in computer science and technology today. □

Acknowledgments

We received support in part from the Air Force Office of Scientific Research, the Army Research Office, and the National Science Foundation. We also wish to thank Cynthia Suchta and Carol Yanakakis for their valuable assistance in preparing the manuscript.

Gail A. Carpenter is a professor in the Dept. of Mathematics of Northeastern University and senior research associate in the Center for Adaptive Systems at Boston University. Her current research interests are in the fields of neural networks, pattern recognition, applied mathematics, and differential equations. She is a member of the founding board of governors of the International Neural Network Society (INNS), is organization chair of the INNS first annual meeting, and serves on the editorial board of the INNS journal, *Neural Networks*.

Carpenter received a BA degree summa cum laude in mathematics from the University of Colorado in 1970, and an MA in 1972 and a PhD in 1974, both from the Mathematics Dept. of the University of Wisconsin.

Stephen Grossberg is founder and director of the Center for Adaptive Systems and a professor of mathematics, psychology, and biomedical engineering at Boston University. His current research interests include vision, cognitive information, processing, sensory-motor control, and speech perception and production. He is a member of the founding board of governors of the International Neural Network Society and currently serves as its president. He was awarded the Norbert Wiener Medal for Cybernetics and the A.P. Sloan Research Fellowship, among other honors.

Grossberg received a BA degree at Dartmouth College in 1961, an MS from Stanford University in 1964, and a PhD from Rockefeller University in 1967.

References

1. G.A. Carpenter and S. Grossberg, "A Massively Parallel Architecture for a Self-Organizing Neural Pattern Recognition Machine," *Computer Vision, Graphics, and Image Processing*, Vol. 37, 1987, pp. 54-115.

2. G.A. Carpenter and S. Grossberg, "ART 2: Self-Organization of Stable Category Recognition Codes for Analog Input Patterns," *Applied Optics*, Dec. 1, 1987, pp. 4919-30.

3. S. Grossberg, ed., *The Adaptive Brain, Vol. I and II*, Elsevier/North-Holland, Amsterdam, 1987.

4. S. Grossberg, ed., *Neural Networks and Natural Intelligence*, MIT Press, Cambridge, Mass., 1988.

5. C. von der Malsburg, "Self-Organization of Orientation Sensitive Cells in the Striate Cortex," *Kybernetik*, Vol. 14, 1973, pp. 85-100.

6. S. Grossberg, "Adaptive Pattern Classification and Universal Recoding, I: Parallel Development and Coding of Neural Feature Detectors," *Biological Cybernetics*, Vol. 23, 1976, pp. 121-134.

7. S. Amari and A. Takeuchi, "Mathematical Theory on Formation of Category Detecting Nerve Cells," *Biological Cybernetics*, Vol. 29, 1978, pp. 127-136.

8. E.L. Bienenstock, L.N. Cooper, and P.W. Munro, "Theory for the Development of Neuron Selectivity: Orientation Specificity and Binocular Interaction in Visual Cortex," *Journal of Neuroscience*, Vol. 2, 1982, pp. 32-48.

9. T. Kohonen, *Self-Organization and Associative Memory*, Springer-Verlag, New York, 1984.

10. D.H. Ackley, G.E. Hinton, and T.J. Sejnowski, "A Learning Algorithm for Boltzmann Machines," *Cognitive Science*, Vol. 9, 1985, pp. 147-169.

11. D.E. Rumelhart, G.E. Hinton, and R.J. Williams, "Learning Internal Representations by Error Propagation," D.E. Rumelhart and J.L. McClelland, eds., *Parallel Distributed Processing*, MIT Press, Cambridge, Mass., 1986.

12. J.S. Denker, ed., *Neural Networks for Computing*, American Institute of Physics, New York, 1986.

13. A.B. Gschwendtner, R.C. Harney, and R.J. Hull, "Coherent IR Radar Technology," D.K. Killinger and A. Mooradian, eds., *Optical and Laser Remote Sensing*, Springer-Verlag, New York, 1983.

14. D. Casasent and D. Psaltis, "Position, Rotation, and Scale Invariant Optical Correlations," *Applied Optics*, Vol. 15, 1976, pp 1793-99.

15. E.L. Schwartz, "Computational Anatomy and Functional Architecture of Striate Cortex: A Spatial Mapping Approach to Perceptual Coding," *Vision Research*, Vol. 20, 1980, pp. 645-669.

Readers may write to the authors at the Center for Adaptive Systems, Boston University, 111 Cummington St., 2nd Floor, Boston, MA 02215.

Neuronlike Adaptive Elements That Can Solve Difficult Learning Control Problems

ANDREW G. BARTO, MEMBER, IEEE, RICHARD S. SUTTON, AND CHARLES W. ANDERSON

Abstract—It is shown how a system consisting of two neuronlike adaptive elements can solve a difficult leaning control problem. The task is to balance a pole that is hinged to a movable cart by applying forces to the cart's base. It is assumed that the equations of motion of the cart-pole system are not known and that the only feedback evaluating performance is a failure signal that occurs when the pole falls past a certain angle from the vertical, or the cart reaches an end of a track. This evaluative feedback is of much lower quality than is required by standard adaptive control techniques. It is argued that the learning problems faced by adaptive elements that are components of adaptive networks are at least as difficult as this version of the pole-balancing problem. The learning system consists of a single *associative search element* (ASE) and a single *adaptive critic element* (ACE). In the course of learning to balance the pole, the ASE constructs associations between input and output by searching under the influence of reinforcement feedback, and the ACE constructs a more informative evaluation function than reinforcement feedback alone can provide. The differences between this approach and other attempts to solve problems using neuronlike elements are discussed, as is the relation of this work to classical and instrumental conditioning in animal learning studies and its possible implications for research in the neurosciences.

Manuscript received August 1, 1982; revised April 20, 1983. This work was supported by AFOSR and the Air Force Wright Aeronautical Laboratory under Contract F33615-80-C-1088.

The authors are with the Department of Computer and Information Science, University of Massachusetts, Amherst, MA 01003.

Reprinted from *IEEE Transactions on Systems, Man, and Cybernetics*, Volume SMC-13, Number 5, September/October 1983, pages 835-846.

I. Introduction

MATHEMATICALLY formulated networks of neuronlike elements have been studied both as models of specific neural circuits and as abstract, though biologically inspired, computational architectures. As models of specific neural circuits, network models can provide theories to explain anatomical and physiological data. As computational architectures, they represent attempts to explore possible substrates for intelligent behavior, both natural and artificial. Networks of this second category are relevant to brain and behavioral science to the extent that their behavior can be related to phenomena of animal behavior for which no plausible mechanisms are known, thereby suggesting novel lines of empirical research. They are relevant to artificial intelligence to the extent that they exhibit forms of problem solving, knowledge acquisition, or data storage that are difficult to achieve by more conventional means.

In this article we illustrate an abstract neural network approach that we believe can have relevance for both neuroscience and computer science. Advances in our appreciation of the complexity of biological cells make it clear that the 35-year old metaphor that places the neuron at the level of the computer logic gate is inadequate. Neurons and synapses have information processing capabilities that make use of both short- and long-term information storage, locally implemented by complex biochemical mechanisms. Biochemical networks within cells are known to perform functions that had previously been attributed to networks of interacting cells. These facts call for new neural metaphors. Moreover, advances in computer science suggest the possibility of achieving sophisticated problem-solving capacity through networks of interacting components that are themselves powerful problem-solving systems (e.g., [1] and [2]). In our approach, network components are neuronlike in their basic structure and behavior and communicate by means of excitatory and inhibitory signals rather than by symbolic messages, but they are much more complex than neuronlike adaptive elements studied in the past. Rather than asking how very primitive components can be interconnected in order to solve problems, we are pursuing questions about how components that are themselves capable of solving relatively difficult problems can interact in order to solve problems that are even more difficult.

This article is devoted to the justification of the design of two types of neuronlike adaptive elements and an illustration of the problem-solving capacities of a system consisting of a single element of each type. We call one element an *associative search element* (ASE) and the other an *adaptive critic element* (ACE). As a vehicle for introducing our adaptive elements, we describe an earlier adaptive problem-solving system, called "boxes," developed by Michie and Chambers [3], [4]. We show that a learning strategy similar to theirs can be implemented by a *single* ASE, and we show how its learning performance can be improved by the addition of a *single* ACE. To illustrate the

problem-solving capabilities of these elements, we use the pole-balancing control problem posed by Michie and Chambers to illustrate their boxes algorithm, and we compare the performance of their system with that of our own. We conclude with a brief discussion of behavioral interpretations of our adaptive elements and their possible implications for neuroscience. A strong analogy exists between the behavior of the ACE and animal behavior in classical conditioning experiments, and parallels can be seen between the behavior of the ASE/ACE system and animal behavior in instrumental learning experiments. The adaptive elements we describe are refinements of those we have discussed previously [5]–[10] and were suggested by the work of Klopf [11], [12]. Our approach also has similarities with the work of Widrow and colleagues [13], [14] on what they called "bootstrap adaptation."

The significance of endowing single adaptive elements with this level of problem-solving capability is twofold. First, we wish to suggest neural metaphors, constrained by the computational demands of problem-solving, that postulate functions for the complex cellular mechanisms that are rapidly being elucidated as the study of the cellular basis of learning progresses. Second, we wish to suggest that if adaptive elements are to learn effectively *as network components*, then they must possess adaptive capabilities at least as robust as those of the elements discussed here. As we argue in the following, the learning problem faced by an adaptive element that is deeply embedded in the interior of a network is characterized by some of the same types of complexities that are present in the pole-balancing task considered here.

Thus, although the algorithms that we implement by means of single adaptive elements can obviously be implemented by networks of many simpler elements, we are attempting to delineate those properties required of components if they are to learn how to function as interconnected, cooperating components of networks. The extensive history of attempts to construct powerful adaptive networks and the generally acknowledged failure of these attempts suggest that network components as simple as those usually considered are not adequate. This lesson from previous theoretical studies, together with our contention that the view of neural function that constrained these studies was too limited, leads us to study elements as complex as the ASE and ACE. Despite our ultimate interest in networks, we do not present results in this paper that show that the elements discussed here are able to learn as components of powerful adaptive networks. However, previous simulation experiments with networks of similar elements have provided preliminary support for our approach to adaptive networks [5], [6], [8], and the research discussed here represents an initial attempt to move toward more difficult learning problems.

Although we intend to raise questions about the level in the functional hierarchy of the nervous system at which neurons can be said to act, we are not claiming that there is necessarily a strict correspondence between single neurons and ACE's and ASE's. Some of the features of these elements clearly are not neuronlike but can be implemented in standard ways by elements more faithful to neural limitations. For example, the ASE can "fire" with both negative and positive output values, but it can be implemented by a pair of reciprocally inhibiting elements, each capable only of positive "spikes." Consequently, by the term "neuronlike element" we do not mean a literal neuron model, and we purposefully exclude well-known neuron properties which would have no clear functional role in the present problem.

Our interest in the pole-balancing problem arises from its convenience as a test bed for exploring a variety of algorithms that may enable elements to learn effectively when embedded in networks. We are not interested in pole balancing *per se*, and our formulation of the problem, following that of Michie and Chambers [3], [4], makes it much more difficult than it would need to be if one were simply interested in controlling this type of dynamical system. We assume that the controller's design must be based upon very little knowledge of the controlled system's dynamics and that the evaluative feedback provided to the controller is of much lower quality than is required by standard adaptive control methods. These constraints produce a difficult learning control problem and reflect some of the conditions that we believe characterize the tasks faced by network components. While a variety of well-developed adaptive control methods can be (and have been) successfully applied to pole balancing, we know of none that are directly applicable to the problem subject to the constraints we impose. Additionally, the algorithm we describe can be applied to nonnumerical problems as well as to problems requiring the control of dynamical systems.

II. LEARNING WITHIN NETWORKS

Many of the previous studies of adaptive networks of neuronlike elements focused on adaptive elements that are capable of solving certain types of pattern classification problems. Elements such as the ADALINE (adaptive linear element [16]) and those employed in the Perceptron [15] perform supervised learning pattern classification (see, for example, [17]). These elements form linear discrimination rules by adjusting a set of "synaptic" weights in an attempt to match their response to each training input pattern with a desired response, or correct classification, that is provided by a "teacher." The resulting discrimination rule can be used to classify new pattern instances (perhaps incorrectly), thereby providing a form of generalization. The algorithms implemented by these adaptive elements are closely related to iterative regression methods used in adaptive control for the identification of unknown system parameters [17].

Unfortunately, a network composed of these types of adaptive elements can only learn if its environment contains a teacher that can supply *each* component adaptive element with its individual desired response for each pattern in a training sequence. This is the Achilles' heel of supervised learning pattern classifiers as network components. In many problem-solving tasks, the network's environment may be able to provide assessments of certain *consequences* of the *collective activity* of all of the network components but the environment cannot know the desired responses of individual elements or even evaluate the behavior of individual elements. To use terms encountered in the artificial intelligence literature (e.g., [18]), the network's internal mechanism is not very "transparent" to the "critic."

Other approaches to the problem of learning within adaptive networks rely on adaptive elements that require neither teachers nor critics. These elements employ some form of unsupervised learning, or clustering, algorithm, often based on Hebb's [19] hypothesis that repeated pairing of pre- and postsynaptic activity strengthens synaptic efficacy. While clustering is likely to play an important role in sophisticated problem-solving systems, it does not by itself provide the necessary means for a system to improve performance in tasks determined by factors external to the system, such as, for example, the task of controlling an environment having initially unknown dynamics. For these types of tasks, a learning system must not just cluster information but must form those clusters that are useful in terms of the system's interaction with its environment. Thus it seems necessary to consider networks that learn under the influence of some sort of evaluative feedback, but this feedback cannot be so informative as to provide individualized instruction to each adaptive element.

These considerations have led us to study adaptive elements that are capable of learning to improve performance with respect to an evaluation function that assesses the consequences, which may be quite indirect, of element actions but does not directly specify these actions. Further, these elements are capable of improving performance under conditions of considerable uncertainty. Since evaluative feedback, or reinforcement feedback, will generally assess the performance of the entire network rather than the performance of individual elements, a high degree of uncertainty is necessarily present in the optimization problem faced by any individual component. Additional uncertainty arises from any delay that might exist between the time of an element's action and the time it receives the resulting reinforcement. The reinforcement feedback received by a network component at any time will generally depend upon factors other than its own action taken some fixed time earlier; it will additionally depend upon the actions of a large number of components taken at a variety of earlier times.

The ASE implements one part of our approach to these problems. Since we assume its environment is unable to provide desired responses, the ASE must *discover* what responses lead to improvements in performance. It employs a trial-and-error, or generate-and-test, search process. In the presence of input signals, it generates actions by a random process. Based on feedback that evaluates the problem-solving consequences of the actions, the ASE "tunes in" input signals to bias the action generation process, conditionally on the input, so that it will more likely generate the actions leading to improved performance. Different actions can be optimal when taken in the presence of different input signals. Actions that lead to improved performance when taken in the presence of certain input signals become associated with those signals in a developing input–output mapping. This type of stochastic search allows the ASE to improve performance under conditions of uncertainty. We have called this general process *associative search* [8] to emphasize both its association formation and generate-and-test search aspects.

In providing elements with these capabilities, we have been guided by the hypothesis of Klopf [11], [12] that neurons implement a strategy for attempting to maximize the frequency of occurrence of one type of input signal and minimize the frequency of occurrence of another type. According to this hypothesis, in other words, neurons can be conditioned in an operant or instrumental manner, where certain types of inputs act as rewarding stimuli and others act as punishing stimuli. A neuron learns how to attain certain types of inputs and avoid others by adjusting the transmission efficacy of its synapses according to the consequences of its discharges as fed back through pathways both internal to the nervous system and external to the animal. The ASE departs in several ways from Klopf's hypothesis, but his underlying idea remains the same.

III. Error Correction Versus Reinforcement Learning

Considerable misunderstanding is evident in the literature about how this type of "reinforcement learning" differs from supervised learning pattern classification as performed, for example, by Perceptrons and ADALINE's. It is important to emphasize these differences before we describe our adaptive elements. Supervised learning pattern classification elements are sometimes formulated in such a manner that the training process occurs as follows. A training pattern is presented to the element which responds as directed by its current set of weights; based on knowledge of the correct response, the element's environment feeds back an error signal giving the difference between the actual and correct resonses; the element uses this error signal to update its weight values. This sequence is repeated for all of the training patterns until the error signals become zero. These error signals are response-contingent feedback to the adaptive element, but it is misleading to view this process as a general form of reinforcement learning.

One important difference between the error-correction process just described and reinforcement learning as implemented by the ASE is that the latter does not rely exclusively on its weight values to determine its actions. Instead, it generates actions by a random process that is merely *biased* by the combination of its weight values and the input patterns. Actions are thus not appropriately viewed strictly as *responses* to input patterns. The random component of the generation process introduces the variety that is necessary to serve as the basis for subsequent selection by

evaluative feedback. The ASE therefore searches in its action space in a manner that supervised learning pattern classification machines do not.

Additionally, significant differences exist between general performance evaluation signals and the signed error signals required by supervised learning pattern classification elements. To supply a signed error signal, the environment must know both what the actual action was and what it should have been.[1] Evaluation of performance, on the other hand, may be based on a relative assessment of certain consequences of the element's actions rather than on knowledge of both the correct and actual actions. Widrow *et al.* [13] used the phrase "learning with a critic" to distinguish this type of process from learning with a teacher, as supervised learning pattern classification is sometimes called.

Very few studies have been made of neuronlike elements capable of learning under reinforcement feedback that is less informative than are signed error signals (Farley and Clark [20]; Minsky [21]; and Widrow *et al.* [13]). Indeed, considerable confusion arises from an unfortunate inconsistency in the usage of the term "error." What psychologists mean by trial-and-error learning is not the same as the error-correction process used by supervised learning pattern classification machines. Like the process employed by our ASE, trial-and-error learning is a "selectional" rather than an "instructional" process (cf. the usage of these terms by Edelman [22], although the selectional mechanism of the ASE is quite different from the one he proposes). Much more could be said about these issues, but we shall let the following example further clarify them. It will be apparent that elements such as Perceptrons and ADALINE's cannot by themselves solve the control problem we will consider.

IV. The Credit Assignment Problem

One can view the uncertainty discussed in the foregoing as a result of a fundamental problem that faces any learning system, whether it is natural or artificial, that has been called the "credit-assignment" problem by artificial intelligence researchers [18], [23]. This is the problem of determining what parts of a complex interacting or interlocking set of mechanisms, decisions, or actions deserve credit (blame) for improvements (decrements) in the overall performance of the system. The credit-assignment problem is especially acute when evaluative feedback to the learning system occurs infrequently, for example, upon the completion of a long series of decisions or actions.

Given the widely acknowledged importance of the credit-assignment problem for adaptive problem-solving systems, it is surprising that techniques for its solution have not been more intensely studied. The most successful,

---

[1]It is thus possible to formulate this training paradigm as one in which the learning machine's environment provides training patterns together with their desired responses (as we have done in Section II), and the system itself determines its error. This formulation does not involve feedback that passes through the machine's environment and more clearly reveals the limited nature of this type of process.

and perhaps the most extensible, solution to date was used in the checkers-playing program written by Samuel [24] more than two decade ago. A few isolated studies using similar techniques have been undertaken (Doran [25]; Holland [26]; Minsky [21], [23]; and Witten [27]), but the current approaches to the credit-assignment problem in artificial intelligence largely rely on providing the critic with domain-specific knowledge [18], [27]. Samuel's method, on the other hand, is one by which the system improves its own internal critic by a learning process.

The ACE implements a strategy most closely related to the methods of Samuel [24] and Witten [27] for reducing the severity of the credit-assignment problem. It adaptively develops an evaluation function that is more informative than the one directly available from the learning system's environment. This reduces the uncertainty under which the ASE must learn. The ACE was developed primarily by Sutton as a refinement of the adaptive element model of classical conditioning introduced by Sutton and Barto [9].

V. A LEARNING CONTROL PROBLEM: POLE BALANCING

Fig. 1 shows a schematic representation of a cart to which a rigid pole is hinged. The cart is free to move within the bounds of a one-dimensional track. The pole is free to move only in the vertical plane of the cart and track. The controller can apply an impulsive "left" or "right" force F of fixed magnitude to the cart at discrete time intervals. The cart–pole system was simulated by digital computer using a very detailed model that includes all of the nonlinearities and reactive forces of the physical system (the Appendix provides details of the cart–pole model and simulations). The cart–pole model has four state variables:

x position of the cart on the track,
θ angle of the pole with the vertical,
$\dot{x}$ cart velocity, and
$\dot{\theta}$ rate of change of the angle.

Parameters specify the pole length and mass, cart mass, coefficients of friction between the cart and the track and at the hinge between the pole and the cart, the impulsive control force magnitude, the force due to gravity, and the simulation time step size.

The control problem we pose is identical to the one studied by Michie and Chambers. We assume that the equations of motion of the cart–pole system are not known and that there is no preexisting controller that can be imitated. At each time step, the controller receives a vector giving the cart–pole system's state at that instant. If the pole falls or the cart hits the track boundary, the controller receives a failure signal, the cart–pole system (but not the controller's memory) is reset to its initial state, and another learning trial begins. The controller must attempt to generate controlling forces in order to avoid the failure signal for as long as possible. No evaluative feedback other than the failure signal is available.

Learning to avoid the failure signal under these constraints is a very different problem than learning to balance

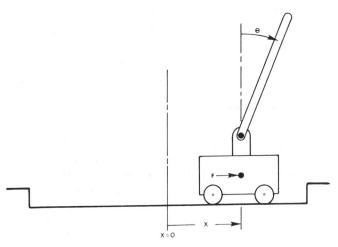

Fig. 1. Cart–pole system to be controlled. Solution of system's equations of motion approximated numerically (see Appendix).

the pole under the conditions usually assumed by control theorists. Since the failure signal will occur only after a long sequence of individual control decisions, a difficult credit-assignment problem arises in the attempt to determine which decisions were responsible for the failure. Neither a continuously available error signal nor a continuously available performance evaluation signal exists, as is the case in more conventional formulations of pole balancing. For example, Widrow and Smith [14] used a linear regression method, implemented by an ADALINE, to approximate the bang-bang control law required for balancing the pole. In order to use this method, however, they had to supply the controller with a signed error signal at each time step whose determination required external knowledge of the correct control decision for that time step. The present formulation of the problem, on the other hand, requires the learning system to discover for itself which control decisions are correct, and in so doing, solve a difficult credit-assignment problem that is completely absent in the usual versions of this problem.

VI. THE BOXES SYSTEM

By first describing Michie and Chambers' [3], [4] boxes system, we can provide much of the justification for the design of our adaptive elements. The strategy of these authors was to decompose the pole-balancing problem into a number of independent subproblems and to use an identical generate-and-test rule for learning to solve each subproblem. They divided the four-dimensional cart–pole state space into disjoint regions (or boxes) by quantizing the four state variables. They distinguished three grades of cart position, six of the pole angle, three of cart velocity, and three of pole angular velocity [4]. We use a similar partition of the state space based on the following quantization thresholds:

1) x: ± 0.8, ± 2.4 m,
2) θ: 0, ± 1, ± 6, $\pm 12°$,
3) $\dot{x}$: ± 0.5, $\pm \infty$ m/s,
4) $\dot{\theta}$: ± 50, $\pm \infty °$/s.

This yields $3 \times 3 \times 6 \times 3 = 162$ regions corresponding to all of the combinations of the intervals. The physical units of these thresholds differ from those used in [3] and [4]. We chose these values and units to produce what seemed like a physically realistic control problem, given our parameterization of the cart–pole simulation (Michie and Chambers did not publish the parameters of their cart–pole simulation. See the Appendix for our parameter values). At present we assume, as Michie and Chambers did, that this quantization is provided from the start (see Section X).

Each box is imagined to contain a *local demon* whose job is to choose a control action (left or right) whenever the system state enters its box. The local demon must learn to choose the action that will tend to be correlated with long system lifetime, that is, a long time until the occurrence of the failure signal. A *global demon* inspects the incoming state vector at each time step and alerts the local demon whose box contains that system state. When a failure signal is received, the global demon distributes it to all local demons. Each local demon maintains estimates of the expected lifetimes of the system following a left decision and following a right decision. A local demon's estimate of the expected lifetime for left is a weighted average of actual system lifetimes over all past occasions that the system state entered the demon's box and the decision left was made. The expected lifetime for the decision right is determined in the same way for occasions in which a right decision was made.

More specifically, upon being signaled by the global demon that the system state has entered its box, a local demon does the following.

1) It chooses the control action left or right according to which has the longest lifetime estimate. The control system emits the control action as soon as the decision is made.

2) It remembers which action was just taken and begins to count time steps.

3) When a failure signal is received, it uses its current count to update the left or right lifetime estimate, depending on which action it chose when its box was entered.

Michie and Chambers' actual algorithm is somewhat more complicated than this, but this description is sufficient for our present purposes. Details are provided in [3] where it is shown that the system is capable of learning to balance the pole for extended periods of time (in one reported run, the pole was balanced for a time approximately corresponding to one hour of real time). Notice that since the effect of a demon's decision will depend on the decisions made by other demons whose boxes are visited during a trial (where a trial is the time period from reset to failure), the environment of a local demon, consisting of the other demons as well as the cart–pole system, does not consistently evaluate the demon's actions.

VII. The Associative Search Element (ASE)

Obviously, many possibilities exist for implementing a system like boxes using neuronlike elements. We know, for example, that any algorithm can be implemented by a network of McCulloch–Pitts abstract neurons acting as logic gates and delay units. Such an implementation would illustrate the neural metaphor resulting from the very earliest contact between neuroscience and digital technology [29]. More recent neural metaphors suggest that each local demon might be implemented by a network of adaptive neurons that would be set into reverberatory activity under conditions corresponding to the demon's box being entered by the state vector. Upon receipt of the failure signal, the magnitude of this reverberatory activity would somehow alter synapses used for triggering control actions. The global demon might be implemented by a neural network responsible for quantizing the system state vectors, conjunctively combining the results, and activating appropriate local demon networks (a neural decoder—see Section X). Finally, an element or network of elements would be required for channeling the action of each local demon network to a common efferent pathway.

In the neuronlike implementation we are pursuing, however, a local demon corresponds to the mechanism of a single synapse (to use the language of neural metaphor), and the output pathway of the postsynaptic element (the ASE) provides the common efferent pathway for control signals. At each synapse of the ASE are both a long-term memory trace that determines control actions and a short-term memory trace that is required to update the long-term trace, a role similar to that of a local demon's counter in the boxes algorithm. To accomplish the global demon's job of activating the appropriate local demon, we assume the existence of a decoder that has four real-valued input pathways (for the system state vector) and 162 binary valued output pathways corresponding to the boxes of Michie and Chambers' system (Fig. 2). The decoder transforms each state vector into a 162-component binary vector whose components are all zeros except for a single one in the position corresponding to the box containing the state vector. This vector is provided as input to the ASE and effectively selects the synapse corresponding to the appropriate box. For the other job of the global demon, that of distributing a failure signal to all of the local demons, we just let the adaptive element receive the failure signal via its reinforcement pathway and distribute the information to all of of its afferent synapses. In this way the entire boxes algorithm can be implemented by a single neuronlike ASE and an appropriate decoder.

In more detail, an ASE is defined as follows. The element has a reinforcement input pathway, n pathways for nonreinforcement input, and a single output pathway (Fig. 2). Let $x_i(t), 1 \leq i \leq n$, denote the real-valued signal on the ith nonreinforcement input pathway at time t, and let $y(t)$ denote the output at time t. Associated with each nonreinforcement input pathway i is a real-valued weight with value at time t denoted by $w_i(t)$.

The element's output $y(t)$ is determined from the input vector $X(t) = (x_1(t), \cdots, x_n(t))$ as follows:

$$y(t) = f\left[\sum_{i=1}^{n} w_i(t) x_i(t) + \text{noise}(t) \right] \quad (1)$$

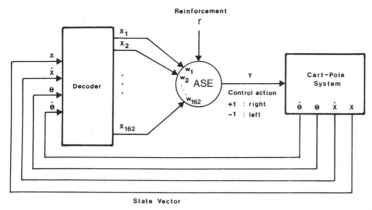

Fig. 2. ASE controller for cart–pole system. ASE's input is determined from current cart–pole state vector by decoder that produces output vector consisting of zeros with single one indicating which of 162 boxes contains state vector. ASE's output determines force applied to cart. Reinforcement is constant throughout trial and becomes -1 to signal failure.

where noise (t) is a real random variable with probability density function d and f is either a threshold, sigmoid, or identity function. For the pole-balancing illustration, d is the mean zero Gaussian distribution with variance σ^2, and f is the following threshold function:

$$f(x) = \begin{cases} +1, & \text{if } x \geqslant 0 \quad \text{(control action right)} \\ -1, & \text{if } x < 0 \quad \text{(control action left)}. \end{cases}$$

This follows the usual linear threshold convention common in adaptive network studies, but our approach does not depend strongly on the specifics of the input/output function of the element.

According to (1), actions are emitted even in the absence of nonzero input signals. The element's output is determined by chance, with a probability biased by the weighted sum of the input signals. If that sum is zero, the left and right control actions are equally probable. Assuming the decoder input shown in Fig. 2, a positive weight w_i, for example, would make the decision right more probable than left when box i is entered by the system state vector. The value of a weight, therefore, plays a role corresponding to the difference between the expected lifetimes for the left and right actions stored by a local demon in the boxes system. However, unlike the boxes system, the weight only determines the probability of an action rather than the action itself. The learning process updates the action probabilities. Also note that an input vector need not be of the restricted form produced by the decoder in order for (1) and the equations that follow to the meaningful.

The weights $w_i, 1 \leqslant i \leqslant n$, change over (discrete) time as follows:

$$w_i(t+1) = w_i(t) + \alpha r(t) e_i(t) \qquad (2)$$

where

α positive constant determining the rate of change of w_i,
$r(t)$ real-valued *reinforcement* at time t, and
$e_i(t)$ *eligibility* at time t of input pathway i.

The basic idea expressed by (2) is that whenever certain conditions (to be discussed later) hold for input pathway i, then that pathway becomes eligible to have its weight modified, and it remains eligible for some period of time after the conditions cease to hold. How w_i changes depends on the reinforcement received during periods of eligibility. If the reinforcement indicates improved performance, then the weights of the eligible pathways are changed so as to make the element more likely to do whatever it did that made those pathways eligible. If reinforcement indicates decreased performance, then the weights of the eligible pathways are changed to make the element more likely to do something else. The term "eligibility" and this weight update scheme are derived from the theory of Klopf [11], [12] and have precursors in the work of Farley and Clark [20], Minsky [21], and others. This general approach to reinforcement learning is related to the theory of stochastic learning automata [30], [31], which has its roots in the work of Bush and Mosteller [32] and Tsetlin [33].

Reinforcement: Positive r indicates the occurrence of a rewarding event and negative r indicates the occurrence of a punishing event.[2] It can be regarded as a measure of the *change* in the value of a performance criterion as commonly used in control theory. For the pole-balancing problem, r remains zero throughout a trial and becomes -1 when failure occurs.

Eligibility: Klopf [11] proposed that a pathway should reach maximum eligibility a short time after the occurrence of a pairing of a nonzero input signal on that pathway with the "firing" of the element. Eligibility should decay thereafter toward zero. Thus, when the consequences of the element's firing are fed back to the element, credit or blame can be assigned to the weights that will alter the firing probability when a similar input pattern occurs in the future. More generally, the eligibility of a pathway reflects the extent to which input activity on that pathway was paired in the past with element output activity. The eligibility of pathway i at time t is therefore a *trace* of the product $y(\tau) x_i(\tau)$ for times τ preceding t. If either or both of the quantities $y(\tau)$ and $x_i(\tau)$ are negative (as they can be for the ASE defined earlier), then credit is assigned

---

[2]A negative value of r is not the same as a psychologists's "negative reinforcement." In psychology, negative reinforcement is reinforcement due to the cessation of an aversive stimulus.

appropriately via (2) if eligibility is a trace of the signed product $y(\tau)x_i(\tau)$.

For computational simplicity, we generate exponentially decaying eligibility traces e_i using the following linear difference equation:

$$e_i(t + 1) = \delta e_i(t) + (1 - \delta)y(t)x_i(t), \qquad (3)$$

where $\delta, 0 \leqslant \delta < 1$, determines the trace decay rate. Note that each synapse has its own local eligibility trace.

Eligibility plays a role analogous to the part of the boxes local-demon algorithm that, when the demon's box is entered and an action has been chosen, remembers what action was chosen and begins to count. The factor $x_i(t)$ in (3) triggers the eligibility trace, a kind of count, or contributes to an ongoing trace, whenever box i is entered ($x_i(t) = 1$). Instead of explicitly remembering what action was chosen, our system contributes a different amount to the eligibility trace depending on what action was chosen (via the term $y(t)$ in (3)). Thus the trace contains information not only about how long ago a box was entered but also about what decision was made when it was entered.

Unlike the count initiated by a local demon in the boxes system, however, the eligibility trace effectively counts down rather than up (more precisely, its magnitude decays toward zero). Recall that reinforcement r remains zero until a failure occurs, at which time it becomes -1. Thus whatever control decision was made when a box was visited will always be made *less* likely when the failure occurs, but the longer the time interval between the decision and the occurrence of the failure signal, the less this decrease in probability will be. From one perspective, this process seems appropriate. Since the failure signal always eventually occurs, the action that was taken may deserve some of the blame for the failure. However, this view misses the point that even though both actions inevitably lead to failure, one action is probably *better* than the other. The learning process defined by (1)–(3) needs to be more subtle to ensure convergence to the actions that yield the least punishment in cases in which only punishment is available. In the present article, we build this subtlety into the ACE rather than into the ASE. Among its other functions, the ACE constructs predictions of reinforcement so that if punishment is less than its expected level, it acts as reward. For the pole-balancing task, the ASE as defined here must operate in conjunction with the ACE.

Although the boxes system and the version of the pole-balancing problem described earlier serve well to make an ASE's design understandable, the ASE does not represent an attempt to duplicate the boxes algorithm in neuronlike form. We are interested in tasks more general than the pole-balancing problem and in learning systems that are more general than the boxes system. An ASE is less restricted than the boxes system in several ways. First, the boxes system is based on the subdivision of the problem space into a finite number of nonoverlapping regions, and no generalization is attempted between regions. It develops a control rule that is effectively specified by means of a lookup table. Although a form of generalization can be easily added to the boxes algorithm by using an averaging process over neighboring boxes (see Section X) it is not immediately obvious how to extend the algorithm to take advantage of the other forms of generalization that would be possible if the controlled system's states could be represented by arbitrary vectors rather than only by the standard unit basis vectors which are produced by a suitable decoder. The ASE can accept arbitrary input vectors and, although we do not illustrate it in this article, can be regarded as a step toward extending the type of generalization produced by error-correction supervised learning pattern classification methods to the less restricted reinforcement learning paradigm (see Section III).

The boxes system is also restricted in that its design was based on the *a priori* knowledge that the time until failure was to serve as the evaluation criterion and that the learning process would be divided into distinct trials that would always end with a failure signal. This knowledge permitted Michie and Chambers to reduce the uncertainty in the problem by restricting each local demon to choosing the same action each time its box was entered during any given trial. The ASE, on the other hand, is capable of working to achieve rewarding events and to avoid punishing events which might occur at any time. It is not exclusively failure-driven, and its operation is specified without reference to the notion of a trial.

VIII. THE ADAPTIVE CRITIC ELEMENT (ACE)

Fig. 3 shows an ASE together with an ACE configured for the pole-balancing task. The ACE receives the externally supplied reinforcement signal which it uses to determine how to compute, on the basis of the current cart–pole state vector, an improved reinforcement signal that it sends to the ASE. Expressed in terms of the boxes system, the job of the ACE is to store in each box a prediction or expectation of the reinforcement that can eventually be obtained from the environment by choosing an action for that box. The ACE uses this prediction to determine a reinforcement signal that it delivers to the ASE whenever the box is entered by the cart–pole state, thus permitting learning to occur throughout the pole-balancing trials rather than solely upon failure. This greatly decreases the uncertainty faced by the ASE. The central idea behind the ACE algorithm is that predictions are formed that predict not just reinforcement but also future predictions of reinforcement.

Like the ASE, the ACE has a reinforcement input pathway, n pathways for nonreinforcement input, and a single output pathway (Fig. 3). Let $r(t)$ denote the real-valued reinforcement at time t; let $x_i(t), 1 \leqslant i \leqslant n$, denote the real-valued signal on the ith nonreinforcement input pathway at time t; and let $\hat{r}(t)$ denote the real-valued output signal at time t. Each nonreinforcement input pathway i has a weight with real value $v_i(t)$ at time t. The output $\hat{r}$ is the improved reinforcement signal that is used by the ASE in place of r in (2).

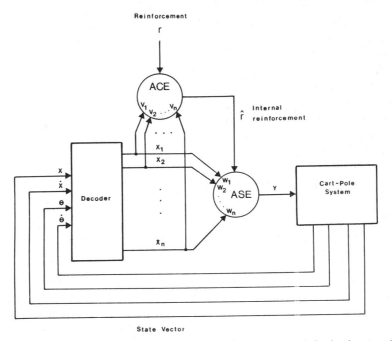

Fig. 3. ASE and ACE configured for pole-balancing task. ACE receives same nonreinforcing input as ASE and uses it to compute an improved or internal reinforcement signal to be used by ASE.

In order to produce $\hat{r}(t)$, the ACE must determine a prediction $p(t)$ of eventual reinforcement that is a function of the input vector $X(t)$ (which in the boxes paradigm, simply selects a box). We let

$$p(t) = \sum_{i=1}^{n} v_i(t)x_i(t) \tag{4}$$

and seek a means of updating the weights v_i so that $p(t)$ converges to an accurate prediction. The updating rule we use is

$$v_i(t+1) = v_i(t) + \beta[r(t) + \gamma p(t) - p(t-1)]\bar{x}_i(t), \tag{5}$$

where β is a positive constant determining the rate of change of v_i; $\gamma, 0 < \gamma \leqslant 1$, is a constant to be explained below; $r(t)$ is the reinforcement signal supplied by the environment at time t; and $\bar{x}_i(t)$ is the value at time t of a *trace* of the input variable x_i.

It is beyond the scope of the present paper to explain the derivation of this learning rule fully (see [7] and [9]). Very briefly, the trace $\bar{x}_i$ acts much like the eligibility trace e_i defined by (3). Here, however, an input pathway gains positive eligibility whenever a nonzero signal is present on that pathway, irrespective of what the element's action is. We compute $\bar{x}_i$ using the following linear difference equation (cf. (3)):

$$\bar{x}_i(t+1) = \lambda \bar{x}_i(t) + (1-\lambda)x_i(t), \tag{6}$$

where $\lambda, 0 \leqslant \lambda < 1$ determines the trace decay rate.

According to (6), an eligible pathways's weight changes whenever the actual reinforcement $r(t)$ plus the current prediction $p(t)$ differs from the value $p(t-1)$ that was predicted for this sum. Closely related to the ADALINE learning rule and related regression techniques, this rule provides a means of finding weight values such that $p(t-1)$ approximates $r(t) + \gamma p(t)$, or, equivalently, such that $p(t)$ approximates $r(t+1) + \gamma p(t+1)$. By attempting to predict its own prediction, the learning rule produces predictions that tend to be the earliest possible indictions of eventual reinforcement. The constant γ, related to Witten's [27] "discount factor," provides for eventual extinction of predictions in the absence of external reinforcement. If $\gamma = 1$, predictions will be self-sustaining in the absence of external reinforcement; whereas if $0 < \gamma < 1$, predictions will decay in the absence of external reinforcement. In our simulations, $\gamma = 0.95$.

The ACE's output, the improved or internal reinforcement signal, is computed from these predictions as follows:

$$\hat{r}(t) = r(t) + \gamma p(t) - p(t-1). \tag{7}$$

This is the same expression appearing in (5). The reader should note that with $\hat{r}$ substituted for r in (2), the weight updating rules for the ASE and ACE ((2) and (5), respectively) differ only in their forms of eligibility traces. The ASE's traces are conditional on its output, whereas the ACE's are not.

Although this process works for arbitrary input vectors, it is easiest to justify (7) by again specializing to the boxes input representation. According to (7), as the cart–pole state moves between boxes without failure occurring (i.e., $r(t) = 0$), the reinforcement $\hat{r}(t)$ sent to the ASE is the difference between the prediction of reinforcement of the current box (discounted by γ) and the prediction of reinforcement of the previous box. Increases in reinforcement prediction therefore become rewarding events (assuming $\gamma = 1$), and decreases become penalizing events.

When failure occurs, the situation is slightly different. Given the way the control problem is represented, when failure occurs the cart–pole state is not in any box. Thus all $x_i(t)$ are equal to zero at failure, and according to (4), so is $p(t)$. Upon failure, then, the reinforcement sent to the ASE is the externally supplied reinforcement $r(t) = -1$, minus the previous prediction $p(t-1)$. Consequently, an unpredicted failure results in $\hat{r}(t)$ being negative. This both punishes the actions made preceding the failure and, via (5), increments the predictions of failure (i.e., decrements the p's) of the boxes entered before the failure. A fully predicted failure generates no punishment. However, when a box with such a high prediction of failure is entered from a box with a lower prediction of failure, the recently made actions are punished and the recent predictions of failure are incremented, just as they were initially upon failure. Similarly, if the cart–pole state moves from a box with a higher prediction of failure to a box with a lower prediction, the recent actions are rewarded and recent predictions of failure are decremented (i.e., the p's are incremented). The system thus learns which boxes are "safe" and which are "dangerous." It punishes itself for moving from any box to a more dangerous box and rewards itself for moving from any box to a safer box. In the following we discuss the relation between the behavior of the ACE and that of animals in classical conditioning experiments.

IX. SIMULATION RESULTS

We implemented the boxes system as described in [3] and [4] as well as our systems shown in Fig. 2 (ASE alone) and Fig. 3 (ASE with ACE). We wanted to determine what kinds of neuronlike elements could attain or exceed the performance of the boxes system. Our results suggest that a system using an ASE with internal reinforcement supplied by an ACE is easily able to outperform the boxes system. We must emphasize at the outset, however, that it is not our intention to criticize Michie and Chambers' program: the boxes system they described was in an initial state of development and clearly could be extended to include a mechanism analogous to our ACE. We make comparisons with the performance of the boxes system because it provides a convenient reference point.

We simulated a series of runs of each learning system attempting to control the same cart–pole simulation (see the Appendix). Each run consisted of a sequence of trials, where each trial began with the cart–pole state $x = 0$, $\dot{x} = 0$, $\theta = 0$, $\dot{\theta} = 0$, and ended with a failure signal indicating that θ left the interval $[-12°, 12°]$ or x left the interval $[-2.4 \text{ m}, 2.4 \text{ m}]$. We also set all the trace variables e_i to zero at the start of each trial. The learning systems were "naive" at the start of each run (i.e., all the weights w_i and v_i were set to zero). At the start of each boxes run, we supplied a different seed value to the pseudorandom number generator that we used to initialize the state of the learning system and to break ties in comparing expected lifetimes in order to choose control actions. We did not reset the cart–pole state to a randomly chosen state at the start of each trial as was done in the experiments reported in [3] and [4]. At the start of each run of an ASE system, we supplied a different seed to the pseudorandom number generator that we used to generate the noise used in (1). We approximated this Gaussian random variable by the usual procedure of summing uniformly distributed random variables (we used an eightfold sum). Since the ASE runs began with weight vectors equal to zero, initial actions for each box were equiprobable, and initial ACE predictions were zero. Except for the random number generator seeds,

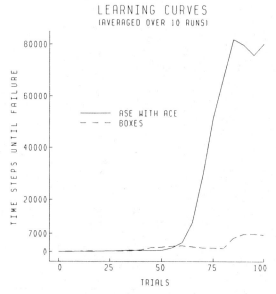

Fig. 4. Simulation results. Performance of boxes system and ASE/ACE system averaged over ten runs. See text for complete explanation.

identical parameter values were used for all runs. Runs consisted of 100 trials unless the run's duration exceeded 500 000 time steps (approximately 2.8 h of simulated real time), in which case the run was terminated. For our implementation of the boxes system, we used the parameter values published in [3]. We experimented with other parameter values without obtaining consistently better performance. We did not attempt to optimize the performance of the systems using the ASE. We picked values that seemed reasonable based on our previous experience with similar adaptive elements.

Figs. 4 and 5 show the results of our simulations of boxes and the ASE/ACE system. The graphs of Fig. 4 are averages of performance over the ten runs that produced the individual graphs shown in Fig. 5. In both figures, a single point is plotted for each bin of five trials giving the number of time steps until failure averaged over those five trials. Almost all runs of the ASE/ACE system, and one run of the boxes system, were terminated after 500 000 time steps before all 100 trials took place (those whose graphs terminate short of 100 trials in Fig. 5). We stopped the simulation before failure on the last trials of these runs. To produce the averages for all 100 trials shown in Fig. 4, we needed to make special provision for the interrupted runs. If the duration of the trial that was underway when the run was interrupted was less than the duration of the immediately preceding (and therefore complete) trial, then we assigned to fictitious remaining trials the duration of that preceding trial. Otherwise, we assigned to fictitious remaining trials the duration of the last trial when it was interrupted. We did this to prevent any short interrupted trials from producing deceptively low averages.

The ASE/ACE system achieved much longer runs than did the boxes system. Fig. 5 shows that the ACE/ASE system tended to solve the problem before it had experienced 100 failures, whereas the boxes system tended not to. Obviously, we cannot make definitive statements about the relative performance of these systems, or about the general utility of the ASE/ACE system solely on the basis of these

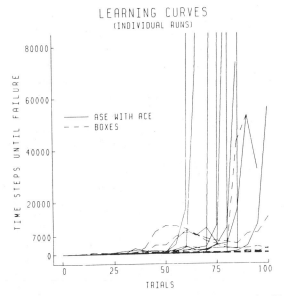

LEARNING CURVES
(INDIVIDUAL RUNS)

—— ASE WITH ACE
- - - BOXES

Fig. 5. Simulation results. Performance of boxes system and ASE/ACE system in individual runs that were averaged to produce Fig. 4. See text for complete explanation.

experiments. However, these results encourage us to continue developing the principles upon which the ASE/ACE system is based.

The parameter values used in producing these results were $\alpha = 1000$, $\beta = 0.5$, $\delta = 0.9$, $\gamma = 0.95$, $\lambda = 0.8$, and $\sigma = 0.01$. Except for one set of extreme values, these were the only values we tried. The large value of α was chosen so that large changes in the weights w_i occurred upon reinforcement. This caused the probability of a rewarded action to become nearly one and the probability of a penalized action to become nearly zero. We did this in an attempt to implement in our system the feature of the boxes system that causes each local demon to choose the same action each time its box is entered in any given trial. This greatly reduces the uncertainty in the problem but would be inappropriate, we think, for problems in which other reinforcing events could occur during trials. The parameters δ and λ determine the durations of the eligibility traces. Their values, 0.9 and 0.8, respectively, cause long, slowly decaying traces to form, as seemed appropriate given the nature of the problem.

The good performance of the ASE/ACE system was almost entirely due to the ACE's supplying reinforcement throughout trials. For the boxes system and for an ASE without an ACE, learning occurs only upon failure, an event that becomes less frequent as learning proceeds. With the ACE in place, an ASE can receive feedback on every time step. The learning produced by this feedback causes the system to attempt to enter particular parts of the state space and to avoid others. We simulated the control problem using an ASE without an ACE, using the same parameter settings that worked well for the ASE/ACE experiments. The ASE was not able to attain the level of performance shown by the boxes system. These shortcomings of the ASE are due to difficulties in the convergence process in tasks involving only penalizing feedback, as

discussed in Section VII. The use of reinforcement computed by the ACE markedly changes this property of the pole-balancing problem. At present, we have little experience with ASE-like elements operating without ACE supplied reinforcement in the pole-balancing problem.

X. THE DECODER

We have assumed the existence of a decoder that effectively divides the cart–pole state space into a number of disjoint regions by transforming each state vector into a vector having 162 components, all but one of which is zero. We call this a decoder after a similar device used in computer memory circuits to transform each memory address into a signal on the wire connected to the physical location having that address. With this decoder providing its input, the ASE essentially fills in a lookup table of control actions. Similarly, the ACE fills in a table of reinforcement predictions. Each item of information is stored by the setting of the value of a single synaptic weight at a given location.

As a consequence of this localized storage scheme, no generalization occurs beyond the confines of a given box. Given the relative smoothness of the cart–pole dynamics, learning would be faster if information stored in a box could be extrapolated to neighboring boxes (using the Euclidean metric). This can be accomplished by using a kind of decoder that produces activity on overlapping sets of output pathways. It is interesting to note that in several theories of sensorimotor learning, it is postulated that the granular layer of the cerebellum implements just this kind of decoder and that Purkinje cells are adaptive elements [34], [35].[3]

Localized extrapolation is not the only type of generalization that can be useful. There has lately been increasing interest in "associative memory networks" that use distributed representations in which dispersed rather than localized patterns of activity encode information [36], [37]. Rather than implementing table-lookup storage, associative memories use weighted summations to compute output vectors from input vectors. This style of information storage provides generalization among patterns according to where they lie with respect to a set of linear discriminant functions. Since the ASE and ACE use weighted summations that are defined for arbitrary input vectors, they implement linear discriminant functions and are capable of forming information storage networks having all of the properties that have generated interest in associative memory networks. Unlike the associative memory networks discussed in the literature, however, networks of ASE-like components are capable of discovering via reinforcement learning what information is useful to store. These aspects

[3]In these theories, the adaptive elements perform supervised learning pattern classification, with climbing fiber input providing the desired responses, and not the type of reinforcement learning with which the present article is concerned. If the adaptive capacity of a Purkinje cell were limited to that postulated in these theories, then a Purkinje cell would not be able to solve the type of problem illustrated by the pole-balancing task described in this article.

of ASE's are emphasized by Barto *et al.* [8] where *associative search* networks are discussed.

Whether environmental states are represented using localized or distributed patterns, the problem remains of how to choose the specifics of the representations in order to facilitate learning. In this article we followed Michie and Chambers in choosing a state–space partition based on special knowledge of the control task. As they point out, it is easy to choose a partition that makes the task impossible [4]. For the next stage of development of the boxes system, Michie and Chambers planned to give the system the ability to change the boundaries of the boxes by the processes of "splitting" and "lumping" [4]. We are not aware of any results they published on these processes, but we were motivated in part by their comments to experiment with layered networks of ASE-like adaptive elements in order to examine the feasibility of implementing a kind of adaptive decoder. Some preliminary results, reported in [5], were encouraging, and we are continuing our investigation in this direction.

XI. Animal Learning

Minsky has pointed out [23] that methods for reducing the severity of the credit-assignment problem like the one used in Samuel's checkers player are suggestive of secondary or conditioned reinforcement phenomena in animal learning studies. A stimulus acquires reinforcing qualities (i.e., becomes a secondary reinforcer) if it predicts either primary reinforcement (e.g., food or shock) or some other secondary reinforcer. It is generally held that higher order classical conditioning, whereby previously conditioned conditioned stimuli (CS's) can act as unconditioned stimuli (US's) for earlier potential CS's, is the basis for the development of secondary reinforcement [38].

The ACE is a refinement of the model of classical conditioning that was presented in [9]. That model's behavior is consistent with the Rescorla–Wagner model of classical conditioning [39]. While not without certain problems, the Rescorla–Wagner model has been the most influential model of classical conditioning for the last ten years [40]. One interpretation of the basic premise of the Rescorla–Wagner model is that the degree to which an event is "unexpected" or "surprising" determines the degree to which it enters into associations with earlier events. Stimuli lose their reinforcing qualities to the extent that they are expected on the basis of the occurrence of earlier stimuli. The model upon which the ACE is based extends the basic mechanism of the Rescorla–Wagner model to

provide for some of the features of higher order conditioning, the influence of relative event timing within trials, and the occurrence of conditioned responses (CR's) that anticipate the US. In these terms, the failure signal r corresponds to the US, the signals x_i from the decoder correspond to potential CS's, and the prediction p corresponds to a component of the CR. We have not yet thoroughly investigated the extent to which the ACE/ASE system is a valid model of animal behavior in instrumental conditioning experiments.

XII. Conclusion

It should be clear that our approach differs from that of the pioneering adaptive neural-network theorists of the 1950's and 1960's. We have built into single neuronlike adaptive elements a problem-solving capacity that in many respects exceeds that achieved in the past by entire simulated neural networks. The metaphor for neural function suggested by this approach provides, at least to us, the first convincing inkling of how nervous tissue could possibly be capable of its exquisite feats of problem solving and control.

We argued that components of powerful adaptive networks must be at least as sophisticated as the components described in this article. If this were true for biological networks as well as for artificial networks, then it would suggest that parallels might exist between neurons and the adaptive elements described here. It would suggest, for example, that 1) there are single neuron analogs of instrumental conditioning and chemically specialized reinforcing neurons that may themselves be adaptive (see [41]); 2) the random component of an instrumental neuron's behavior is necessary for generating variety to serve as the basis for subsequent selection; and 3) mechanisms exist for maintaining relatively long-lasting synaptically local traces of activity that modulate changes in synaptic efficacy. Although some of these implications are supported in varying degrees by existing data, there are no data that provide direct support for the existence of the specific mechanisms used in our adaptive elements. By showing how neuronlike elements can solve genuinely difficult problems that are solved routinely by many animals, we hope to stimulate interest in the relevant experimental research.

Appendix
Details of the Cart–Pole Simulation

The cart–pole system is modeled by the following nonlinear differential equations (see [42]):

$$\ddot{\theta}_t = \frac{g \sin \theta_t + \cos \theta_t \left[\dfrac{-F_t - ml\dot{\theta}_t^2 \sin \theta_t + \mu_c \, \text{sgn} \, (\dot{x}_t)}{m_c + m} \right] - \dfrac{\mu_p \dot{\theta}_t}{ml}}{l \left[\dfrac{4}{3} - \dfrac{m \cos^2 \theta_t}{m_c + m} \right]}$$

$$\ddot{x}_t = \frac{F_t + ml \left[\dot{\theta}_t^2 \sin \theta_t - \ddot{\theta}_t \cos \theta_t \right] - \mu_c \, \text{sgn} \, (\dot{x}_t)}{m_c + m}$$

where

$g = -9.8 \text{ m/s}^2$, acceleration due to gravity,
$m_c = 1.0$ kg, mass of cart
$m = 0.1$ kg, mass of pole,
$l = 0.5$ m, half-pole length,
$\mu_c = 0.0005$, coefficient of friction of cart on track,
$\mu_p = 0.000002$, coefficient of friction of pole on cart,
$F_t = \pm 10.0$ newtons, force applied to cart's center of mass at time t.

We initially used the Adams–Moulton predictor–corrector method to approximate numerically the solution of these equations, but the results reported in this article were produced using Euler's method with a time step of 0.02 s for the sake of computational speed. Comparisons of solutions generated by the Adams–Moulton methods and the less accurate Euler method did not reveal discrepencies that we deemed significant for the purposes of this article.

ACKNOWLEDGMENT

We thank A. H. Klopf for bringing to us a set of ideas filled with possibilities. We are grateful also to D. N. Spinelli, M. A. Arbib, and S. Epstein for their valuable comments and criticisms; to D. Lawton for first making us aware of Michie and Chambers' boxes system; to D. Politis and W. Licata for pointing out an important error in our original cart–pole simulations; and to S. Parker for essential help in preparing the manuscript.

REFERENCES

[1] B. Chandrasekaran, "Natural and social system metaphors for distributed problem solving: Introduction to the issue," *IEEE Trans. Syst., Man., Cybern.*, vol. SMC-11, pp. 1–5, 1981.

[2] V. R. Lesser and D. D. Corkill, "Functionally-accurate, cooperative distributed systems," *IEEE Trans. Syst., Man, Cybern.*, vol. SMC-11, pp. 81–96, 1981.

[3] D. Michie and R. A. Chambers, "BOXES: An experiment in adaptive control," in *Machine Intelligence 2*, E. Dale and D. Michie, Eds. Edinburgh: Oliver and Boyd, 1968, pp. 137–152.

[4] D. Michie and R. A. Chambers, "'Boxes' as a model of pattern-formation," in *Towards a Theoretical Biology*, vol. 1, *Prolegomena*, C. H. Waddington, Ed. Edinburgh: Edinburgh Univ. Press, 1968, pp. 206–215.

[5] A. G. Barto, C. W. Anderson, and R. S. Sutton, "Synthesis of nonlinear control surfaces by a layered associative search network," *Biol. Cybern.*, vol. 43, pp. 175–185, 1982.

[6] A. G. Barto and R. S. Sutton, "Landmark learning: An illustration of associative search," *Biol. Cybern.*, vol. 42, pp. 1–8, 1981.

[7] ____, "Simulation of anticipatory responses in classical conditioning by a neuron-like adaptive element," *Behavioral Brain Res.*, vol. 4, pp. 221–235, 1982.

[8] A. G. Barto, R. S. Sutton, and P. S. Brouwer, "Associative search network: A reinforcement learning associative memory," *Biol. Cybern.*, vol. 40, pp. 201–211, 1981.

[9] R. S. Sutton and A. G. Barto, "Toward a modern theory of adaptive networks: Expectation and prediction," *Psychol. Rev.*, vol. 88, pp. 135–171, 1981.

[10] ____, "An adaptive network that constructs and uses an internal model of its world," *Cognition and Brain Theory*, vol. 4, pp. 213–246, 1981.

[11] A. H. Klopf, "Brain function and adaptive systems—A heterostatic theory," Air Force Cambridge Res. Lab. Res. Rep., AFCRL-72-0164, Bedford, MA, 1972. (A summary appears in *Proc. Int. Conf. Syst., Man, Cybern.*, 1974).

[12] A. H. Klopf, *The Hedonistic Neuron: A Theory of Memory, Learning, and Intelligence.* Washington, DC: Hemisphere, 1982.

[13] B. Widrow, N. K. Gupta, and S. Maitra, "Punish/reward: learning with a critic in adaptive threshold systems," *IEEE Trans. Syst., Man, Cybern.*, vol. SMC-3, pp. 455–465, 1973.

[14] B. Widrow and F. W. Smith, "Pattern-recognizing control systems," in *Computer and Information Sciences*, J. T. Tow and R. H. Wilcox, Eds. Clever Hume Press, 1964, pp. 288–317.

[15] F. Rosenblatt, *Principles of Neurodynamics.* New York: Spartan, 1962.

[16] B. Widrow and M. E. Hoff, "Adaptive switching circuits," in *1960 WESCON Conv. Record*, part IV, 1960, pp. 96–104.

[17] R. O. Duda and P. E. Hart, *Pattern Classification and Scene Analysis.* New York: Wiley, 1973.

[18] P. R. Cohen and E. A. Feigenbaum, *The Handbook of Artificial Intelligence*, vol. 3. Los Altos, CA: Kauffman, 1982.

[19] D. O. Hebb, *Organization of Behavior.* New York: Wiley, 1949.

[20] B. G. Farley and W. A. Clark, "Simulation of self-organizing systems by digital computer," *IRE Trans. Inform. Theory*, vol. PGIT-4, pp. 76–84, 1954

[21] M. L. Minsky, "Theory of neural-analog reinforcement systems and its application to the brain-model problem," Ph.D. dissertation, Princeton Univ., Princeton, NJ, 1954.

[22] G. M. Edelman, "Group selection and phasic reentrant signaling: A theory of higher brain function," in *The Mindful Brain: Cortical Organization and the Group-Selective Theory of Higher Brain Function*, G. M. Edelman and V. B. Mountcastle, Eds. Cambridge, MA: MIT Press, 1978.

[23] M. L. Minsky, "Steps toward artificial intelligence," *Proc. IRE*, vol. 49, pp. 8–30, 1961.

[24] A. L. Samuel, "Some studies in machine learning using the game of checkers," *IBM J. Res. Develop.*, vol. 3, pp. 210–229, 1959.

[25] J. Doran, "An approach to automatic problem solving," in *Machine Intelligence*, vol. 1, E. L. Collins and D. Michie, Eds. Edinburgh: Oliver and Boyd, 1967, pp. 105–123.

[26] J. H. Holland, "Adaptive algorithms for discovering and using general patterns in growing knowledge-bases," *Int. J. Policy Anal. Inform. Syst.*, vol. 4, pp. 217–240, 1980.

[27] I. H. Witten, "An adaptive optimal controller for discrete-time Markov environments," *Inform. Contr.*, vol. 34, pp. 286–295, 1977.

[28] T. D. Dietterich and B. G. Buchanan, "The role of the critic in learning systems," Stanford Univ. Tech. Rep., STAN-CS-81-891, 1981.

[29] W. S. McCulloch and W. H. Pitts, "A logical calculus of the ideas immanent in nervous activity," *Bull. Math. Biophys.*, vol. 5, pp. 115–133, 1943.

[30] K. S. Narendra and M. A. L. Thatachar, "Learning automata—A survey," *IEEE Trans. Syst., Man, Cybern.*, vol. SMC-4, pp. 323–334, 1974.

[31] S. Lakshmivarahan, *Learning Algorithms Theory and Applications.* New York: Springer-Verlag, 1981.

[32] R. R. Bush and F. Mosteller, *Stochastic Models for Learning.* New York: Wiley, 1958.

[33] M. L. Tsetlin, *Automaton Theory and Modelling of Biological Systems.* New York: Academic, 1973.

[34] J. A. Albus, *Brains, Behavior, and Robotics.* Peterborough, NH: BYTE Books, 1981.

[35] D. Marr, "A theory of cerebellar cortex," *J. Physiol.*, vol. 202, pp. 437–470, 1969.

[36] G. E. Hinton and J. A. Anderson, Eds., *Parallel Models of Associative Memory.* Hillsdale, NJ: Erlbaum, 1981.

[37] T. Kohonen, *Associative Memory: A System Theoretic Approach.* Berlin, Germany: Springer, 1977.

[38] R. A. Rescorla, *Pavlovian Second-Order Conditioning: Studies in Associative Learning.* Hillsdale, NJ: Erlbaum, 1980.

[39] R. A. Rescorla and A. R. Wagner, "A theory of Pavlovian conditioning: Variations in the effectiveness of reinforcement and nonreinforcement," in *Classical Conditioning II: Current Research and Theory*, A. H. Black and W. R. Prokasy, Eds. New York: Appleton-Century-Crofts, 1972.

[40] A. Dickinson, *Contemporary Animal Learning Theory.* Cambridge: Cambridge Univ. Press, 1980.

[41] L. Stein and J. D. Belluzzi, "Beyond the reflex arc: A neuronal model of operant conditioning," in *Changing Concepts of the Nervous System.* New York: Academic, 1982.

[42] R. H. Cannon, *Dynamics of Physical Systems.* New York: McGraw-Hill, 1967.

On the Use of Backpropagation
in Associative Reinforcement Learning

Ronald J. Williams
College of Computer Science
Northeastern University
Boston, MA 02115

Abstract—This paper describes several ways that backpropagation can be useful in training networks to perform associative reinforcement learning tasks. One way is to train a second network to model the environmental reinforcement signal and to then backpropagate through this network into the first network. This technique has been proposed and explored in various forms by others. Another way, implicit in earlier work of this author, is based on the use of the REINFORCE algorithm and amounts to backpropagating through deterministic parts of the network while performing a correlation-style computation where the behavior is stochastic. A third way, which is an extension of the second, allows backpropagation through the stochastic parts of the network as well. The mathematical validity of this third technique rests on the use of continuous-valued stochastic units. Some implications of this result for using supervised learning to train networks of stochastic units are noted, and it is also observed that such an approach even permits a seamless blend of associative reinforcement learning and supervised learning within the same network.

Introduction

The backpropagation learning algorithm (Rumelhart, Hinton, & Williams, 1986) has been found to be a very effective method for performing supervised learning in tasks involving the training of hidden units. This has led to some investigations of its potential use in other types of learning problem as well, including unsupervised learning (by means of autoassociation, or learning of identity maps) and associative reinforcement learning. This paper explores various ways that backpropagation can be used as a means of computing (or estimating) gradient information in networks facing associative reinforcement learning tasks. We begin by defining this class of learning problem.

Associative reinforcement learning. In the associative reinforcement learning paradigm a network and its training environment interact in the following manner: The network receives a time-varying vector of inputs from the environment and sends a time-varying vector of outputs (also called *actions*) to the environment. In addition, it receives a time-varying scalar signal, called *reinforcement*, from the environment. The objective of learning is for the network to try to maximize some function of this reinforcement signal, such as the expectation of its value on the upcoming time step or the expectation of some integral of its values over all future time, as appropriate for the particular task. The precise nature of the computation of reinforcement by the environment can be anything appropriate for the particular problem and is assumed to be unknown to the learning system. In general, it is some function, deterministic or stochastic, of the input patterns produced by the environment and the output patterns it receives from the network. Figure 1 depicts the interaction between a network and its environment in an associative reinforcement learning situation.

This formulation should be contrasted with the *supervised learning* paradigm, in which the network receives a time-varying vector signal, indicating *desired output*, from the environment, rather than the

---

This research was supported by the National Science Foundation under grant IRI-8703566.

94

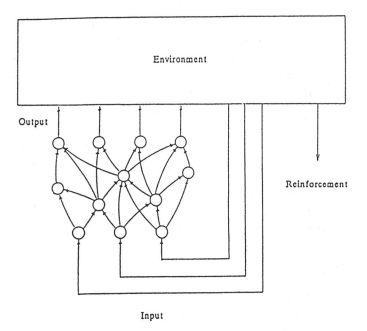

Figure 1. A connectionist network and its training environment for the associative reinforcement learning problem. The precise manner in which the reinforcement signal is used by the individual units depends on the learning algorithm to be applied. In the simplest case, the reinforcement signal is simply broadcast to all units, but the use of additional units or interconnections designed to help in the learning process is also possible.

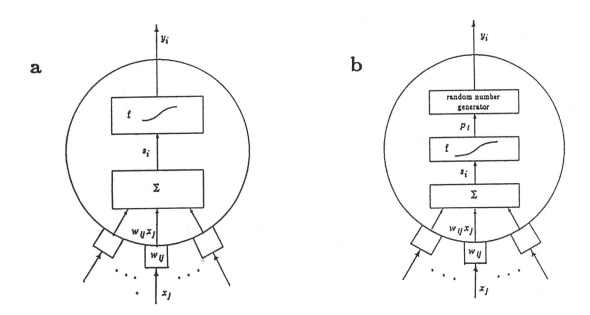

Figure 2. (a) The computation performed by a *semilinear unit*, as used, for example, in most implementations of the backpropagation learning algorithm (Rumelhart et al., 1986). (b) The computation performed by a *stochastic semilinear unit*, as introduced in Williams (1986). The random number generator produces a value according to a distribution determined by the single parameter p_i. In both cases it is assumed that the squashing function f is differentiable. Not shown are additional computational mechanisms required to support learning, which causes changes to the weights w_{ij}.

scalar reinforcement signal, and the objective is for the network's output to match the desired output as closely as possible. This distinction is sometimes summarized by saying that the feedback provided to the network is *instructive* in the case of supervised learning and *evaluative* in the case of reinforcement learning. Later we note a more revealing and mathematically precise characterization of the distinction between these two learning paradigms which applies in many cases.

Another important aspect of the reinforcement learning paradigm is the need for a source of variation in the manner in which actions are chosen by the network, to allow exploration of alternative actions. To this end, it is generally assumed that (at least some of) the units in such a network compute their output as a *stochastic* function of their inputs. Such an assumption has been made by Barto and colleagues (e.g., Barto, 1985; Sutton, 1984; Anderson; 1986) throughout their work and is consistent with assumptions made in the closely related theory of *stochastic learning automata* (Narendra & Thathatchar, 1974). We follow suit here and also make this assumption. In contrast, the supervised learning formulation does not require this exploratory behavior (nor does it rule it out). Thus a supervised learning problem may be posed to a network consisting of any mix of deterministic and stochastic units.

Backpropagation. The term *backpropagation* is often used to mean an entire supervised learning algorithm, complete with particular choice of unit transfer functions (e.g., semilinear, with logistic squashing function), error function (e.g., mean-square error), and weight update rule (e.g., using *momentum*). On the other hand, it is often convenient to use it in a more restrictive sense to mean the single component of this algorithm which determines relevant partial derivatives by means of the backward pass. In this sense it is simply a computational implementation of the chain rule. Throughout this paper the term *backpropagation* will generally be used in this more restricted sense, with the term *backpropagation learning algorithm* intended to mean an entire supervised learning algorithm which uses backpropagation to compute partial derivatives.

Notation. Let y_i denote the output of the ith unit in the network, and let $\mathbf{x}^i$ denote the pattern of input to that unit. Note that $\mathbf{x}^i$ is a tuple whose individual elements are either the outputs of certain units in the network (those sending their output directly to the ith unit) or certain inputs from the environment (if that unit happens to be connected so that it receives input directly from the environment). If the unit is deterministic, the output y_i is computed as a function of $\mathbf{x}^i$ and a set of parameters $\{w_{ij}\}$, where j ranges over an appropriate index set. If the unit is stochastic, the output y_i is drawn from a distribution depending on $\mathbf{x}^i$ and a corresponding set of parameters $\{w_{ij}\}$. In either case, for each i, let $\mathbf{w}^i$ denote the tuple consisting of all the parameters w_{ij}. Then let $\mathbf{W}$ denote the tuple consisting of all the parameters w_{ij} for the network.

These definitions are intended to be completely general, but it might be helpful to think of them in terms of more conventional neural networks, in which w_{ij} is the *weight* on the connection from the jth unit to the ith unit, $\mathbf{w}^i$ is the *weight vector* for the ith unit, and $\mathbf{W}$ is the *weight matrix* for the network. Figure 2 shows block diagrams of the computation performed in two common examples of units used in neural networks, one deterministic and one stochastic.

If the ith unit is stochastic and produces discrete-valued output, it is useful to define $g_i(\xi, \mathbf{w}^i, \mathbf{x}^i) = Pr\{y_i = \xi \mid \mathbf{w}^i, \mathbf{x}^i\}$, so that g_i is the probability mass function determining the value of y_i as a function of the parameters of the unit and its input. If the ith unit is stochastic and produces continuous-valued output, we correspondingly let $g_i(\xi, \mathbf{w}^i, \mathbf{x}^i)$ represent the probability density function determining the value of y_i as a function of the parameters of the unit and its input.

To use the REINFORCE algorithm described below, we assume that $\dfrac{\partial g_i}{\partial w_{ij}}$ exists for all j, but no further restrictions need be imposed. Buried within this simple formulation are an extremely wide variety of possible stochastic computational schemes, including stochastic binary units, or *Bernoulli units* (Williams, 1986), as well as units whose output is computed using a normal distribution.

Finally, we let r denote the reinforcement signal delivered by the environment.

Optimization of expected reinforcement. A natural measure of performance for a reinforcement learning system is

$$J(\mathbf{W}) = E\{r \mid \mathbf{W}\}$$

the expected value of the reinforcement signal r for the given setting of the parameters $\mathbf{W}$. The goal of learning is thus to find $\mathbf{W}$ maximizing this function. Note that the actual reinforcement signal r received on any given trial represents an unbiased estimate of $J(\mathbf{W})$.

Now, for the moment, consider an arbitrary learning algorithm, which amounts to a prescription for computing the collection of parameter increments $\Delta \mathbf{W}$ to be added to the current values of the parameters $\mathbf{W}$ after each trial, and consider also an arbitrary performance measure J. One reasonable criterion for this learning algorithm weaker than asking that it actually succeed in optimizing J is to ask that it continue to improve the value of J as learning proceeds, at least on average. This is the motivation behind the following definition: We will say a learning procedure satisfies the *stochastic hillclimbing property* with respect to the performance measure J if the inner product of $E\{\Delta \mathbf{W} \mid \mathbf{W}\}$ and $\nabla_{\mathbf{W}} J$ is always positive except where $\nabla_{\mathbf{W}} J$ is zero. Note that one would expect such an algorithm, if it converges at all, to converge to a local maximum of J. To analytically derive the actual asymptotic properties of many of the learning algorithms which have been found useful in practice is often quite difficult. Thus it is methodologically attractive to settle for establishing weaker but more analytically tractable properties such as the one suggested here, allowing simulation studies to be used to help fill the gaps in analytic understanding.

Backpropagating Through a Model

One of the proposals for incorporating backpropagation into a reinforcement learning problem is to train a second network, to serve as an *internal model* of the environmental reinforcement. Here we give a broad overview of this approach and make some general observations about it.

The particular scheme described here is essentially identical to that proposed and studied by Munro (1987). Another use of these ideas, suitably extended to handle what amounts to a delayed reinforcement task, was investigated by Jordan (1988) to train a network to find a time-optimal control strategy. Work of Anderson (1986) bears a more distant relationship but also involved the use of backpropagation as one component of a reinforcement learning task.

In this scheme, the internal model can be viewed as a feedforward network undergoing supervised learning. It receives as its input the input to the learning network as well as a copy of the output produced by the learning network. (The reader may find it useful to refer to Figure 1 while following this discussion.) The internal model network has a single output unit, and it receives as desired output the reinforcement signal produced by the environment. The actual output of the internal model network can be viewed as a prediction of reinforcement about to be received. The objective of the supervised learning task faced by the internal model network is to learn to duplicate the environmental reinforcement signal, by minimizing the prediction error. The weights in this network are thus trained accordingly using a backpropagation learning algorithm.

On the other hand, the original learning network is trained by backpropagating certain partial derivative information through the internal model network into the learning network (without making any weight changes in the internal model network). In this case the partial derivatives being computed are those of the actual output value of the internal model network. The objective of learning in the original net is to maximize the model's predicted reinforcement value. The weights in the two networks are thus trained differently, and the links in the internal model net are used to backpropagate two different kinds of information: prediction errors, which are used to train the internal model's weights, and predicted reinforcement, which is used to train the learning network's weights.

This approach is an interesting one and is certainly worthy of further study. From the point of view of the approach taken in this paper, it would be worthwhile to perform an analytic investigation of its relationship to the other forms of reinforcement learning algorithm discussed here. Also, it would be interesting to compare the relative learning speeds of these various approaches. One insight into this technique is the following: It amounts to attempting to optimize a function by first finding a member of a parameterized family of functions best fitting observed values of the given function and then using gradient information based on this best-fit approximation to the function.

REINFORCE Algorithms

A general class of reinforcement learning algorithms was introduced in Williams (1987a, 1987b). These algorithms prescribe parameter increments of the form

$$\Delta w_{ij} = \alpha_{ij}(r - b_{ij})e_{ij},$$

where α_{ij} is a *learning rate factor*, b_{ij} is a *reinforcement baseline*, and $e_{ij} = \dfrac{\partial \ln g_i}{\partial w_{ij}}$ is called the *characteristic eligibility* of w_{ij}. The factor $r - b_{ij}$ is called a *reinforcement offset*. The reinforcement baseline b_{ij} is assumed to be conditionally independent of y_i, given $\mathbf{W}$ and $\mathbf{x}^i$, and the rate factor α_{ij} is assumed to be nonnegative and to satisfy some other conditions, the most notable of which is that it not depend on the input $\mathbf{x}^i$ to the unit. REINFORCE is an acronym for *REward Increment = Nonnegative Factor × Offset Reinforcement × Characteristic Eligibility*, which describes the particular form of the algorithm.

A key result, proved in Williams (1987a) is that any REINFORCE algorithm in which all the α_{ij} are greater than zero satisfies the stochastic hillclimbing property with respect to the performance measure $E\{r \mid \mathbf{W}\}$. It was also shown in that paper and in Williams (1986) that certain algorithms studied elsewhere belong to this class, including the reward-inaction variant of Barto's (1985) reward-penalty algorithm, some stochastic learning automata algorithms (Narendra & Thathatchar, 1974), and variants of these in which Sutton's (1984) reinforcement comparison methods are used.

It should be noted that this and other reinforcement learning algorithms built around the use of stochastic units work essentially by measuring the correlation between variations in local behavior and the resulting variations in global performance, as measured by the reinforcement signal. REINFORCE algorithms are a particular approach designed to provide unbiased estimates of gradients.

However, it should also be noted that backpropagation is implicitly called for even within a REINFORCE algorithm. The reason is that the computation of the characteristic eligibility of a parameter, which is a partial derivative, can be carried out by means of the chain rule. For example, in the stochastic semilinear unit depicted in Figure 2b, $\dfrac{\partial \ln g_i}{\partial w_{ij}}$ can be computed as the product $\dfrac{\partial \ln g_i}{\partial p_i} \dfrac{\partial p_i}{\partial s_i} \dfrac{\partial s_i}{\partial w_{ij}}$, which amounts to computing the characteristic eligibility of the parameter p_i and then backpropagating through the sub-units consisting of the "squasher" and the "summer" depicted in that figure. This suggests how a REINFORCE algorithm must work in any network containing a mixture of stochastic and deterministic units. One simply performs the correlation-style REINFORCE computation at stochastic units, using backpropagation through deterministic units to compute the eligibilities of the individual parameters. This technique works because backpropagation is an entirely general computational technique for computing partial derivatives whenever a particular variable is a deterministic differentiable function of other variables. Such an algorithm, consisting of an apparent mix of REINFORCE and backpropagation, satisfies the stochastic hillclimbing property because it is really just a REINFORCE algorithm, so the result cited above automatically applies to it.

Backpropagating Through Random Number Generators

Continuing the discussion of the previous section, note that the REINFORCE algorithm calls for a correlation-style computation whenever it is necessary to obtain partial derivative information on the input side of a random number generator. Suppose instead that it were possible to somehow "backpropagate through a random number generator," which would mean, for example, being able to compute $\frac{\partial J}{\partial p_i}$ from knowledge of $\frac{\partial J}{\partial y_i}$ for the unit depicted in Figure 2b. Of course, because of the randomness, we could not expect there to be a deterministic relationship between these quantities. A more reasonable property to ask for is that $\frac{\partial E\{J \mid p_i\}}{\partial p_i}$ be determined by $E\left\{\frac{\partial J}{\partial y_i} \Big| p_i \right\}$.

Unfortunately, it is not hard to show that even this property fails to hold in general. To see this, let the random number generator generate 0's and 1's, with p_i representing the probability of generating a 1. In this case it is simple to observe that whenever J is a nonlinear function of y_i there need be no particular relationship between these two quantitities.

However, if a continuous distribution is used instead, the situation is very much more favorable. In particular, consider the following: Suppose that a random number generator has as its density function

$$\phi(y,\mu,\sigma) = \frac{1}{\sigma} H'(\frac{y-\mu}{\sigma}),$$

where μ and σ are the inputs to this random number generator and y is its output. Note that the corresponding cumulative distribution function has the form $H(\frac{y-\mu}{\sigma})$. This use of notation is suggestive of that used for the normal distribution, where μ denotes the mean and σ the standard deviation, but the intent here is for μ to represent an arbitrary translation parameter for the distribution, not necessarily its mean, while σ represents an arbitrary scaling parameter for the distribution, not necessarily its standard deviation.

Two special cases of this general formulation are the normal distribution, for which $H'(z) = \frac{1}{\sqrt{2\pi}} e^{-z^2/2}$, and the logistic distribution, for which $H(z) = \frac{1}{1+e^{-z}}$.

It can be shown that the following result holds for any such random number generator:

Theorem. If J is bounded and $\hat{J}_y$ is an unbiased estimate of $\frac{\partial J}{\partial y}$, then $\hat{J}_y$ is also an unbiased estimate of $\frac{\partial J}{\partial \mu}$ and $\hat{J}_y \frac{y-\mu}{\sigma}$ is an unbiased estimate of $\frac{\partial J}{\partial \sigma}$.

This result implies that we can compute unbiased estimates of all the partial derivatives in a network whose only stochastic components have the form given above by means of a backpropagation computation, where backpropagation through deterministic components is performed via the chain rule and backpropagation through such random number generators is performed as follows: When passing partial derivative information from the y branch to the μ branch, multiply by 1; when passing this information to the σ branch, multiply by $\frac{y-\mu}{\sigma}$. Any learning algorithm designed to always make weight changes having positive inner product with the resulting gradient estimate will then satisfy the stochastic hillclimbing property with respect to this performance measure J.

Discussion

Application to supervised learning. While the results of the last section have been presented in the context of the associative reinforcement learning problem, it is worthwhile to note that they are immediately relevant to the question of constructing stochastic hillclimbing algorithms for supervised learning in networks containing stochastic units. A standard formulation of the supervised learning problem is the minimization of some error measure J based on all the input-output pairs p the system could be tested on. Typically, one defines an error measure J_p for each such pair and then sets $J = E\{J_p\}$. For our purposes, note that with each pattern presentation, backpropagation permits the computation of $\nabla_W J_p$ when the network is deterministic. Furthermore, when the conditions of the theorem of the last section are met, backpropagation permits the unbiased estimation of $\nabla_W J_p$ even in the stochastic case. Thus, in either case, backpropagating according to all the values obtained on a particular trial is guaranteed to lead to an unbiased estimate of $\nabla_W J$.

Based on this discussion, along with observations made earlier, the following unifying relationship between associative reinforcement learning and supervised learning should be evident: *The associative reinforcement learning problem can be formulated as the problem of optimizing a function given unbiased estimates of its values, while the supervised learning problem can be formulated as the problem of optimizing a function given unbiased estimates of its gradient (assuming that backpropagation is possible).* One might imagine situations in which only function values can be observed at some times but gradient information can be observed at others, in what amounts to a mixture of the two learning paradigms. The approach described here allows the creation of algorithms able to take advantage of both types of information.

Search properties using continuous multiparameter distributions. It has been suggested elsewhere (Williams, 1987b) that the use of random number generators having separate control over their mean and variance as the stochastic components of units might lead to interesting search properties because of the ability to provide separate control of the location being searched and the breadth of the search around that location For example, consider a single unit whose output y is drawn from the normal distribution. We assume that there is no input to the unit and that its adjustable parameters are its mean μ and its standard deviation σ. Preliminary simulations of such a system using both an appropriate REINFORCE algorithm and an algorithm based on the backpropagation method described in the previous section have demonstrated that both of these lead to reasonable behavior when searching for the maximum of a function. The details of the algorithms used will be omitted except that it should be noted that the REINFORCE algorithm gives the most reasonable behavior when reinforcement comparison is used, so that the reinforcement baseline represents a reasonable measure of what the reinforcement has been in the recent past. Likewise, the details of the simulation results will be omitted in favor of a brief discussion of the qualitative properties of the behavior of these algorithms.

Either algorithm adapts the mean as one might expect. In the REINFORCE algorithm, if a value y is sampled which leads to a higher function value than has been obtained in the recent past, then μ moves toward y; similarly, μ moves away from points giving lower function values. Using backpropagation, μ simply moves in the direction indicated by the slope at the sampled point y.

What is more interesting is how these algorithms adapt σ. First, consider the REINFORCE algorithm and assume that the sampled point y gives rise to a higher function value than has been obtained in the recent past. In this case, σ will decrease if $|y-\mu| < \sigma$ but increase if $|y-\mu| > \sigma$. The change made to σ corresponds to that required to make the re-occurence of y more likely. There is corresponding behavior in the opposite direction if the sampled point leads to a lower value. In terms of a search, this amounts to narrowing the search around μ if a better point is found suitably close to the mean or a worse point is found suitably far from the mean, while broadening the search around μ if a worse point is found suitably close to the mean or a better point is found suitably far from the mean. Since the sampled points y are roughly twice as likely to lie within one standard deviation of the mean, it follows that whenever μ sits at the top of a local hill (of sufficient breadth with respect to σ), then σ narrows down to allow convergence to the local maximum. However it is also true that if the local maximum is very flat on top, σ will decrease to the point where sampling worse values becomes extremely unlikely and then stop changing.

For backpropagation, σ decreases if $y - \mu$ and the derivative at y have opposite signs and increases if they have the same sign. In terms of a search, this means that the search is narrowed around μ if, based on the derivative at y, the value at y appears to be lower than the value at μ, and it is broadened around μ if the opposite is true. A consequence of this is that the search is narrowed around μ whenever μ sits at the top of a hill, allowing convergence to a local maximum. Correspondingly, the search is widened whenever μ sits at the bottom of a valley, in some sense allowing exploration of both neighboring hills.

References

Anderson, C. W. (1986). *Learning and problem solving with multilayer connectionist systems.* Ph.D. Dissertation, Dept. of Computer and Information Science, University of Massachusetts, Amherst, MA.

Barto, A. G. (1985). Learning by statistical cooperation of self-interested neuron-like computing elements. *Human Neurobiology, 4,* 229-256.

Jordan, M. I. (1988). *Sequential dependencies and systems with excess degrees of freedom* (COINS Tech. Rept. 88-23). Dept. of Computer and Information Science, University of Massachusetts, Amherst, MA.

Munro, P. (1987) A dual back-propagation scheme for scalar reward learning *Proceedings of the Ninth Annual Conference of the Cognitive Science Society*, Seattle, WA, 165-176.

Narendra, K. S. & Thathatchar, M. A. L. (1974). Learning automata—a survey. *IEEE Transactions on Systems, Man, and Cybernetics, 4,* 323-334.

Rumelhart, D. E., Hinton, G. E., & Williams, R. J. (1986). Learning internal representations by error propagation. In: Rumelhart, D. E. & McClelland, J. L. (Eds.) *Parallel Distributed Processing: Explorations in the Microstructure of Cognition. Vol. 1: Foundations.* Cambridge: MIT Press/Bradford Books,

Sutton, R. S. (1984). *Temporal credit assignment in reinforcement learning.* Ph.D. Dissertation (available as COINS Tech. Rept. 84-02), Dept. of Computer and Information Science, University of Massachusetts, Amherst, MA.

Williams, R. J. (1986). *Reinforcement learning in connectionist networks: a mathematical analysis.* (Tech. Rept. 8605). La Jolla: University of California, San Diego, Institute for Cognitive Science.

Williams, R. J. (1987a). *Reinforcement-learning connectionist systems* (Tech. Rept. NU-CCS-87-3). College of Computer Science, Northeastern University, Boston, MA.

Williams, R. J. (1987b). A class of gradient-estimating algorithms for reinforcement learning in neural networks. *Proceedings of the First Annual International Conference on Neural Networks*, San Diego, CA, Vol. II, 601-608.

A learning rule for asynchronous perceptrons with feedback in a combinatorial environment

Luis B. Almeida

INESC, R. Alves Redol, 9-2, 1000 Lisboa, Portugal

Abstract

A learning rule for feedforward, multilayer perceptron-like structures (which we shall call feedforward perceptrons) was introduced by Rumelhart et al. in 1985. This rule is based on a "backward error propagation" technique. It is not clear how it could be applied to perceptrons with feedback, since error propagation around loops would then have to be performed. In this work, we interpret this rule in terms of the transposed, linearized perceptron network. We then introduce the main result of this paper, the generalization of this rule to perceptrons with feedback.

The stability of the backward error propagation network, and of the perceptron itself, are then studied. The error propagation network is shown to be always stable during training. For the perceptron network, a sufficient condition for stability is derived, and an interesting relationship with Boltzmann machines and Hopfield nets is established. Multistability is also discussed. Finally, some experimental results on perceptrons with feedback are presented.

1 – Introduction

Single layer perceptrons, with their learning rule, were introduced by Rosenblatt [1], and rose a great interest as devices that could learn from experience. Later, however, Minsky and Papert [2] showed the strong limitations of single layer systems, and expressed doubts that a learning theorem would ever be found for multiple layer systems. This caused the interest on perceptrons to progressively die.

Recently, however, Rumelhart, Hinton and Williams [3] introduced a learning rule (the "generalized delta rule", or "backward error propagation rule") for multilayer perceptron-like structures. The only difference between these structures and Rosenblatt's perceptron, apart from being multilayer, is that they use a smooth, sigmoid input-output characteristic, instead of Rosenblatt's step function. This difference does not seem to introduce any significant limitation, and in fact it even allows these systems to operate in an analog manner, when needed. On the other hand, the multilayer structure removes the limitations pointed out by Minsky and Papert to single layer systems. Since these multilayer structures are very much perceptron-like, we shall still call them perceptrons, in this paper.

The backward error propagation rule of [3] is only applicable to **feedforward** perceptrons (i.e., those in which interconnections between units do not form any loops). An extension of this rule to sequential, non-feedforward perceptrons was made, still in [3], following an idea by Minsky and Papert [2], by transforming these systems into iterative feedforward ones. Two remarks are of importance here, however: (1) these systems implicitly assume the existence of a sample and hold operation, which is performed simultaneously on the outputs of all units; they can thus be called **synchronous**; and (2) application of the learning rule now demands the existence of unlimited memory in each unit (memory with the length of the input sequence, whatever it may be), which imposes limitations on its practical applicability.

Reprinted from *Proceedings of IEEE International Conference on Neural Networks*. Copyright ©1987 by The Institute of Electrical and Electronics Engineers, Inc. All rights reserved.

In this work, a somewhat different class of perceptrons is considered. They are non-feedforward (and we shall thus designate them as "**feedback perceptrons**"), and they are **asynchronous**, in the sense that no sample-and-hold is assumed to exist at the outputs of the units. Instead, the inputs of the system are held constant long enough for it to reach an equilibrium state (if it ever does so), and the outputs in this state are compared to the desired outputs. Also, a **combinatorial** framework is considered, i.e., the desired outputs are assumed to depend only on present inputs (and not on past ones).

The main result of this paper is the derivation of a learning rule for this class of perceptrons. This rule is a generalization of the backward error propagation used for feedforward systems. It is **local**, meaning that the data needed for the update of each coefficient can be obtained from the two units that it connects (this is a very useful property when hardware implementation is envisaged), and it demands no memory.

The problem of stability is also addressed, and a sufficient condition for stability is derived. This is done through the use of an energy function, which bears an interesting relationship to the one used in Boltzmann machines [4] and Hopfield nets [5]. The error propagation network is shown to always be stable during training. The problem of multistability of the perceptron is also discussed, though only in an intuitive way. Finally, some practical examples using feedback perceptrons are presented.

2 - Applying a bit of network theory

Consider a multilayer perceptron, with units that have smooth input-output characteristics, that we shall designate by S_i (the index i means that the I/O characteristic may vary from one unit to another). In perceptron simulations, a sigmoid S_i has generally been used [3]. Let a_{ij} be the weight in the connection from unit i to unit j, b_{kj} the weight in the connection from external input k to unit j, and c_j the constant term in unit j. If there are N units and K external inputs, we can write the result of the sum performed in unit j as

$$s_j = \sum_{i=1}^{N} a_{ij} y_i + \sum_{k=1}^{K} b_{kj} x_k + c_j \qquad j = 1,...,N \qquad (1)$$

where x_k is the k-th external input, and y_i is the output of unit i, given by

$$y_i = S_i(s_i) \qquad i = 1,...,N \qquad (2)$$

The solutions of these equations, for each input vector $[x_k]$, give the values of the y_i and s_i at the equilibrium states that correspond to that input vector (whether these states are stable or unstable, shall not concern us for the moment). If we designate by O the set of units that produce external outputs, the values of these outputs will be given by

$$o_p = y_p \qquad p \in O \qquad (3)$$

The perceptron network generally is nonlinear, due to the nonlinearity of the S_i. We can linearize it around a given equilibrium state. The equations of the linearized network (for which we will use primed variables) are

$$s'_j = \sum_{i=1}^{N} a_{ij} y'_i + \sum_{k=1}^{K} b_{kj} x'_k \qquad j = 1,...,N \qquad (4)$$

$$y'_i = D_i(s_i) s'_i \qquad i = 1,...,N \qquad (5)$$

$$o'_p = y'_p \qquad p \in O \qquad (6)$$

where D_i is the derivative of S_i. Note that, in terms of the linearized network, $D_i(s_i)$ is just a constant coefficient.

Now consider the transpose [6] of this linearized network, and denote its variables by a double prime. The inputs of this network will be located at the outputs of the previous one, and will thus be denoted o''_p ($p \in O$). The equations of this new network will be

$$
y''_j = \begin{cases} \displaystyle\sum_{i=1}^{N} a_{ji} s''_i + o''_j & \text{if } j \in O \\[2em] \displaystyle\sum_{i=1}^{N} a_{ji} s''_i & \text{if } j \in O \end{cases} \tag{7}
$$

$$
s''_i = D_i(s_i) y''_i \qquad\qquad i = 1,\dots,N \tag{8}
$$

$$
x''_k = \sum_{i=1}^{N} b_{ki} s''_i \qquad\qquad k = 1,\dots,K \tag{9}
$$

In the case of a feedforward perceptron, the transposed network also is feedforward (though it propagates in the reverse direction) and it is just the backward error propagation network, for the generalized delta rule. In fact, if the desired outputs of the perceptron are d_p ($p \in O$), the output errors are

$$
e_p = o_p - d_p \qquad\qquad p \quad O \tag{10}
$$

and the global, quadratic error is

$$
E = \sum_{p \in O} e_p^2 \tag{11}
$$

It is easy to see that, if we make $o''_p = e_p$, equations (7) and (8) are just the backward error propagation equations, as given in [3]. The components of the gradient of the error relative to the perceptron weights are given by

$$
\frac{\partial E}{\partial a_{ij}} = 2 y_i s''_j \qquad\qquad i,j = 1,\dots,N \tag{12a}
$$

$$
\frac{\partial E}{\partial b_{kj}} = 2 x_k s''_j \qquad\qquad k = 1,\dots,K \quad j = 1,\dots,N \tag{12b}
$$

$$
\frac{\partial E}{\partial c_j} = 2 s''_j \qquad\qquad j = 1,\dots,N \tag{12c}
$$

In an actual hardware implementation of a feedforward perceptron, one would also have to include the transposed network, as part of the training circuitry. An important advantage of the backward error propagation rule, in terms of implementation, is that it is local in character, as can be seen from equations (12).

Given these equations, expressing the gradient of E in terms of variables of the feedforward perceptron and of the transposed network, one is naturally led to wonder if they generalize to feedback perceptrons, in which loops exist both in the perceptron itself and in the transposed network. We shall prove in the next section that this is indeed true.

3 – Gradient learning in feedback perceptrons

The partial derivative of E relative to a weight $\overset{\bullet}{a}_{mn}$ is given by

$$\overset{\bullet}{E} = \sum_{p \in O} \frac{\partial E}{\partial o_p} \overset{\bullet}{o}_p = 2 \sum_{p \in O} e_p \overset{\bullet}{o}_p \tag{13}$$

(denoting by a dot the derivatives relative to a_{mn}). Let us differentiate both sides of eqs. (1-3) relative to a_{mn}.

$$\overset{\bullet}{s}_j = \begin{cases} \sum\limits_{i=1}^{N} a_{ij} \overset{\bullet}{y}_i + y_m & \text{if } j = n \\[2em] \sum\limits_{i=1}^{N} a_{ij} \overset{\bullet}{y}_i & \text{if } j \neq n \end{cases} \tag{14}$$

$$\overset{\bullet}{y}_i = D_i(s_i) \overset{\bullet}{s}_i \qquad\qquad i = 1,...,N \tag{15}$$

$$\overset{\bullet}{o}_p = \overset{\bullet}{y}_p \qquad\qquad p \in O \tag{16}$$

These equations are just those of the direct, linearized network (eqs. 4-6) with a single input y_m applied at node s'_n (with a unit weight). Denote by t'_{np} the transfer ratio of the direct, linearized network, from an input at node s'_n to output o'_p, i.e.,

$$\overset{\bullet}{o}_p = y_m t'_{np} \qquad\qquad p \in O, \quad m,n = 1,...,N \tag{17}$$

which we can always do because this network is linear. We know, from the transposition theorem [6], that t'_{np} is equal to the transfer ratio t''_{pn}, from o''_p to s''_n, in the transposed network. Thus,

$$\overset{\bullet}{o}_p = \overset{\bullet}{y}_m t''_{pn} \qquad\qquad p \in O, \quad m,n = 1,...,N \tag{18}$$

and replacing $\overset{\bullet}{o}_p$ in eq. (13),

$$\overset{\bullet}{E} = 2 y_m \sum_{p \in O} e_p t''_{pn} \qquad\qquad m,n = 1,...,N \tag{19}$$

Finally, since the transposed circuit is linear, the sum in the right hand side of this equation is the value that will be obtained at node s''_n if we apply the errors e_p at the inputs o''_p. We thus have, as in eq. (12a)

$$\frac{\partial E}{\partial a_{mn}} = 2 y_m s''_n \qquad\qquad m,n = 1,...,N \tag{20}$$

This result, together with similar derivations relative to b and c coefficients, allows us to conclude that the transposed, linearized network is still the appropriate network for backward error propagation in feedback perceptrons, and that the corrections to be applied to the weights are still based on eqs. (12). Note that no assumptions have been made on the functions S_i, other than that they are differentiable. As in the feedforward case, equations (12) mean that the learning rule is local in character, and thus that it is of relatively easy implementation in hardware.

4 – Stability

We shall address three stability issues, in the following sections. First, the stability of the error propagation network will be analysed (sec. 4.1). Then, the stability of the perceptron network itself will be discussed (sec. 4.2). Finally, we will discuss the problem of multistability of the perceptron network (sec. 4.3).

4.1 - Stability of the error propagation network

In a feedback perceptron, the backward error propagation network also has feedback, and thus the problem of its stability becomes essential: if it is not stable, it cannot be used in practice. We shall demonstrate that, when training is performed, the transposed network is stable, and thus that it can always be used for error propagation.

It is known from works on stability (e.g. [7]) that the stability of a nonlinear dynamical system at an equilibrium state is equivalent to the stability of the dynamical system obtained through linearization around that state (under very broad assumptions, that we shall not detail here). On the other hand, it is very easy to show that the stability of a dynamical system is equivalent to the stability of its transpose. In fact, stability of a linear dynamical system depends on the eigenvalues of the system matrix [7], and the eigenvalues of a matrix are equal to the eigenvalues of its transpose. We can conclude that, if the perceptron network is stable, the backward error propagation network also is. Thus, if we always let the perceptron reach stable equilibrium before performing training, the error propagation network will always be stable when training is performed. This is true if the error propagation network is the transpose of the linearized perceptron network, not only in static, but also in dynamical terms. In an actual implementation, this means that the dynamical properties of the error propagation network should closely match those of the perceptron network itself.

4.2 - Stability of the perceptron network

The stability of a perceptron network will depend not only on the static input-output characteristics of its units, but also on their dynamical properties. Equations (1-3), which only concern the static values of the perceptron variables, are not adequate for studying stability. For this purpose, we need to make some assumptions about the dynamical characteristics of the perceptron units.

One of the simplest, realistic dynamical behaviors that one can assume for the perceptron units corresponds to the circuit of fig. 1, where the adder and the S-function block are assumed to be instantaneous, and the latter is also assumed to have zero output impedance.

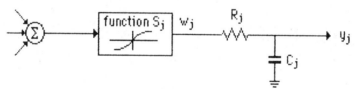

Fig. 1 - Circuit corresponding to the assumed dynamical behavior of a perceptron unit

The equation relating y_j to w_j will then be

$$\frac{dy_j}{dt} = \frac{1}{R_j C_j} (w_j - y_j) = \tau_j^{-1} (w_j - y_j) \tag{21}$$

where $\tau_j = R_j C_j$. We can also write

$$\frac{dy_j}{dt} = \tau_j^{-1} [S_j(\sum_{i=1}^{N} a_{ij} y_i + \sum_{k=1}^{K} b_{kj} x_k + c_j) - y_j] \tag{22}$$

We shall now prove that a sufficient condition for the stability of such a perceptron is that there exist positive coefficients μ_j such that

$$\mu_i a_{ji} = \mu_j a_{ij} \tag{23}$$

The proof will be achieved through the use of an energy function W, defined as

106

$$W = -\frac{1}{2} \sum_{i=1}^{N} \sum_{j=1}^{N} \mu_j a_{ij} y_i y_j - \sum_{k=1}^{K} \sum_{j=1}^{N} \mu_j b_{kj} x_k y_j - \sum_{j=1}^{N} \mu_j c_j y_j + \sum_{j=1}^{N} \mu_j U_j(y_j) \quad (24)$$

where U_j is a primitive of the inverse of function S_j, i.e.,

$$\frac{d}{dy} U_j(y) = S_j^{-1}(y) \quad (25)$$

with

$$S_j^{-1}[S_j(y)] = y \quad (26)$$

(we shall assume that all the functions S_j are strictly increasing, and hence that they are invertible; the proof can be easily extended to the case where there exist μ_j, not necessarily positive, such that for all j, $\mu_j S_j$ is strictly increasing). Note that if S_j is a sigmoid function, U_j will be a U-shaped function (see fig. 2).

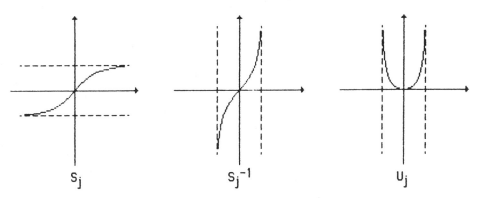

$$S_j \qquad\qquad S_j^{-1} \qquad\qquad U_j$$

Fig. 2 - Examples of functions S, S^{-1} and U

The time derivative of the energy is

$$\frac{dW}{dt} = \sum_{j=1}^{N} \frac{\partial W}{\partial y_j} \frac{dy_j}{dt} \quad (27)$$

and

$$\frac{\partial W}{\partial y_j} = -\frac{1}{2} \sum_{i=1}^{N} (\mu_j a_{ij} + \mu_i a_{ji}) y_i - \sum_{k=1}^{K} \mu_j b_{kj} x_k - \mu_j c_j + \mu_j S_j^{-1}(y_j) \quad (28)$$

but using (23), and defining $z_j = S_j^{-1}(y_j)$

$$\frac{\partial W}{\partial y_j} = -\mu_j [(\sum_{i=1}^{N} a_{ij} y_i + \sum_{k=1}^{K} b_{kj} x_k + \mu_j c_j) - z_j] \quad (29)$$

On the other hand, from (22)

$$\frac{dy_j}{dt} = \tau_j^{-1} [S(\sum_{i=1}^{N} a_{ij} y_i + \sum_{k=1}^{K} b_{kj} x_k + \mu_j c_j) - S(z_j)] \quad (30)$$

Comparing eqs. (29) and (30), and reminding ourselves that S_j is strictly increasing and that μ_j and τ_j are positive, we see that the derivatives $\partial W/\partial y_j$ and dy_j/dt always have opposite signs (or are both equal to zero), and thus that W can only decrease with time (or be constant, in which case all the y_j also are, and the system is at an equilibrium state). Hence, the perceptron cannot oscillate: it can only converge toward some equilibrium point, or diverge toward infinite. However, divergence toward infinite cannot occur with the functions S_j normally used in perceptrons, since they are bounded, and thus put bounds on the values of the y_j.

As a consequence, the perceptron must always converge toward some equilibrium point (in terms of the surface W, it must always descend toward some stationarity point). In theory, it can stop at an unstable equilibrium state, corresponding to a saddle point of W (or even to a local maximum, if it was initialized there). However, in any real analog implementation, residual noise will move it away from any unstable point, into some local minimum of W. In digital implementations, a very small amount of noise can be added on purpose, if desired, for the same effect.

In summary, a sufficient condition for stability is that the S_j be strictly increasing, and that there exist positive μ_i such that $\mu_i a_{ji} = \mu_j a_{ij}$. This condition is valid if the perceptron units have a dynamical behavior corresponding to fig. 1.

Some remarks are due at this point. First of all, note that the stability condition includes weight symmetry, i.e., $a_{ij} = a_{ji}$ as a special case (where we can make all the $\mu_i = 1$). However, the stability condition certainly is still too restrictive — as an example the feedforward perceptron, which is always stable, does not obey condition (25). Finally, we should note that in the experiments reported ahead in this paper, unstable situations never arose, even without imposing any condition on the weights; in experiments with other problems, not reported here, some unstable situations were actually met, though very infrequently, when conditions for stability were not imposed.

An interesting relationship can be established between feedback perceptrons and Boltzmann machines [4] and Hopfield nets [5]. In these systems, weight symmetry is always imposed, and the diagonal elements a_{ii} are always zero (in [5], the constant terms c_j also are always zero, but this is not essential). On the other hand, these systems have no external inputs, in the sense used in this paper (instead, their internal variables are clamped to values supplied from the outside world). To mirror these restrictions, we shall consider a perceptron where $a_{ij} = a_{ji}$, $a_{ii} = 0$ and $b_{kj} = 0$, for all i, j, k (as a consequence, condition (23) is verified, with all the $\mu_i = 1$). The outputs of the units of Boltzmann machines and Hopfield nets can only take two discrete values. This can be mirrored by making all the S_i approach a step function. In the limit, the U_i will become constant, between their vertical asymptotes (cf. fig. 2). Since the U_i were defined as primitives, they have arbitrary additive constants, and we can make them all equal to zero between their asymptotes. As a result, the energy function becomes

$$W = -\frac{1}{2} \sum_{i=1}^{N} \sum_{j=1}^{N} a_{ij} y_i y_j - \sum_{j=1}^{N} c_j y_j \qquad (31)$$

which is exactly the energy function used in Boltzmann machines and Hopfield nets. We can thus conclude that, in the limit, as the S_i approach a step function, the perceptron, in its operation, minimizes the same energy function as a Boltzmann machine or a Hopfield net with the same weights.

4.3 - Multistability

The perceptron network being nonlinear, it can exhibit more than one stable state, for a given input vector. The state that the perceptron will converge to, upon presentation of that input vector, will depend on its previous state, and thus the behavior of the perceptron can be sequential. This could be advantageous for handling sequential problems, but no learning rule is known for asynchronous perceptrons in a sequential framework. In a combinatorial framework, as concerns us in this paper, sequential behavior generally is undesirable. Though we do not know of any general condition for the existence of a single stable state, some intuitive reasoning can be made on this subject. We will only consider a bistable system, but the reasoning would apply equally well to a system with more than two stable states.

Suppose that, at a certain time in the course of the training process, the perceptron being considered has two stable states, for a given input vector. Two cases may arise:

(1) With any of the initial conditions that can appear in practice, the perceptron will always "fall" into a single one of those states, when that specific input vector is presented. Then, the perceptron will behave as if it had only a single stable state: the existence of the other state does not affect its normal operation.

(2) Some of the possible initial conditions will lead the perceptron to one of the stable states, and other conditions will lead it to the other state. Then, during training (which is assumed to be representative of actual operating conditions), both states will be visited, and weight adjustment will tend to move them both toward positions in which their outputs are close to the desired ones. The two atates may merge or stay separated, but even in this case the behavior of the perceptron may be perfectly acceptable, since the two states will produce similar outputs.

Of course, during training the system may alternate between the two cases above, without affecting these considerations. However, training for other input vectors may in some cases tend to move one or both stable states away from producing the desired outputs, thus weakening somewhat the above reasoning. But the same effect can arise even with a single stable state. Simulations done so far by the author, seem to confirm that the problem of multistability actually is not severe.

5 - Experimental results

Various experimental tests were performed on feedback perceptrons; for lack of space, we will only describe three of them, in a very brief manner.

The first test is an example of a situation where feedback brought only a small improvement, relative to feedforward structures. A single analog input $x \in [-1,1]$ was used, and the desired output was $d = x^2$. Table I summarizes the results (root mean squared errors) obtained with three different structures. For each structure, 10 independent trainings were performed, starting from independent, randomly generated, initial weight values.

Table I

Results for $d = x^2$, $x \in [-1,1]$

Structure	no. of weights	RMS error
2 units, feedforward	5	.25
2 units, feedback	8	.17
3 units, feedforward	9	.11

The improvement in the 2-unit structure with feedback, relative to the feedforward one, is not very large, and a 3-unit feedforward structure, which has just one more weight, seems to make a better use of its degrees of freedom. Other similar problems (e.g. $d = x^2$ with $x \in [0,1]$, and $d = x_1 x_2$ with $x_1, x_2 \in [-1,1]$) produced similar results.

In the second test, there were three analog inputs, $x_1, x_2, x_3 \in [-1,1]$, and three outputs o_1, o_2 and o_3. We desired o_i to be positive if and only if x_i was the largest of the three inputs. Table II summarizes the results obtained with various structures. Note that in one of them, symmetry was imposed as a means to ensure stability. However, as mentioned in section 4.2, no unstable situations were encountered, even when symmetry was not imposed.

Table II

Results for the "largest of 3 inputs" problem

Structure	no. of independent weights	Average error rate, per output
3 units, feedforward	15	5.9%
4 » »	22	5.5%
5 » »	30	3.5%
6 » »	39	3.6%
3 » feedback, unconstrained	21	1.7%
3 » » symmetrical	18	1.4%

These results suggest that feedback is essential to improve the performance of the perceptron, in this problem: even with 6 units, and 39 independent weights, feedforward perceptrons make more than twice the errors made by 3-unit feedback perceptrons, with only 18 or 21 independent weights. The feedback perceptrons always develop strong negative weights between their three units, in what amounts to a kind of "lateral inhibition", that allows them to achieve a significant improvement relative to feedforward perceptrons. The slightly better results obtained when symmetry was imposed are not surprising, since the problem to be solved is symmetrical, and thus the optimal solution probably also is. The solutions developped by the unconstrained perceptron were always almost symmetrical.

The third test concerned a pattern completion problem. Ten random binary vectors, with 10 components each, were generated (these vectors stayed fixed throughout the test). The problem consisted in trying to fill the values of two, randomly selected, missing components, given the other eigth. In this kind of problem, external connections act sometimes as inputs and sometimes as outputs. Thus, feedforward perceptrons, with their clearly defined inputs and outputs, are not very appropriate for pattern completion. However, we included one 10-input, 10-output feedforward structure in the test: the missing inputs were set to a value midway between the two binary values, and only the outputs corresponding to the missing components were tested. In the structures with feedback, no external inputs (in the sense used above, in this paper) were employed. Instead, a clamping technique was used, similar to the one generally utilized in Boltzmann machines and Hopfield nets: the outputs of the units corresponding to known components were clamped to the component values, and the other units were left free. Once again, 10 different random initializations were tried for each structure. Table III summarizes the results of this test.

Table III

Results of pattern completion problem

Structure	no. of independent weights	average error rate, per missing component
10 units, feedforward	155	4.50%
10 » feedback, unconstrained	110	.89%
10 » » symmetrical	65	.86%

Once again, the improvement in performance, obtained through the use of feedback, is quite large, and in this case, this is accompanied by a decrease in the number of independent weights, confirming that feedback structures are much better adapted to this kind of problem. The slight improvement in performance, obtained when symmetry was imposed, probably is not very significant. What is significant, and somewhat surprising, is that the symmetry constraint did not impair the perceptron's performance in this problem. It is not obvious, in this case, that the optimal solution should be symmetrical, and in fact the solutions developed by the unconstrained structures were, in general, quite unsymmetrical. One should also note that the unconstrained structure never led to unstable situations, in this test, as previously mentioned.

The results of the tests described above suggest two basic conclusions, which are also supported, by other tests performed by the author:

- there are problems in which the use of feedback can be quite advantageous, while in other problems the improvement may be only marginal;

- the symmetry constraint, as a means for ensuring stability, often will not impair the perceptron's performance significantly. However, in many problems, even if one imposes no such constraint, unstability will arise only very infrequently.

6 - Conclusions

A learning rule for feedback perceptrons was derived. This rule is a generalization of the backward error propagation rule for feedforward perceptrons, introduced in [3]. It is local, in the sense that the information needed for the adaptation of each weight can be obtained from the two units that it connects.

The backward error propagation network was shown to always be stable when training is performed. On the other hand, a sufficient condition for the stability of the perceptron network itself was derived; in this context, an interesting relationship with Boltzmann machines and Hopfield nets was developped. The problem of multistability was also discussed.

Finally, experimental results were presented, illustrating cases where feedback is advantageous, as well as other cases where the advantage of feedback is only marginal.

References

[1] - F. Rosenblatt, "Principles of Neurodynamics", New York: Spartan, 1962.

[2] - M. Minsky and S. Papert, "Perceptrons", Cambridge, MA: MIT Press, 1969.

[3] - D. Rumelhart, G. Hinton and R. Williams, "Learning Internal Representations by Error Propagation", ICS Report 8506, Institute for Cognitive Science, Univ. California, S. Diego, CA, 1985.

[4] - G. Hinton, T. Sejnowski and D. Ackley, "Boltzmann Machines: Constraint Satisfaction Networks that Learn", Tech. Report CMU-CS-84-119, Carnegie-Mellon University, Pittsburgh, PA, 1984.

[5] - J. Hopfield, "Neuronal Networks and Physical Systems with Emergent Collective Computational Abilities", Proc. Nat. Acad. Sci. USA, Vol. 79, pp. 2554-2558, April 1982.

[6] - A. Oppenheim and R. Schafer, "Digital Signal Processing", Englewood Cliffs, NJ: Prentice-Hall, 1975.

[7] - J. L. Willems, "Stability Theory of Dynamical Systems", London: Thomas Nelson and Sons Ltd., 1970.

Attractor dynamics and parallelism in a connectionist sequential machine

Michael I. Jordan
Department of Computer and Information Science
University of Massachusetts

ABSTRACT

Fluent human sequential behavior, such as that observed in speech production, is characterized by a high degree of parallelism, fuzzy boundaries, and insensitivity to perturbations. In this paper, I consider a theoretical treatment of sequential behavior which is based on data from speech production. A network is discussed which is essentially a sequential machine built out of connectionist components. The network relies on distributed representations and a high degree of parallelism at the level of the component processing units. These properties lead to parallelism at the level at which whole output vectors arise, and constraints must be imposed to make the performance of the network more sequential. The sequential trajectories that are realized by the network have dynamic properties that are analogous to those observed in networks with point attractors (Hopfield, 1982): learned trajectories generalize, and attractors such as limit cycles can arise.

INTRODUCTION

One of the arguments for "connectionist" or "parallel, distributed processing" networks has been that they have properties that seem to reflect processes at which humans are most naturally proficient (Hinton & Anderson, 1981; Rumelhart & McClelland, 1986). These properties include the ability to generalize from instances, the ability to deal with partial information, and insensitivity to noise. It has been suggested that it might be advisable to base theories on such primitives rather than on those associated with sequential, symbolic processing. These arguments have been made mostly in the context of models dealing with the interpretation of incoming data, or with mappings from one set of data to another. However, one need only consider the fluency of human speech to see that humans are also very good at certain kinds of sequential behavior. Furthermore, such behavior is often characterized by a high degree of parallelism, fuzzy boundaries, and insensitivity to perturbations — properties which are difficult to capture in a formalism in which the underlying primitive is a sequential processor, but which are more natural in a connectionist system. In this paper, I consider the problem of parallelism in speech production and suggest a connectionist architecture that can exhibit behavior similar to that shown in speech. My approach is based on the recent work on learning by Rumelhart, Hinton, and Williams (1986) and is related to previous work by Henke (1966), Kohonen, Lehtio, and Oja (1981), and Rumelhart and Norman (1982).

COARTICULATION

Much of the complexity of describing sequential processes in speech production comes from the fact that speech gestures associated with nearby phonemes can overlap in time. Such overlap, or *coarticulation*, is ubiquitous in utterances and can be quite complex, given the many degrees of freedom of the speech apparatus. It is possible to see gestures that anticipate future phonemes, referred to as *forward coarticulation*, as well as perseveratory gestures, or *backward coarticulation*. The overall effect of coarticulation is to make the utterance more smooth by merging nearby phonemes and to allow speech to proceed faster than would otherwise be possible by taking advantage of opportunities for the parallel execution of movements.

Several studies have investigated coarticulation by recording articulator trajectories during utterances. Moll and Daniloff (1971) showed that in an utterance such as "freon", the velar opening for the nasal /n/ can begin as early as the first vowel, thereby nasalizing the vowels. [1] Benguerel and Cowan (1974) studied phrases such as "une sinistre structure," in which there is a string of the six consonants /strstr/ followed by the rounded vowel /y/. [2] They showed that lip-rounding for the /y/ can begin as early as the first /s/, an example of forward coarticulation over six phonemes.

One way to characterize these examples is to say that if certain degrees of freedom are not being used in the production of a particular sound, then they may anticipate or perseverate aspects of other phonemes in the utterance so that performance becomes more parallel. However, such a conception of coarticulation ignores the constraints which must be imposed on the parallelism. Certain anticipatory gestures, for example, would inflict too much change on the sound currently being produced, and there must therefore be a way to prevent such coarticulations while allowing others. In the case of "freon", for example, the velum is allowed to open during the production of the vowels because the language being spoken is English. In a language such as French, in which nasal vowels

---

[1] The velum is a muscular tissue that opens to allow air to pass between the pharynx and the nasal cavities.

[2] The vowel /y/ is the "u" in "tu", and is somewhat like pronouncing the English sound "ee" with rounded lips.

are different phonemically from non-nasal vowels, the velum would not be allowed to coarticulate. Thus the articulatory control system cannot blindly anticipate articulations, but must be sensitive to phonemic distinctions in the language being spoken.

The implementation of constraints on parallelism is complicated by the fact that the constraints cannot be encoded as relations between whole phonemes, but must be specific to particular phonemic structure. For example, in the case of /strstry/, the *rounding* of the /y/ can be anticipated during the preceding consonants, but the *voicing* of the /y/ cannot, because that would change the phonemic identities of the consonants (for example, the /s/ would become a /z/). Other features of the /y/, such as those specifying tongue position, may be more or less constrained, depending on the particular allowable variations of the consonants. Again, such knowledge cannot come from consideration of strategies of articulation, but must reflect higher-level phonemic constraints.

Thus, speech presents an interesting control problem in which constraints of various kinds are imposed on the particular patternings of parallelism and sequentiality that can be obtained in an utterance. What I wish to discuss in the remainder of this paper is an approach to this problem based on connectionist mechanisms.

CONNECTIONIST NETWORKS

General discussions of connectionist networks can be found in Feldman and Ballard (1982) and Rumelhart and McClelland (1986). For present purposes, the main features of the networks that are relevant involve distributed representations, nonlinearities, and learning.

A one layer network with no recurrent connections computes a function from the vector of activation of its input units to the vector of activation of its output units. It is possible for such a network to learn to make associations between input vectors and output vectors. This can be done by an error-correcting learning rule that changes the weights coming in to each output unit in proportion to the difference between the actual output of that unit and the desired output (Widrow & Hoff, 1960).

An important property of such networks, which is due to the weighted sums that units form in determining their activations, is that similar input vectors tend to produce similar output vectors. Many connectionist approaches take advantage of this property by representing entities as distributed patterns of activation, so as to achieve a kind of automatic generalization between similar patterns (Hinton & Anderson, 1981).

A one layer network has only a single weight matrix and is restricted to linear mappings. By allowing more layers, with nonlinear activation functions on intermediate units, it is possible to implement arbitrary nonlinear mappings. Until recently, the learning rules in these networks were restricted to the single layer case. However, several rules have now been developed for multilayer networks that allow essentially arbitrary associations to be formed (Ackley, Hinton, & Sejnowski, 1985; Barto & Anandan, 1985; Rumelhart, Hinton, & Williams, 1986). The back-propagation rule of Rumelhart, Hinton, and Williams has been used in simulations of the network discussed in this paper. The back-propagation rule is an error-correction procedure that generalizes the Widrow-Hoff rule. As before, errors are generated at the output units by comparing the actual outputs to the desired outputs, and these errors are used to change the weights of the output units. The errors are then propagated back into the network to provide intermediate units with error signals so that they can change their weights.

A NETWORK ARCHITECTURE FOR SEQUENTIAL PERFORMANCE

Let there be some sequence of *actions* $x_1, x_2, \ldots, x_s$, which are to be produced in order in the presence of a *plan* p. Each action is a vector in a feature or parameter space, and the plan can be treated as an action produced by a higher level of the system. The plan is assumed to remain constant during the production of the sequence, and serves primarily to designate the particular sequence which is to be performed.

We wish to construct a network that can perform arbitrary sequences by taking a plan as input and producing the corresponding sequence. One approach is to explicitly represent the state of a sequential machine as an activation vector and to produce actions by evaluating a function from states to actions. At each moment in time, an action is chosen based on the current state s, and the state is then updated to allow the next action to be chosen. Thus, there is a function f which determines the output action x_n at time n,

$$x_n = f(s_n, p)$$

and a function g which determines the state s_{n+1},

$$s_{n+1} = g(s_n, p), \tag{1}$$

where both functions depend on the constant plan vector as well as the current state vector. Following the terminology of automata theory (Booth, 1969), f will be referred to as the *output* function, and g will be referred to as the *next-state* function. [3]

The basic network architecture is shown in Figure 1. The entities in the state equations — plans, states, and outputs — are all assumed to be represented as distributed patterns

---

[3]From the definition, it can be seen that the plan p plays the role of the input symbol in a sequential machine. The use of the term "plan" is to emphasize the assumption that p remains constant during the production of the sequence. That is, we are not allowed to assume temporal order in the input to the system.

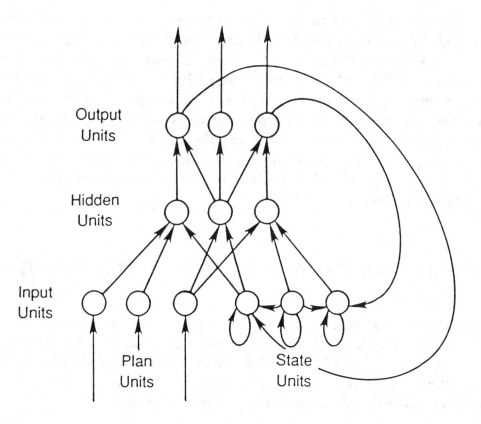

Figure 1: Basic network architecture. (Not all connections are shown).

of activation on separate pools of processing units. The plan units and the state units together serve as the input units for a multilayer network. This network implements the output function through weighted connections from the plan and state units to the output units. The output function is generally nonlinear, as will be discussed below, therefore it is also necessary to have hidden units in the path from the plan and state units to the output units. Finally, the next-state function is implemented with recurrent connections from the state units to themselves, and from the output units to the state units. This allows the current state to depend on the previous state and on the previous output (which is itself a function of the previous state and the plan).

The network can learn to produce sequences of actions by changing the weights in the network. Assume that the recurrent connections implementing the next-state function are given fixed values (particular choices for these values are discussed below). At each time step, an activation vector composed of the plan and the state is present on the input units, and an association can be learned from this input vector to a desired output vector. Clearly, one requirement for the network to be able to learn arbitrary sequences is that the next-state function produce distinguishable state vectors at each time step. It is not necessary that these vectors be different between sequences, because the plan serves to distinguish the sequences. A second requirement is that there be no restrictions on the form of the associations that can be learned (such as a linearity restriction). This requirement is met by using the back-propagation learning rule. Note that the ability to learn arbitrary sequences does not imply that all sequences are equally easy to learn; indeed, the network will have more difficulty in learning and performing sequences when distinctions must be made similar states and plans.

A further requirement must be imposed on the next-state function so that the results on parallelism will hold: *State vectors at nearby points in time must be similar.* There are many ways to choose the recurrent connections so as to achieve this continuity property. One particular choice, which has been used in many of the simulations of the network, is based on a conception of the state as representing the *temporal context* of actions. Consider the case of a sequence with a repeated subsequence or a pair of sequences with a common subsequence. It seems appropriate, given the positive transfer which can occur in such situations as well as the phenomena of capture errors (Norman, 1981), that the state should be similar during the performance of similar subsequences. One way to achieve this is to define the state in terms of the actions being produced. However, the representation must provide an extensive enough temporal context so that there are no ambiguities in cases involving repeated subsequences. If the state were to be defined as a function of the last n outputs, for example, then the system would be unable to perform sequences with repeated subsequences of length n, or to distinguish between pairs of sequences with a common subsequence of length n. To avoid such problems, the state can be defined as an exponentially weighted average of past outputs, so that the arbitrarily distant past has some representation in the state, albeit with ever-diminishing strength. This representation of the state can be obtained if each output unit feeds back to a state unit with a weight of one, if each state unit feeds back to itself with a weight μ, and if the state units are linear. [4] In this case, the state at time n is given by

$$
\begin{aligned}
\mathbf{s}_n &= \mu \mathbf{s}_{n-1} + \mathbf{x}_{n-1} \\
&= \sum_{r=1}^{n-1} \mu^{r-1} \mathbf{x}_{n-r}.
\end{aligned}
$$

Since this representation of the state is an average, it tends to have the desired property that states nearby in time are similar. The similarity depends on the particular actions that are added in at each time step and on the value of μ. In general, however, with sufficiently large values of μ, the similarity extends forward and backward in time, growing weaker with increasing distance.

Other possible representations of the state are discussed in Jordan (1985). The major differences between different representations is in the particular metrics they induce on the

---

[4] The linearity assumption gives the state a simple interpretation and also gives the state units a more extended dynamic range, but is not essential for the operation of the network.

difficulty of learning and performing particular sequences and also the kinds of generalizations that can be made between sequences. It is also possible to consider learning of the next-state function. Indeed, the back-propagation algorithm applies to the case of recurrent networks, although in a more complex form, requiring units to store histories of their activations (Rumelhart, Hinton, & Williams, 1986). However, in the current framework, there is little to be gained by learning the next-state function; all the hard work can be done in learning the output function.

LEARNING AND PARALLELISM

The network as described thus far would appear to be strictly sequential: there is no overlap between neighboring actions. This is indeed the case and it is necessary to modify the form in which desired output vectors are specified to see that the network is in fact capable of highly parallel performance.

The form that desired output vectors are assumed to take is a generalization of the approach used in traditional error-correction schemes (Duda & Hart, 1973; Rosenblatt, 1961; Rumelhart, Hinton, & Williams, 1986; Widrow & Hoff, 1960). Rather than assuming that a value is specified for each output unit, it is assumed that in general there are *constraints* specified on the values of the output units. Constraints may specify a range of values which an output unit may have, a particular value, or no value at all. This latter case is referred to as a "don't-care condition." It is also possible to consider constraints which are defined among output units. For example, the sum of the activations of a set of units may be required to have a particular value.

Constraints enter into the learning process in the following way: If the activation of an output unit fits the constraints on that unit, then no error corrections are instigated from that unit. If, however, a constraint is not met, then the error is defined as a proportion of the degree to which that constraint is not met, and this error is used in the normal way to change weights towards a configuration in which the constraint is met. An example of this process is shown in Figure 2 for a desired output vector with three specified values and two don't-care conditions (represented by stars). As shown in the figure, errors are propagated from only those units where constraints are imposed. In the case of constraints among units, it is possible to impose constraints on units having fixed connections from the output units. Errors generated at these units are propagated back to the output units. This process is sketched in Figure 3, where the constraints $x_1 + x_2 = .6$ and $x_2 + x_3 = .4$ are imposed. Note that if many constraints are imposed on the same unit, the errors are simply added together, and the network will eventually find an activation value for the unit that satisfies all of the constraints (given that such a value exists).

Consider now the case in which desired output vectors specify values for only a single

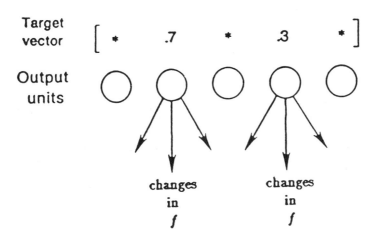

$$\mathbf{x}_i = \begin{bmatrix} * \\ .7 \\ * \\ .3 \\ * \end{bmatrix}$$

Target vector $\begin{bmatrix} * & .7 & * & .3 & * \end{bmatrix}$

Output units

changes in f changes in f

Figure 2: Learning with don't-care conditions.

output unit. This is essentially the case of local representations for actions, in which the network is essentially being instructed to activate its output units in a particular order. Suppose, for example, that a network with three output units is learning the sequence

$$\begin{bmatrix} 1 \\ * \\ * \end{bmatrix}, \begin{bmatrix} * \\ 1 \\ * \end{bmatrix}, \begin{bmatrix} * \\ * \\ 1 \end{bmatrix}.$$

At each time step, errors are propagated from only a single output unit, so that activation of that unit becomes associated to the current state. Associations are learned from s_1 to activation of the first output unit, from s_2 to activation of the second output unit, and from s_3 to activation of the third output unit. [5]

---

[5] where s_i denotes the activation of the state units at time i. I am ignoring the plan vector to simplify the exposition.

$$\mathbf{x}_i \quad = \quad \begin{bmatrix} x_1 + x_2 = .6 \\ \\ x_2 + x_3 = .4 \end{bmatrix}$$

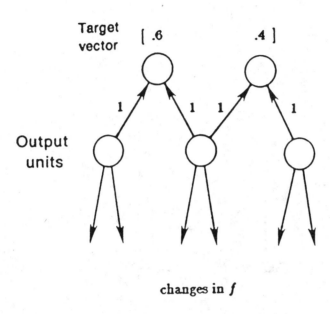

Figure 3: Learning with constraints among units.

After learning, the presence of s_1 on the state units will activate the first output unit. It will also partially activate the second and third output units, even though no associations from s_1 to these units have been learned. This occurs because s_1 is similar to s_2 and s_3 (given the requirement made of the next-state function) and similar inputs tend to produce similar outputs in these networks. The associations made to s_2 and s_3 also generalize, so that after learning, the network will likely produce a sequence such as

$$\begin{bmatrix} 1 \\ .8 \\ .6 \end{bmatrix}, \begin{bmatrix} .8 \\ 1 \\ .8 \end{bmatrix}, \begin{bmatrix} .6 \\ .8 \\ 1 \end{bmatrix},$$

where at each time step, there are parallel activations of all output units. If the network is driving a set of articulators that must travel a certain distance, or have a certain inertia, then it will be possible to go faster with these parallel control signals than with signals where only one output unit can be active at a time.

The foregoing example is simply the least constrained case and further constraints can be added. Suppose, for example, that the second output unit is not allowed to be active during the first action. This can be encoded in the constraint vector for the first action so that the network is instructed to learn the sequence

$$\begin{bmatrix} 1 \\ 0 \\ * \end{bmatrix}, \begin{bmatrix} * \\ 1 \\ * \end{bmatrix}, \begin{bmatrix} * \\ * \\ 1 \end{bmatrix}.$$

After learning, the output sequence will likely be as follows:

$$\begin{bmatrix} 1 \\ 0 \\ .6 \end{bmatrix}, \begin{bmatrix} .8 \\ 1 \\ .8 \end{bmatrix}, \begin{bmatrix} .6 \\ .7 \\ 1 \end{bmatrix},$$

where the added constraint is now met. In this example, the network must block the generalization that is made from s_2 to s_1. In general, the ability to block generalizations in this manner implies the need for a nonlinear output function.

As further constraints are added, there are fewer generalizations across nearby states that are allowed, and performance becomes less parallel. Minimal parallelism will arise when neighboring actions specify conflicting values on all output units, in which case the performance will be strictly sequential. Maximal parallelism should be expected when neighboring actions specify values on non-overlapping sets of output units. Note that there is no need to invoke a special process to program in the parallelism. Essentially, the system generalizes naturally across similar state vectors, and given that state vectors nearby in time are similar, the generalizations act so as to spread actions in time. In most cases, it will be more difficult for the system to learn in the more sequential case when there are more constraints imposed on the system which block the generalizations. These observations are summarized in Figure 4, which shows the relationships between constraint vectors and parallelism.

ATTRACTOR DYNAMICS

The properties of the system that lead to parallel performance also make the system relatively insensitive to perturbations. Suppose that the system has learned a particular sequence and that during performance of the sequence the state is perturbed somewhat. Given that similar states tend to produce similar outputs, the output of the system will not be greatly different from the unperturbed case. This would suggest that the network will perform a sequence which is a "shifted" version of the learned sequence. However, a stronger property appears to hold: The learned sequences become attractors for nearby

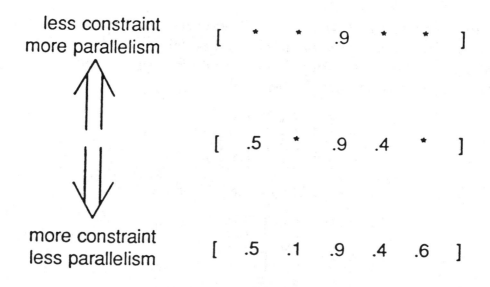

less constraint
more parallelism

[*   *   .9   *   *]

[.5   *   .9   .4   *]

more constraint
less parallelism

[.5   .1   .9   .4   .6]

Figure 4: Relationships between constraint and parallelism.

regions of the state space and perturbed trajectories return to the learned trajectories. This property is demonstrated in Figures 5 and 6. A network with two output units learned to follow a square in the two-dimensional space which corresponds to the activations of the output units. As shown in the figures, when the network was started at other points in the space, the trajectories moved toward the square. This occurred whether the trajectories began inside or outside the square, showing that the square is a *limit cycle* for the system. For a dynamical system to have limit cycles, it is necessary that the system be nonlinear (Hirsch & Smale, 1974), which further demonstrates the need for the output function to be nonlinear.

More globally, a network which has learned to produce several different cyclical sequences may have several regions of the state space which are attractor basins for the learned cycles. If the network is started in one of these basins, then the performed trajectory will approach the learned cycle, with the part of the cycle which first appears depending on where in the basin the network is started relative to the configuration of the cycle. The network can be regarded as a generalization of a content-addressable memory (cf. Hopfield, 1982) in which the memories correspond to cycles or other dynamic trajectories rather than static points.

Constraints on the output units in general define regions through which trajectories can pass. The network is free to choose a particular trajectory within the region, and this tends to be done in a way so as to avoid sharp changes in the trajectory. Whatever trajectory is chosen by the network, it will tend to generalize so as to become an attractor

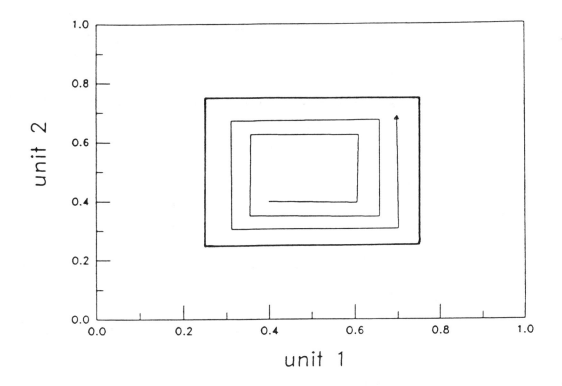

Figure 5: The activations of the two output units plotted with time as a parameter. The square is the trajectory that the network learned, and the spiral trajectory is the path that the network followed when started at the point (.4, .4).

for the surrounding space.

APPLICATIONS TO SPEECH PRODUCTION

In the case of speech, the constraint lists used by the learning process can be taken to encode knowledge about the phonetic structure of the language, and it is natural to identify these constraint lists with phonemes. Thus, in the current framework, the role of phonemes is to constrain the dynamical process that produces utterances by changing parameters of the process until the constraints are met. The constraints that define phonemes are themselves independent of context: They specify in what ways a phoneme can be altered by its context, without specifying values for particular contexts. During the learning process, parallel interactions between nearby phonemes can arise as long as they do not

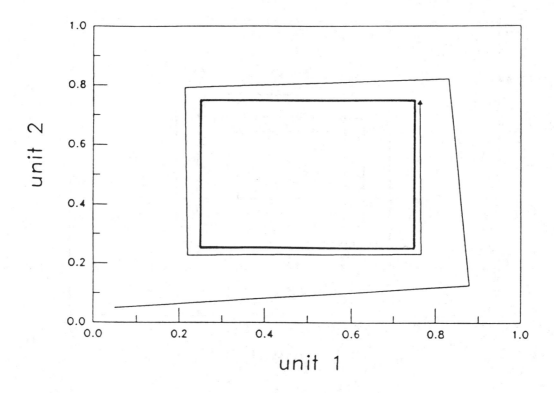

Figure 6: The activations of the two output units plotted with time as a parameter. The square is the trajectory that the network learned, and the spiral trajectory is the path that the network followed when started at the point (.05, .05).

violate the constraints.

I have elsewhere presented simulations that show that the network can mimic coarticulation data such as those presented earlier (Jordan, 1986). Several predictions were also made on the basis of these simulations. The simulations show that there can be non-adjacent interactions, so that, for example, the degree of anticipation of a feature can depend on what follows the feature. It is also the case that there is more coarticulation in the simulation over strings with homogeneous phonemic structure than over strings with heterogeneous phonemic structure.

Finally, it should be noted that it is consistent with the current approach to treat the state equations as discrete versions of a continuous process. In this case, the constraint vectors can still be applied at discrete epochs during learning. Thus, the approach would seem to have some promise for resolving some of the theoretical problems that arise at the interface between discrete phonemic representations and continuous articulatory processes

(Fowler, 1980).

DISCUSSION

One of the important problems that arises in the temporal domain is that there can be interactions both forward and backward in time. One approach to this problem is to represent actions explicitly in a spatial buffer, use relaxation techniques to allow interactions between buffer positions, and then map space into time by gating connections between actions (Feldman & Ballard, 1982). The present paper demonstrates a second approach. In the proposed network, there is no explicit representation of temporal order and no explicit representation of action sequences. There is only one set of output units for the network, therefore output vectors must arise as a dynamic process. Representing actions as distributed patterns on a common set of processing units has the virtue that partial activations can blend together in a simple way to produce the output of the system. Likewise, the representation of states as distributed patterns on a single set of units has the advantage that similarity between states has a natural functional representation in terms of the overlap of patterns. It is the similarity between nearby states that is responsible for interactions in time and this similarity has no time arrow associated with it, so that forward and backward interactions are both possible.

REFERENCES

Ackley, D. H., Hinton, G. E., & Sejnowski, T. J. (1985). A learning algorithm for Boltzmann machines. *Cognitive Science, 9*, 147-169.

Barto, A. G. & Anandan, P. (1985). Pattern recognizing stochastic learning automata. *IEEE Transactions on Systems, Man, and Cybernetics, 15*, 360-375.

Benguerel, A.- P. & Cowan, H. A. (1974). Coarticulation of upper lip protusion in French. *Phonetica, 30*, 41-55.

Booth, T. L. (1967). *Sequential machines and automata theory*. New York: Wiley.

Duda, R. O. & Hart, P. E. (1973). *Pattern classification and scene analysis.* New York: Wiley.

Feldman, J. A. & Ballard, D. H. (1982). Connectionist models and their properties. *Cognitive Science, 6,* 205-254.

Fowler, C. A. (1980). Coarticulation and theories of extrinsic timing. *Journal of Phonetics, 8,* 113-133.

Henke, W. L. (1966). *Dynamic articulatory model of speech production using computer simulation.* Massachusetts Institute of Technology.

Hinton, G. E. & Anderson, J. A. (Eds.) (1981). *Parallel models of associative memory.* Hillsdale, NJ: Erlbaum.

Hirsch, M. W. & Smale, S. (1974). *Differential equations, dynamical systems and linear algebra.* New York: Academic Press.

Hopfield, J. J. (1982). Neural networks and physical systems with emergent collective computational abilities. *Proceedings of the National Academy of Science, 79,* 2554-2558

Jordan, M. I. (1986). *Serial order: A parallel, distributed processing approach.* (Technical Report 8604). La Jolla, CA: University of California, San Diego, Institute for Cognitive Science.

Kohonen, T., Lehtio, P. & Oja, E. (1981). Storage and processing of information in distributed associative memory systems. In: G. E. Hinton and J. A. Anderson (Eds), *Parallel models of associative memory.* Hillsdale, NJ: Erlbaum.

Moll, K. L. & Daniloff, R. G. (1971). Investigation of the timing of velar movements during speech. *Journal of the Acoustical Society of America, 50,* 678-684.

Norman, D. A. (1981). A psychologist views human processing: Human errors and other phenomena suggest processing mechanisms. In: *Proceedings of the Seventh IJCAI.* Vancouver, BC.

Rosenblatt, F. (1961). *Principles of neurodynamics: Perceptrons and the theory of brain mechanisms.* Washington, D.C.: Spartan Books.

Rumelhart, D. E., Hinton, G. E., & Williams, R. J. (1986). Learning internal representations by error propagation. In: D. E. Rumelhart and J. L. McClelland (Eds.), *Parallel distributed processing: Explorations in the microstructure of cognition, Vol.1: Foundations.* Cambridge, MA: Bradford Books/MIT Press.

Rumelhart, D. E. & McClelland, J. L. (1986). *Parallel distributed processing: Explorations in the microstructure of cognition, Vol.1: Foundations.* Cambridge, MA: Bradford Books/MIT Press.

Rumelhart, D. E. & Norman, D. A. (1982). Simulating a skilled typist: A study of skilled cognitive-motor performance. *Cognitive Science, 6,* 1-36.

Widrow, B. & Hoff, M. E. (1960). Adaptive switching circuits. *WESCON Convention Record Part IV,* 96-104.

Deterministic Boltzmann Learning Performs Steepest Descent in Weight-Space

Geoffrey E. Hinton

Department of Computer Science, University of Toronto,
10 King's College Road, Toronto M5S 1A4, Canada

The Boltzmann machine learning procedure has been successfully applied in deterministic networks of analog units that use a mean field approximation to efficiently simulate a truly stochastic system (Peterson and Anderson 1987). This type of "deterministic Boltzmann machine" (DBM) learns much faster than the equivalent "stochastic Boltzmann machine" (SBM), but since the learning procedure for DBM's is only based on an analogy with SBM's, there is no existing proof that it performs gradient descent in any function, and it has only been justified by simulations. By using the appropriate interpretation for the way in which a DBM represents the probability of an output vector given an input vector, it is shown that the DBM performs steepest descent in the same function as the original SBM, except at rare discontinuities. A very simple way of forcing the weights to become symmetrical is also described, and this makes the DBM more biologically plausible than back-propagation (Werbos 1974; Parker 1985; Rumelhart et al. 1986).

1 Introduction

The promising results obtained by Peterson and Anderson (Peterson and Anderson 1987) using a DBM are hard to assess because they present no mathematical guarantee that the learning does gradient descent in any error function (except in the limiting case of a very large net with small random weights). It is quite conceivable that in a DBM the computed gradient might have a small systematic difference from the true gradient of the normal performance measure for each training case, and when these slightly incorrect gradients are added together over many cases their resultant might bear little relation to the resultant of the true case-wise gradients (see Fig. 1).

2 The Learning Procedure for Stochastic Boltzmann Machines

A Boltzmann machine (Hinton and Sejnowski 1986) is a network of symmetrically connected binary units that asynchronously update their states according to a *stochastic* decision rule. The units have states of 1 or 0 and the probability that unit i adopts the state 1 is given by

$$p_i = \sigma(\frac{1}{T} \sum_j s_j w_{ij}) \tag{2.1}$$

where s_j is the state of the jth unit, w_{ij} is the weight on the connection between the jth and the ith unit, T is the "temperature" and σ is a smooth non-linear function defined as

$$\sigma(x) = \frac{1}{1 + e^{-x}} \tag{2.2}$$

If the binary states of units are updated asynchronously and repeatedly using equation 2.1, the network will reach "thermal equilibrium" so that the relative probabilities of global configurations are determined by their energies according to the Boltzmann distribution:

$$\frac{P_\alpha}{P_\beta} = \frac{e^{-E_\alpha/T}}{e^{-E_\beta/T}} \tag{2.3}$$

where P_α is the probability of a global configuration and E_α is its energy defined by

$$E_\alpha = -\sum_{i<j} s_i^\alpha s_j^\alpha w_{ij} \tag{2.4}$$

where s_i^α is the binary state of unit i in the αth global configuration, and bias terms are ignored because they can always be treated as weights on connections from a permanently active unit.

At any given temperature, T, the Boltzmann distribution is the one that minimizes the Helmholtz free energy, F, of the distribution. F is defined by the equation

$$F = \langle E \rangle - TH \tag{2.5}$$

where $\langle E \rangle$ is the expected value of the energy given the probability distribution over configurations and H is the entropy of the distribution. It

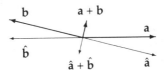

Figure 1: The true gradients of the performance measure are **a** and **b** for two training cases. Even fairly accurate estimates, **â** and **b̂**, can have a resultant that points in a very different direction.

can be shown that minima of F (which will be denoted by F^*) satisfy the equation

$$e^{-F^*/T} = \sum_\alpha e^{-E_\alpha/T} \tag{2.6}$$

In a stochastic Boltzmann machine, the probability of an output vector, O_β, given an input vector, I_α is represented by

$$P^-(O_\beta|I_\alpha) = \frac{e^{-F_{\alpha\beta}^*/T}}{e^{-F_\alpha^*/T}} \tag{2.7}$$

where $F_{\alpha\beta}^*$ is the minimum free energy with I_α and O_β clamped, and F_α^* is the minimum free energy with just I_α clamped. A very natural way to observe $P^-(O_\beta|I_\alpha)$ is to allow the network to reach thermal equilibrium with I_α clamped, and to observe the probability of O_β. The key to Boltzmann machine learning is the simple way in which a small change to a weight, w_{ij}, affects the free energy and hence the log probability of an output vector in a network at thermal equilibrium.

$$\frac{\partial F^*}{\partial w_{ij}} = -\langle s_i s_j \rangle \tag{2.8}$$

where $\langle s_i s_j \rangle$ is the expected value of $s_i s_j$ in the minimum free energy distribution. The simple relationship between weight changes and log probabilities of output vectors makes it easy to teach the network an input-output mapping. The network is "shown" the mapping that it is required to perform by clamping an input vector on the input units and clamping the required output vector on the output units (with the appropriate conditional probability). It is then allowed to reach thermal equilibrium at $T = 1$, and at equilibrium each connection measures how often the units it connects are simultaneously active. This is repeated for all input-output pairs so that each connection can measure $\langle s_i s_j \rangle^+$, the expected probability, averaged over all cases, that unit i and unit j are simultaneously active at thermal equilibrium when the input and output vectors are both clamped. The network must also be run in just the same way but without clamping the output units to measure $\langle s_i s_j \rangle^-$, the expected probability that both units are active at thermal equilibrium when the output vector is determined by the network. Each weight is then updated by

$$\Delta w_{ij} = \epsilon(\langle s_i s_j \rangle^+ - \langle s_i s_j \rangle^-) \tag{2.9}$$

It follows from equation 2.7 and equation 2.8 that if ϵ is sufficiently small this performs steepest descent in an information theoretic measure, G, of the difference between the behavior of the output units when they are clamped and their behavior when they are not clamped.

$$G = \sum_{\alpha,\beta} P^+(I_\alpha, O_\beta) \log \frac{P^+(O_\beta \mid I_\alpha)}{P^-(O_\beta \mid I_\alpha)} \tag{2.10}$$

where I_α is a state vector over the input units, O_β is a state vector over the output units, P^+ is a probability measured at thermal equilibrium when both the input and output units are clamped, and P^- is a probability measured when only the input units are clamped.

Stochastic Boltzmann machines learn slowly, partly because of the time required to reach thermal equilibrium and partly because the learning is driven by the *difference* between two noisy variables, so these variables must be sampled for a long time at thermal equilibrium to reduce the noise. If we could achieve the same simple relationships between log probabilities and weights in a deterministic system, learning would be much faster.

3 Mean field theory

Under certain conditions, a stochastic system can be approximated by a deterministic one by replacing the stochastic binary variables of equation 2.1 by deterministic real-valued variables that represent their mean values

$$p_i = \sigma(\frac{1}{T} \sum_j p_j w_{ij}) \tag{3.1}$$

We could now perform discrete, asynchronous updates of the p_i using equation 3.1 or we could use a synchronous, discrete time approximation of the set of differential equations

$$\frac{dp_i}{dt} = -p_i + \sigma(\frac{1}{T} \sum_j p_j w_{ij}) \tag{3.2}$$

We shall view the p_i as a representation of a probability distribution over all binary global configurations. Since many different distributions can give rise to the same mean values for the p_i we shall assume that the distribution being represented is the one that maximizes the entropy, subject to the constraints imposed on the mean values by the p_i. Equivalently, it is the distribution in which the p_i are treated as the mean values of *independent* stochastic binary variables. Using equation 2.5 we can calculate the free energy of the distribution represented by the state of a DBM (at $T = 1$).

$$F = -\sum_{i<j} p_i p_j w_{ij} + \sum_i [p_i \log(p_i) + (1 - p_i) \log(1 - p_i)] \qquad (3.3)$$

Although the dynamics of the system defined by equation 3.2 do not consist in following the gradient of F, it can be shown that it always moves in a direction that has a positive cosine with the gradient of $-F$ so it settles to one of the minima of F (Hopfield 1984).

Mean field systems are normally viewed as approximations to systems that really contain higher order statistics, but they can also be viewed as exact systems that are strongly limited in the probability distributions that they can represent because they use only N real values to represent distributions over 2^N binary states. Within the limits of their representational powers, they are an efficient way of manipulating these large but constrained probability distributions.

4 Deterministic Boltzmann machine learning

In a DBM, we shall define the representation of $P^-(O_\beta|I_\alpha)$ exactly as in equation 2.7, but now $F^*_{\alpha\beta}$ and F^*_α will refer to the free energies of the particular minima that the network actually settles into. Unfortunately, in a DBM this representation is no longer equivalent to the obvious way of defining $P^-(O_\beta|I_\alpha)$ which is to clamp I_α on the input units, settle to a minimum of F_α, and interpret the values of the output units as a representation of a probability distribution over output vectors, using the maximum entropy assumption.

The reason for choosing the first definition rather than the second is this: Provided the stable states that the network settles to do not change radically when the weights are changed slightly, it can now be shown that the mean field version of the Boltzmann machine learning procedure changes each weight in proportion to the gradient of $\log P^-(O_\beta|I_\alpha)$, which is exactly what is required to perform steepest descent in the performance measure G defined in equation 2.10.

When w_{ij} is incremented by an infinitessimal amount $\epsilon p_i p_j$ two things happen to F^* (see Fig. 2). First, the mean energy of the probability distribution represented by the state of the DBM is decreased by $\epsilon p^2_i p^2_j$ and, to first order, the mean energy of all nearby states of the DBM is decreased by the same amount. Second, the values of the p_i at which F is minimized change slightly so the stable state moves slightly. But, to first order, this movement of the minimum has *no* effect on the value of F because we are at a stable state in which $\partial F/\partial p_i = 0$ for all i. Hence the effect of incrementing w_{ij} by $\epsilon p_i p_j$ is simply to create a new, nearby stable state which, to first order, has a free energy that is $\epsilon p_i^2 p_j^2$ lower than the old stable state. So, assuming $T = 1$, if all weights are incremented by $\epsilon p_i^+ p_j^+$ in the stable state that has I_α and O_β clamped and are decremented by $\epsilon p_i^- p_j^-$ in the stable state that has only I_α clamped we have, from equation 2.7

$$\Delta w_{ij} = \epsilon(p_i^+ p_j^+ - p_i^- p_j^-) = \epsilon \frac{\partial \log P^-(O_\beta|I_\alpha)}{\partial w_{ij}} \qquad (4.1)$$

This ensures that by making ϵ sufficiently small the learning procedure can be made to approximate steepest descent in G arbitrarily closely.

The derivation above is invalid if, with the same boundary conditions, a small change in the weights causes the network to settle to a stable state with a very different free energy. This can happen with energy landscapes like the one shown in figure 3. A small weight change caused by some other training case can cause a free energy barrier that prevents the network finding the deeper minimum. In simulations that repeatedly sweep through a fixed set of training cases, it is easy to avoid this phenomenon by always starting the network at the stable state that was found using the same boundary conditions on the previous sweep. This has the added advantage of eliminating almost all the computation required to settle on a stable state, and thus making a settling almost as fast as a forward pass of the back-propagation procedure.

Unfortunately, starting from the previous best state does not eliminate the possibility that a small free-energy barrier will disappear and a much better state will then be found when the network is running with the output units unclamped. This can greatly increase the denominator in equation 2.7 and thus greatly decrease the network's representation of the probability of a correct output vector. It should also be noted that it is conceivable that, due to local minima in the free energy landscape, F_α^* may actually be higher than $F_{\alpha\beta}^*$, in which case the network's representation of $P^-(O_\beta|I_\alpha)$ will exceed 1. In practice this does not seem to be a problem, and DBM's compare very favorably with back-propagation in learning speed.

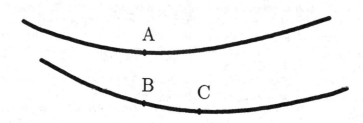

Figure 2: The effect of a small weight increment on a free energy minimum. To first order, the difference in free energy between A and C is equal to the difference between A and B. At a minimum, small changes in the distribution (sideways movements) have negligible effects on free energy, even though they may have significant (and opposite) effects on the energy and the entropy terms.

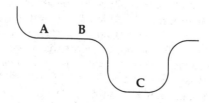

Figure 3: A small increase in the free energy of B can prevent a network from settling to the free energy minimum at C. So small changes in weights occasionally cause large changes in the final free energy.

5 Symmetry of the Weights

We have assumed that the weight of the connection from i to j is the same as the weight from j to i. If these weights are asymmetric, the learning procedure will automatically symmetrize them provided that, after each weight update, each weight is decayed slightly towards zero by an amount proportional to its magnitude. This favors "simple" networks that have small weights, and it also reduces the energy barriers that create local minima. Weight-decay always reduces the difference between w_{ij} and w_{ji}, and since the learning rule specifies weight changes that are exactly symmetrical in i and j, the two weights will always approach one another. Williams (1985) makes a similar argument about a different learning procedure. Thus the symmetry that is required to allow the network to compute its own error derivatives is easily achieved, whereas achieving symmetry between forward and backward weights in back-propagation networks requires much more complex schemes (Parker 1985).

6 Acknowledgments

I thank Christopher Longuet-Higgins, Conrad Galland, Scott Kirkpatrick, and Yann Le Cun for helpful comments. This research was supported by grants from the Ontario Information Technology Research Center, the National Science and Engineering Research Council of Canada, and DuPont. Geoffrey Hinton is a fellow of the Canadian Institute for Advanced Research.

References

Hinton, G.E. and T.J. Sejnowski. 1986. Learning and relearning in Boltzmann machines. *In:* Parallel Distributed Processing: Explorations in the Microstructure of Cognition, Volume 1: Foundations, eds. D.E. Rumelhart, J.L. McClelland, and the PDP group. Cambridge, MA: MIT Press.

Hopfield, J.J. 1984. Neurons with Graded Response Have Collective Computational Properties like Those of Two-state Neurons. *Proceedings of the National Academy of Sciences U.S.A.* **81**, 3088–3092.

Parker, D.B. 1985. *Learning-logic.* Technical Report TR-47, Sloan School of Management, Massachusetts Institute of Technology, Cambridge, MA.

Peterson, C. and J.R. Anderson. 1987. A Mean Field Theory Learning Algorithm for Neural Networks. *Complex Systems* **1**, 995–1019.

Rumelhart, D.E., G.E. Hinton, and R.J. Williams. 1986. Learning Representations by Back-propagating Errors. *Nature* **323**, 533–536.

Werbos, P.J. 1974. *Beyond Regression: New Tools for Prediction and Analysis in the Behavioral Sciences.* PhD Thesis, Harvard University, Cambridge, MA.

Williams, R.J. 1985. *Feature Discovery through Error-correction Learning.* Technical Report ICS-8501, Institute for Cognitive Science, University of California, San Diego, La Jolla, CA.

Received 5 December; accepted 15 December 1988.

Communicated by Scott Kirkpatrick ━━━━━━━━━━━━

About the Author

Joachim Diederich is a senior scientist at the German National Research Center for Computer Science (GMD) in St. Augustin (FRG) and the University of California in Davis. His research interests include learning in artificial neural networks and natural language processing.

He received his doctoral degree in computational linguistics from the University of Bielefeld (FRG) and his diploma degree in psychology from the University of Muenster (FRG). His current address is: German National Research Center for Computer Science (GMD), Schloss Birlinghoven, P.O. Box 1240, D-5205 Sankt Augustin 1, Germany.

Index

IEEE Computer Society

IEEE Computer Society Press Publications

Monographs: A monograph is an authored book

Tutorials: A tutorial is a collection of original materials prepared by the editors and reprints of the best articles published in a subject area. They must contain at least five percent original material (15 to 20 percent original material is recommended).

Reprint Books: A reprint book is a collection of reprints divided into sections with a preface, table of contents, and section introductions that discuss the reprints and why they were selected. It contains less than five percent original material.

(Subject) Technology Series: Each technology series is a collection of anthologies of reprints, each with a narrow focus on a subset of a particular discipline, such as networks, architecture, software, robotics.

Submission of proposals: For guidelines on preparing CS Press Books, write Editor-in-Chief, IEEE Computer Society, P.O. Box 3014, 10662 Los Vaqueros Circle, Los Alamitos, CA 90720-1264 (telephone 714-821-8380).

Purpose

The IEEE Computer Society advances the theory and practice of computer science and engineering, promotes the exchange of technical information among 100,000 members worldwide, and provides a wide range of services to members and nonmembers.

Membership

Members receive the acclaimed monthly magazine *Computer*, discounts, and opportunities to serve (all activities are led by volunteer members). Membership is open to all IEEE members, affiliate society members, and others seriously interested in the computer field.

Publications and Activities

Computer. An authoritative, easy-to-read magazine containing tutorial and in-depth articles on topics across the computer field, plus news, conferences, calendar, interviews, and new products.

Periodicals. The society publishes six magazines and four research transactions. Refer to membership application or request information as noted above.

Conference Proceedings, Tutorial Texts, Standards Documents. The Computer Society Press publishes more than 100 titles every year.

Standards Working Groups. Over 100 of these groups produce IEEE standards used throughout the industrial world.

Technical Committees. Over 30 TCs publish newsletters, provide interaction with peers in specialty areas, and directly influence standards, conferences, and education.

Conferences/Education. The society holds about 100 conferences each year and sponsors many educational activites, including computing science accreditation.

Chapters. Regular and student chapters worldwide provide the opportunity to interact with colleagues, hear technical experts, and serve the local professional community.

Other IEEE Computer Society Press Texts

Monographs

Analyzing Computer Architecture
Written by J.C. Huck and M.J. Flynn
(ISBN 0-8186-8857-2); 206 pages

Desktop Publishing for the Writer: Designing, Writing, Developing
Written by Richard Ziegfeld and John Tarp
(ISBN 0-8186-8840-8); 380 pages

Integrating Design and Test: Using CAE Tools for ATE Programming
Written by K.P. Parker
(ISBN 0-8186-8788-6 (case)); 160 pages

JSP and JSD: The Jackson Approach to Software Development (Second Edition)
Written by J.R. Cameron
(ISBN 0-8186-8858-0); 560 pages

National Computer Policies
Written by Ben G. Matley and Thomas A. McDannold
(ISBN 0-8186-8784-3); 192 pages

Physical Level Interfaces and Protocols
Written by Uyless Black
(ISBN 0-8186-8824-6); approximately 272 pages

Protecting Your Proprietary Rights in the Computer and High Technology Industries
Written by Tobey B. Marzouk, Esq.
(ISBN 0-8186-8754-1); 224 pages

Tutorials

Advanced Computer Architecture
Edited by D.P. Agrawal
(ISBN 0-8186-0667-3); 400 pages

Advanced Microprocessors and High-Level Language Computer Architectures
Edited by V. Milutinovic
(ISBN 0-8186-0623-1); 608 pages

Advances in Distributed System Reliability
Edited by Suresh Rai and Dharma P. Agrawal
(ISBN 0-8186-8907-2); 352 pages

Computer Architecture
Edited by D.D. Gajski, V.M. Milutinovic, H. Siegel, and B.P. Furht
(ISBN 0-8186-0704-1); 602 pages

Computer Communications: Architectures, Protocols, and Standards (Second Edition)
Edited by William Stallings
(ISBN 0-8186-0790-4); 448 pages

Computer Graphics (2nd Edition)
Edited by J.C. Beatty and K.S. Booth
(ISBN 0-8186-0425-5); 576 pages

Computer Graphics Hardware: Image Generation and Display
Edited by H.K. Reghbati and A.Y.C. Lee
(ISBN 0-8186-0753-X); 384 pages

Computer Graphics: Image Synthesis
Edited by Kenneth Joy, Max Nelson, Charles Grant, and Lansing Hatfield
(ISBN 0-8186-8854-8); 384

Computer and Network Security
Edited by M.D. Abrams and H.J. Podell
(ISBN 0-8186-0756-4); 448 pages

Computer Networks (4th Edition)
Edited by M.D. Abrams and I.W. Cotton
(ISBN 0-8186-0568-5); 512 pages

Computer Text Recognition and Error Correction
Edited by S.N. Srihari
(ISBN 0-8186-0579-0); 364 pages

Computers for Artificial Intelligence Applications
Edited by B. Wah and G.-J. Li
(ISBN 0-8186-0706-8); 656 pages

Database Management
Edited by J.A. Larson
(ISBN 0-8186-0714-9); 448 pages

Digital Image Processing and Analysis: Volume 1: Digital Image Processing
Edited by R. Chellappa and A.A. Sawchuk
(ISBN 0-8186-0665-7); 736 pages

Digital Image Processing and Analysis: Volume 2: Digital Image Analysis
Edited by R. Chellappa and A.A. Sawchuk
(ISBN 0-8186-0666-5); 670 pages

Digital Private Branch Exchanges (PBXs)
Edited by E.R. Coover
(ISBN 0-8186-0829-3); 400 pages

Distributed Computing Network Reliability
Edited by Suresh Rai and Dharma P. Agrawal
(ISBN 0-8186-8908-0); 368 pages

Distributed Control (2nd Edition)
Edited by R.E. Larson, P.L. McEntire, and J.G. O'Reilly
(ISBN 0-8186-0451-4); 382 pages

Distributed Database Management
Edited by J.A. Larson and S. Rahimi
(ISBN 0-8186-0575-8); 580 pages

Distributed-Software Engineering
Edited by S.M. Shatz and J.-P. Wang
(ISBN 0-8186-8856-4); 304 pages

DSP-Based Testing of Analog and Mixed-Signal Circuits
Edited by M. Mahoney
(ISBN 0-8186-0785-8); 272 pages

Fault-Tolerant Computing
Edited by V.P. nelson and B.D. Carroll
(ISBN 0-8186-0677-0 (paper) 0-8186-8667-4 (case)); 432 pages

Gallium Arsenide Computer Design
Edited by V.M. Milutinovic and D.A. Fura
(ISBN 0-8186-0795-5); 368 pages

Human Factors in Software Development (2nd Edition)
Edited by B. Curtis
(ISBN 0-8186-0577-4); 736 pages

Integrated Services Digital Networks (ISDN) (Second Edition)
Edited by W. Stallings
(ISBN 0-8186-0823-4); 404 pages

For Further Information:

IEEE Computer Society, 10662 Los Vaqueros Circle, P.O. Box 3014,
Los Alamitos, CA 90720-1264

IEEE Computer Society, 13, Avenue de l'Aquilon, 2,
B-1200 Brussels, BELGIUM

IEEE Computer Society,
Ooshima Building, 2-19-1 Minami-Aoyama,
Minato-ku, Tokyo 107, JAPAN

Interconnection Networks for Parallel and Distributed Processing
Edited by C.-L. Wu and T.-Y. Feng
(ISBN 0-8186-0574-X); 500 pages

Local Network Equipment
Edited by H.A. Freeman and K.J. Thurber
(ISBN 0-8186-0605-3); 384 pages

Local Network Technology (3rd Edition)
Edited by W. Stallings
(ISBN 0-8186-0825-0); 512 pages

Microprogramming and Firmware Engineering
Edited by V. Milutinovic
(ISBN 0-8186-0839-0); 416 pages

Modeling and Control of Automated Manufacturing Systems
Edited by A.A. Desrochers
(ISBN 0-8186-8916-1); 384 pages

Modern Design and Analysis of Discrete-Event Computer Simulations
Edited by E.J. Dudewicz and Z. Karian
(ISBN 0-8186-0597-9); 486 pages

New Paradigms for Software Development
Edited by William Agresti
(ISBN 0-8186-0707-6); 304 pages

Object-Oriented Computing--Volume 1: Concepts
Edited by Gerald E. Peterson
(ISBN 0-8186-0821-8); 214 pages

Object-Oriented Computing--Volume 2: Implementations
Edited by Gerald E. Peterson
(ISBN 0-8186-082108); 214 pages

Office Automation Systems (Second Edition)
Edited by H.A. Freemand and K.J. Thurber
(ISBN 0-8186-0822-6); 324 pages

Parallel Architectures for Database Systems
Edited by A. R. Hurson, L.L. Miller, and S.H. Pakzad
(ISBN 0-8186-8838-6); 478 pages

Programming Productivity: Issues for the Eighties (Second Edition)
Edited by C. Jones
(ISBN 0-8186-0681-9); 472 pages

Recent Advances in Distributed Database Management
Edited by C. Mohan
(ISBN 0-8186-0571-5); 500 pages

Reduced Instruction Set Computers (Second Edition)
Edited by W. Stallings
(ISBN 0-8186-8943-9); 448 pages

Reliable Distributed System Software
Edited by J.A. Stankovic
(ISBN 0-8186-0570-7); 400 pages

Robotics Tutorial (2nd Edition)
Edited by C.S. G. Lee, R.C. Gonzalez, and K.S. Fu
(ISBN 0-8186-0658-4); 630 pages

Software Design Techniques (4th Edition)
Edited by P. Freeman and A.I. Wasserman
(ISBN 0-8186-0514-0); 736 pages

Software Engineering Project Management
Edited by R. Thayer
(ISBN 0-8186-0751-3); 512 pages

Software Maintenance
Edited by G. Parikh and N. Zvegintzov
(ISBN 0-8186-0002-0); 360 pages

Software Management (3rd Edition)
Edited by D.J. Reifer
(ISBN 0-8186-0678-9); 526 pages

Software-Oriented Computer Architecture
Edited by E. Fernandez and T. Lang
(ISBN 0-8186-0708-4); 376 pages

Software Reusability
Edited by Peter Freeman
(ISBN 0-8186-0750-5); 304 pages

Software Risk Management
Edited by B.W. Boehm
(ISBN 0-8186-8906-4); 508 pages

Standards, Guidelines, and Examples on System and Software Requirements Engineering
Edited by Merlin Dorfman and Richard H. Thayer
(ISBN 0-8186-8922-6); 626 pages

System and Software Requirements Engineering
Edited by Richard H. Thayer and Merlin Dorfman
(ISBN 0-8186-8921-8); 740 pages

Test Generation for VLSI Chips
Edited by V.D. Agrawal and S.C. Seth
(ISBN 0-8186-8786-X); 416 pages

VSLI Technologies: Through the 80s and Beyond
Edited by D.J. McGreivy and K.A. Pickar
(ISBN 0-8186-0424-7); 346 pages

VLSI Testing and Validation Techniques
Edited by H. Reghbati
(ISBN 0-8186-0668-1); 616 pages

Reprint Collections

Dataflow and Reduction Architectures
Edited by S.S. Thakkar
(ISBN 0-8186-0759-9); 460 pages

Expert Systems: Software Methodology
Edited by Peter Raeth
(ISBN 0-8186-8904-8); 476 pages

Logic Design for Testability
Edited by C.C. Timoc
(ISBN 0-8186-0573-1); 324 pages

Microprocessors and Microcomputers (3rd Edition)
Edited by J.T. Cain
(ISBN 0-8186-0585-5); 386 pages

Software (3rd Edition)
Edited by M.V. Zelkowitz
(ISBN 0-8186-0789-0); 440 pages

VLSI Technologies and Computer Graphics
Edited by H. Fuchs
(ISBN 0-8186-0491-3); 490 pages

Artifical Neural Networks Technology Series

Artificial Neural Networks: Concept Learning
Edited by J. Diederich
(ISBN 0-8186-2015-3); 140 pages

Artificial Neural Networks: Electronic Implementation
Edited by Nelson Morgan
(ISBN 0-8186-2029-3); approximately 192 pages

Artificial Neural Networks: Theoretical Concepts
Edited by V. Vemuri
(ISBN 0-8186-0855-2); 160 pages

Software Technology Series

Computer-Aided Software Engineering (CASE)
Edited by E.J. Chikofsky
(ISBN 0-8186-1970-8); 110 pages

Communications Technology Series

Multicast Communication in Distributed Systems
Edited by Mustaque Ahamad
(ISBN 0-8186-1970-8); 110 pages

Robotic Technology Series

Multirobot Systems
Edited by Rajiv Mehrotra and Murali R. Varanasi
(ISBN 0-8186-1977-5); 122 pages